Social Work with Lesbians & Gay Men

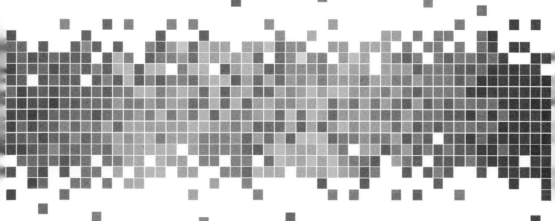

Helen Cosis Brown & Christine Cocker

SAGE

Los Angeles | London | New Delhi
Singapore | Washington DC

SAGE Publications Ltd
1 Oliver's Yard
55 City Road
London EC1Y 1SP

SAGE Publications Inc.
2455 Teller Road
Thousand Oaks, California 91320

SAGE Publications India Pvt Ltd
B 1/I 1 Mohan Cooperative Industrial Area
Mathura Road
New Delhi 110 044

SAGE Publications Asia-Pacific Pte Ltd
33 Pekin Street #02-01
Far East Square
Singapore 048763

Library of Congress Control Number: 2010926586

British Library Cataloguing in Publication data

A catalogue record for this book is available from the British Library

ISBN 978-1-84787-390-3
ISBN 978-1-84787-391-0 (pbk)

Typeset by C&M Digitals (P) Ltd, Chennai, India
Printed in India at Replika Press Pvt Ltd
Printed on paper from sustainable resources

Social Work with Lesbians & Gay Men

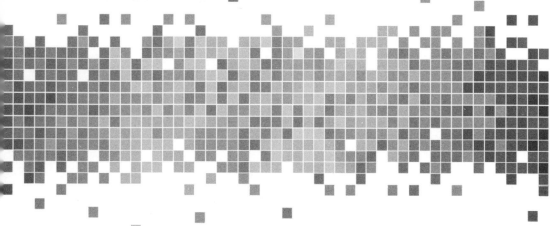

SAGE has been part of the global academic community since 1965, supporting high quality research and learning that transforms society and our understanding of individuals, groups, and cultures. SAGE is the independent, innovative, natural home for authors, editors and societies who share our commitment and passion for the social sciences.

Find out more at: **www.sagepublications.com**

This book is dedicated to:

Helen Cosis Brown: Aaron Brown, Casey Ryan and Rebecca Swift

Christine Cocker: Adi Cooper, Frania Cooper, Rivka Cocker and Shane Cocker.

Contents

Acknowledgements

We would like to thank Adi Cooper, Frania Cooper, Trish Hafford-Letchfield, Stephen Hicks, Ruth Hunt, Joy Trotter, the staff at the British Library and Gay's the Word bookshop, and colleagues and students at Middlesex University. Our particular thanks to our editors at Sage, Emma Paterson and Zoe Elliott-Fawcett and other Sage staff for their patience and helpfulness throughout.

Writing a book with someone else is never easy but we remain good friends. Copious coffee and tea drinking at the Spence café in Stoke Newington and Wiveton Hall in North Norfolk were essential parts of the creative process.

Introduction

This book is about social work with lesbians and gay men. It considers knowledge and practice, because their interconnectedness is necessary and fundamental to what is described as social work; 'theory and practice cannot be separated in any obvious way – the two dimensions are interdependent' (Gray and Webb, 2009: 5).

Three previous books in the UK have specifically examined social work with lesbians and gay men: Hart and Richardson (1981); Brown (1998a) and Jones and Ward (2009). Other books, published in the last ten years, also look at social work with lesbians and gay men, but as part of wider considerations of sexuality (Bywater and Jones, 2007; Myers and Milner, 2007) or within broader arenas of health and social care practice (Wilton, 2000; Fish, 2006). Since the publication in 1998 of *Social Work and Sexuality: Working with Lesbians and Gay Men* (Brown, 1998a) the legal landscape occupied by lesbians and gay men is virtually unrecognisable. We therefore decided to re-visit this area of practice to consider this changed landscape and examine social work's continuing role within it. Given that there are existing texts that consider sexuality in its broadest sense, including heterosexuality, bisexuality and transgender issues, we have chosen to focus exclusively on homosexuality: social work with lesbians and gay men.

However, the terms sexuality, lesbian and gay are contested terms. Historically the meaning ascribed to 'sexuality' has been influenced by a number of different factors which have affected whether it is seen as biologically determined, culturally and socially located, defined by specific physical acts, influenced by religious morality or a combination of all of the above and more! In the past, biology and gender have largely determined how sexuality was understood. Foucault (1978), in his work describing the history of sexuality, identifies the nineteenth century as the beginning of a discourse of sexuality that moved away from the influence of religious morals and principles to be replaced by notions of 'normal' and 'abnormal' sexual behaviour defined through a medical and biological lens. This biologically determined and fixed medicalisation of sexuality is referred to as 'essentialism', and remains influential in some contemporary understandings of sexuality.

Labelling and categorising people's sexuality is problematic. We acknowledge that by using the terms 'lesbian' and 'gay' throughout the book, we may appear to collude with this simplistic categorisation. However, social workers' understanding of sexual issues outside of a heteronormative framework is variable. To provide clarity about whom we are referring to (i.e., women who have intimate sexual relationships with other women and men who have intimate sexual relationships with other men), we will still use these terms. As Bianco comments, '[T]hese categories of identification are, in short, limiting, but, at the same time, they are all that we have' (Bianco, 2008). These labels are problematic because of the fluid nature of sexual identities and relationships: for example, some lesbians and gay men can and do have sex with people of a different gender and continue to refer to themselves as lesbian or gay.

Lesbians and gay men are not a homogeneous group. Despite some positive changes in public opinion (Park et al., 2010) and current protective legislation, they are still subject to some continuing negativity. Within this book we focus on lesbians and gay men in part because there have only been three previous books in the UK that exclusively consider this area, and because the Sexual Orientation Regulations 2007 require the re-consideration of social work practice with lesbians and gay men. If social work is to avoid negatively discriminating against lesbians and gay men in its provision of services and practice, we need to review our practice to ensure it is fit for purpose in this new legal context. Indeed, the Equality Act 2010 means social work has to now engage in equality promotion for lesbians and gay men as it currently does for women, Black communities and people with disabilities.

Social work with lesbians and gay men attracts little academic and practice debate. Indeed, social work has had a troubled relationship with lesbians and gay men and has historically engaged in their oppression (Milligan, 1975; Hart, 1980; Hart and Richardson, 1981; Rights of Women Lesbian Custody Group, 1986; Brown, 1998a; Hicks, 2005a, 2005b). This history does not mean that social work is currently consciously oppressive towards lesbians and gay men or that it will be in the future. However, despite changes in the legislative landscape and because of its conscious and unconscious assumptions of heterosexuality, social work can still fail to meet the needs of lesbians and gay men because it remains a marginalised area of practice, research and teaching.

The book explores a number of topics including: theory informing practice; history; the legal and policy context; the re-appraisal of the meanings and dominance of 'anti-discriminatory practice'; religion; and relationship based social work. The book is structured so that theory and ideas relevant to all social work practice with lesbians and gay men are covered (Chapters 1–5), before specific areas of practice are addressed (Chapters 6–8).

In Chapter 1, we outline the historical and theoretical context for social work with lesbians and gay men. We start the book with this chapter as we believe history is a neglected area in social work and social policy, and is necessary in order to understand the present and inform the future. In addition, we argue that social work practice must be theoretically informed. We look at a range of ideas that are problematic and facilitative for this area of practice, and comment on the tensions therein. We posit the specificity of knowledge as always being historically, geographically, socially and culturally constructed and located. This understanding of 'knowledge' leads us to consider the applicability of ideas that have historically been used oppressively against lesbians and gay men rather than argue for their automatic discard. In considering theory we do not think that it can provide either answers or certainty but can help us to ask apposite questions that should inform research and practice. We also value theory as essential to facilitate thinking and debate. We believe social work is itself an uncertain profession, operating in an uncertain world where professional judgement and decision-making has to be well informed in order to be executed effectively, but it can never deliver truth or certainty.

Chapter 2 outlines the historical and current legal and policy context in which social work takes place. Society's relationship with homosexuality and the turbulent nature of that relationship is clearly demonstrated within the changing legal landscape of the past 20 years. Social work is enmeshed within this dynamic.

In Chapter 3 we discuss social work values and ethical practice and consider what lies beyond anti-discriminatory and anti-oppressive practice. We examine the legacy of the Radical Social Work literature and look at what can be drawn from it that is of use to us today. We look at the development of the anti-discriminatory and anti-oppressive practice literature and consider its positive legacy as well as some of its inherent problems.

Chapter 4 addresses the importance of understanding the meanings of family and kinship for lesbians, gay men and social work practitioners.

We consider research informing debates about the nature of 'family' and 'kinship' and look at the application of some ideas within the literature to social work.

Chapter 5 addresses the relationship between homosexuality, religion and social work practice. We examine the literature in this area of practice, consider dilemmas and tackle areas that create anxiety for social workers. We argue that within the current UK legal context social workers have to be able to work effectively with lesbians and gay men as well as with people of different faiths irrespective of their own sexuality or their religion or beliefs.

Chapters 6, 7 and 8 move on to explore social work practice. Within these chapters we examine research and literature relevant to lesbians and gay men in the service delivery areas of: older adults, adults with learning disabilities and adults with physical disabilities (Chapter 6); mental health (Chapter 7) and children and families (Chapter 8). We argue that it is essential for social workers to seek out specific knowledge, for example knowledge about the mental health of lesbians and gay men, as well as utilising social work knowledge, including research, more broadly. We consider the legal and policy contexts for each of the three areas of service delivery and argue that the legal context for social work with lesbians and gay men is currently ahead of social work practice and that there is a need for social work to 'catch up' to enable lesbians and gay men to receive facilitative and effective social work. In all three 'practice' chapters (6–8) we emphasise the importance of the relationship between social worker and client. Without this relationship effective social work practice is not possible.

In this book we argue for a new radicalism: a radicalism that challenges the status quo and social work theory and practice to enable lesbian and gay social work clients and carers to realise their individual and collective potential.

1

Overview of the historical and contemporary discourses influencing social work with lesbians and gay men

Introduction

Social work is by its very nature a politically and socially constructed activity. When considering social work with lesbians and gay men it is therefore necessary to locate it within its historical, political and social context as social work tends to reflect the ideological moment. Because social work is a practice dependent on the use of language as one of its key activities/skills in engaging with people, thought needs to be given to how different discourses relating to sexuality have impacted upon social work theory and practice. In this chapter we therefore discuss the historical, social and political context and discourses and ideas that we think are significant to this area of social work practice before we look at the detail of social work with lesbians and gay men.

The meaning of 'sexuality' has changed over time. In this chapter we give an overview of lesbian and gay history relevant to understanding the position of lesbians and gay men in the UK. We also examine a number of different theoretical perspectives from psychoanalysis, social constructionism and post-modernism that we argue have been and are currently relevant to social work practice with lesbians and gay men.

Historically, some of these ideas have been used as tools to 'liberate' and 'oppress' lesbians and gay men and therefore a closer analysis is required. The influence of this social, political and theoretical history is then considered in terms of current discourses and the impact of this on social work practice.

A brief overview of lesbian and gay history relevant to social work

Others have recorded the details of lesbian and gay history in the UK (Blasius and Phelan, 1997; Stryker and Whittle, 2006; Cook et al., 2007; Jennings, 2007) and offer a full and interesting commentary. It is not our intention to attempt to replicate such endeavours but rather to note key moments that have impacted on social work (Brown, 1998a).

Chapter 2 notes the development of both criminalising and oppressive legislation towards lesbians and gay men and the development of equalities legislation since the turn of the century. Legislation and social policy initiatives are dependent on their historical context and this is clearly illustrated in this arena.

A key moment in the history of lesbian and gay rights was the event known as 'Stonewall' in 1969. Although this took place in Greenwich Village, New York, it had international ramifications. 'Stonewall' refers to three days of rioting that resulted from a police raid on a club in Greenwich Village. These raids were commonplace at the time but the resistance that the New York police encountered on this particular occasion was not. This event was important symbolically as it signified the 'beginning' of gay pride and lesbian and gay resistance. A subsequent meeting at the London School of Economics arranged by Aubrey Walker and Bob Mellors, both of whom had been influenced by events in America, signalled the birth and development of the Gay Liberation Front (GLF) in the UK. The GLF had an explicit 'left' agenda and incorporated both socialist and feminist ideas.

If Stonewall is associated with the radical politicisation of lesbians and gay men and the development of the GLF in the UK in the 1960s, the publication of the Wolfenden Report in 1957 (Wolfenden, 1957) is associated with the development of 'liberal reformist' lesbian and gay politics in the UK. This report was the outcome of a Home Office committee's findings on homosexuality and prostitution. After three years of deliberations the Report recommended the decriminalisation of consensual sex between men over 21. It took another ten years before this was enacted in the Sexual Offences Act 1967 which made sex between consenting men in private legal. The Homosexual Law Reform Society was formed in 1958 to agitate for reform to enable the Wolfenden recommendations to be realised. Another such group, the Committee for Homosexual Equality, was formed in 1969 (changing its name from Committee to Campaign (CHE) in 1971) and was a predominately gay male organisation arguing for equality. Mills et al. describe the CHE as being more 'respectable' than the GLF with a tighter structure and a broader political base (2007: 183). The main difference between the CHE and the GLF was that the CHE was both a social and liberal campaigning organisation using more traditional methods whilst the GLF was an organisation associated with left liberation politics:

> Within lesbian and gay activist politics, there has always been and there still remains the polarised binary positions of reformism versus liberation; lobbying versus 'in your face' direct action; reasoned passion versus raw passion. In Britain, these different positions were held in the 1970s by the Campaign for Homosexual Equality (CHE) representing reasoned lobbying, while the Gay Liberation front (GLF) held the mantle of passionate direct action. (Brown, 1998a: 31)

A similar pattern emerged in the 1990s in the UK with the organisation 'Outrage' associated with transformationalist politics, and the political lobbying group Stonewall associated with reformist politics. Brown has argued elsewhere that 'this is just a particular construction of a set of complex realities'(1998a: 31). However:

> Crudely, the 'reformist' position argued for equal rights for lesbians and gay men and access to the same rights as heterosexuals, while the 'transformationists' argued for the deconstruction of notions of gender and sexuality. (1998a: 31)

We would argue that with the exception of Hicks (2000; 2005a) much of the writing about social work with lesbians and gay men has been within the 'reformist' tradition, arguing for equitable treatment rather than the transformation of the accepted orthodoxies associated with sexuality, relationships and the construction of the family. We maintain that for the realisation of social and political change both the radical and liberal positions are necessary.

Outrage was symbolically important as it signified a particular quality of resistance and celebratory politics (reminiscent of some of the GLF activities), responding to a specific historical moment associated with a number of factors. Firstly, a Conservative Government came to power in 1979 and focused attention through a number of social policy debates on lesbians and gay men as symbols of 'the decay of civilisation' (see Chapter 2). Secondly, Outrage responded to the homophobia unleashed by the association of HIV/AIDS with gay male sexuality. Thirdly, Outrage represented a practical interpretation and application of Queer politics. Queer theory/politics has been influential in gender and sexualities studies within higher education from the late 1980s. The reclamation of the term 'Queer' was linked to Queer theory and is associated more generally with post-modernism. Whilst post-modernism has had some impact on social work knowledge (Healy, 2000; 2005; Fook, 2002; Hicks, 2005a), Queer politics has mostly passed social work by.

Another major factor in the development of lesbian and gay politics and organisation was the impact of the second wave of the women's movement from the 1960s onwards (Jennings, 2007). This movement brought together lesbian and feminist political discourses. It was within this area that much of the radical thinking about social work and feminism as well as social work with lesbians and gay men took place. The women and social work conferences held in the 1980s had a significant focus on lesbian and gay issues in social work. This was mirrored within the Lesbian and Gay NALGO conferences during the 1980s where much of the discussions had a specific feminist and socialist flavour. However, although conference discussions were concerned about such debates, this didn't always translate into social work publications of the time. Brown comments that 'recent feminist social work literature has had little, beyond generalities to say about lesbians' (1992: 204). In fact, some of the most sophisticated writing about social work with lesbians and gay men came out of the Radical Social Work tradition of the 1970s and early 1980s (Hart and Richardson, 1981; Hart, 1980).

The lesbian and gay NALGO conferences were important in that their content did not differentiate the position of worker and client but sought to emphasise their commonalities as lesbians and gay men. Healy comments:

> Critical practice discourses frequently refer to 'workers' and 'service users' as though each identity group is homogeneous and entirely distinct, thus neglecting the differences within each category and the commonalities across them. (Healy, 2000: 40)

The 1980s NALGO conferences were an example of an exception to this.

From 1979 the 'New Right' Conservative Government placed great emphasis on trying to marginalise lesbians and gay men and this was acted out through various social policy debates and initiatives. This is covered in Chapter 2. During this time there were a number of positive developments within local government that were to impact on social work. Cooper (1994) has documented the rise of lesbian and gay political influence and organisation:

> Municipal lesbian and gay work emerged at the intersection of several different processes: the growing size and confidence of Britain's lesbian and gay communities; the institutionalisation of the new urban left; identity politics; and the developing influence of feminism within local politics. More particularly, the policies were precipitated by the work of lesbian and gay activists in the Labour party, in local government employment, and as elected council members. (Cooper, 1994: 2)

Although these political and social processes were not a priority for many Local Authorities, those that did take on board the quality of employment and service delivery to lesbians and gay men did have an influence on both social work and social policy more generally. However, it was many years before some of these initiatives were translated into protective legislation in the form of the Equality Act 2006 and the Sexual Orientation Regulations 2007.

One of the most significant local government developments relevant to social work with lesbians and gay men in the 1980s were the initiatives taken by the Greater London Council (GLC). Under the leadership of Ken Livingstone, the GLC disseminated good practice guidelines for the delivery of public services to lesbians and gay men. Some of the comments made in these publications about the poor quality of social work with lesbians and gay men are as relevant today as they were when they were first published (GLC, 1986; GLC and the GLC Gay Working Party, 1985).

These municipal developments and the increasing visibility of lesbians and gay men in the trade union movement meant that the question of equitable treatment of lesbians and gay men started to be seriously addressed within some Local Authorities. This took place in the context of other communities also arguing for autonomous organisations within trade unions and within the Labour party.

Lesbians and gay men within the trade union movement began to make links with other groups' industrial actions which increased their visibility as well as enabled some degree of mainstreaming. This was best demonstrated when 'miners and their families led the Gay Pride March in 1985, the biggest yet with over 15,000 participants. The same year, the TUC passed resolutions on gay and lesbian rights in the workplace' (Cook et al., 2007: 186). This period of activity meant that some Local Authorities started to include 'sexual orientation' within their equal opportunities policies. Post the Equality Act 2006 and the decriminalisation of all gay male sexual activities, this might not seem important. However, during the 1980s this was highly significant as it was the only protection that lesbian and gay employees, carers and clients were afforded. It also signified the advanced nature of Labour-led local authority thinking in this arena compared with the overt hostility that the Conservative Government exhibited.

The rising visibility of lesbians and gay men we refer to above is probably most obvious in their increasing presence within popular culture, entertainment and commerce. Although there is still some stereotyping of lesbians and gay men in media portrayals, the economic significance of lesbians and gay men has been demonstrated through commercial developments. This commercial presence, for example in Old Compton Street in London and Canal Street in Manchester, has meant that the public has been more exposed to lesbians and gay men, their varied and various lifestyles as well as their ordinariness. This commercial presence has ensured that lesbians and gay men have entered the public consciousness as more than two dimensional stereotypes.

Against the above backdrop, in 1997 the Labour Government utilised and built upon fertile ground already developed through lesbian and gay commercial, political and social activity that stretched back many decades. However, the impact was somewhat muted by the delays in legislative changes related to the rights of lesbians and gay men until some years after their election. The social policy and legislative changes initiated and realised by New Labour will be covered in Chapter 2. Broadly, this legal and policy framework specifically relevant to lesbians and gay men included: opportunities to parent and have that parenting protected and recognised; to have their intimate relationship commitments recognised and protected, and the decriminalisation of male same-sex sexual activities.

Some of these social policy and legislative developments have exposed, through public and policy debates, the nature and strength of continuing hostility and ambivalence towards lesbian and gay equality. Social work at the end of the first decade of the twenty-first century is in a different position than it was 20 years ago. It could be argued that social work in the 1980s was one of the professions at the forefront of arguing for lesbian and gay equality as demonstrated through social workers' involvement within trade union as well as labour and community activism (Brown, 1998a). Social work in 2011 sits within a changed legislative landscape which is unrecognisable from the one it occupied in the 1980s or indeed the 1990s. This changed landscape places social work in a fundamentally different position. Having been at the forefront of considerations of equitable treatment of lesbians and gay men, having historically been a major player in the oppression of them, we argue that social work is now in need of serious reflection on its practices to make it at least compliant with current legislative requirements. Creative, innovative and imaginative social work should enable the possibility of practice that addresses the individuality and specificity of every client and carer whilst acknowledging their cultural, racial, familial, social and political location.

Discourses on sexuality influencing social work practice with lesbians and gay men

Hicks (2005a: 151) argues that 'social work practitioners should think about a range of theories of sexuality … and develop a reflexive approach' to their understanding of sexuality in practice. We present an overview of ideas about sexuality, including contributions from Queer theory, sexuality studies, sociology and psychology, which have influenced current understanding of social work with lesbians and gay men. We cover a variety of ideas and thinkers that we consider to have been influential on social work's conceptualisation of homosexuality. As well as considering some aspects of the work of Freud, Marx, Foucault and Butler, we also identify relevant discourses of the past 20 years, such as feminism, Queer theory and post-modernism and discuss how they have influenced the debate and development of ideas relating to sexuality and social work.

What is discourse?

Parton defines discourses as:

> structures of knowledge, claims and practices through which we understand, explain and decide things … they also define obligations and determine the distribution of responsibilities and authorities for different categories of

persons such as parents, children, social workers, doctors, lawyers and so on. They are impersonal forms, existing independently of any of these persons as individuals … they are frameworks or grids of social organisations that make some social actions possible while precluding others. (1994: 13)

Foucault wrote that, 'there is no reality outside of discourse' (1981: 67). He identified four salient elements. Firstly, discourses are produced by specific conventions and procedures that exist within particular periods of time and cultural contexts. We contend that ideas are historically, geographically, politically and socially located and understanding the specificity of this is crucial to avoiding 'throwing the baby out with the bath water'. Ideas influence the language we use to describe situations, circumstances and people, and change over time; for example, it was commonplace to hear the term 'client' used 20 years ago whereas currently 'service user' is seen as the accepted term with little understanding of the different discourses surrounding the two expressions. Changing terminology does not in and of itself alter power relations (Ryan with Thomas, 1987; McLaughlin, 2009).

Secondly, discourses and power are interrelated, and therefore knowledge cannot ever be objective, or seen as 'truth', but is defined by power relations. An example of this is the importance that government agencies are placing on interventions underpinned by behavioural ideas, as they are seen to be 'evidenced based' and 'outcome focused'. Such application of 'knowledge' includes the embedded nature of social learning theories in aspects of the 'Care Matters' White Paper (DfES, 2007) such as the Multi-Dimensional Treatment Foster Care programme.

Thirdly, discourses are irregular and incongruous, conflicting and opposing. Discourses are complex and contradictory. Foucault challenged the belief that development of ideas over time is progressive and linear. In terms of application to social work, Healy states that:

the discourses of social work or medicine a century ago bear little resemblance to their contemporary forms. Even so, social workers are not more 'free' now than they were in a previous historical epoch; rather, they have different possibilities for action. (2000: 41)

Fourthly, rather than seeking any hidden truth or deeper meaning from discourses separate from their practical manifestation, the tangible productions and effects of discourses are vitally important. It is in this practical manifestation, 'the principle of exteriority', that the structure and shape and limitations are exposed, including inherent power relationships (Healy, 2000: 40–1).

Healy (2005) identifies three key discourses within social work: 'dominant' discourses (including biomedicine, economics and the law); 'service' discourses (including discourses from psychology and sociology); and 'alternative service' discourses (including those from consumer rights movements, religion and spirituality). A number of psychological and sociological discourses pertaining to sexuality will be examined in this chapter. Chapters 2 and 5 address legal areas and religious issues relevant to social work and sexuality respectively.

The analysis of discourse is therefore concerned with highlighting the ways in which our use of language is constructed and how it reflects hidden ideologies in terms of how we acquire specific knowledge and the meaning we give to it. Discourses influence our understanding about who we are and our relationship with others. In terms of sexuality for example, heteronormativity (an assumption that heterosexuality is the norm) is a dominant discourse within our society, which permeates everything about language, the way our society is organised and what is given social value. However, there are other discourses which challenge heteronormativity as a given reality and present different views about the value of not being heterosexual, and indeed question the need for identity labels at all. We will explore these later in the chapter.

Essentialism, social constructionism and post-modernism: Marx, Freud, Lacan, Derrida, Foucault, Butler and Weeks

We have already highlighted some of the difficulties in defining the term 'sexuality' in the introduction to this book. Developments in discourses about sexuality are not linear. Alongside the expansion of post-modernist thought, pockets of 'biological determinism' are still located in arguments over the causes of homosexuality. There are two positions that have been posited in relation to biological causation of homosexuality that remain influential: hormonal and neurological. Myers and Milner (2007) outline some of the research findings that both support and refute these positions. They argue that, 'biomedical understandings of sex and gender have tended to be dominant in Western thinking and these have influenced social work and social care practices' (2007: 15). The degree of certainty that such a position affords has proved to be attractive as it enables certainty in an area of ambiguity. These ideas have been attractive to conservative thinkers and policy makers but also to some lesbians and gay men. The argument is that if people's sexual orientation is biomedically determined and that lesbians and gay men are

a minority, then they should be afforded protection and rights accordingly. However attractive this certainty of 'we can't help being gay – we
were born that way' might appear, there are limits to this position in
terms of the political ground that is occupied by such attempts at biological unification. Seidman comments that 'many activists and intel-
lectuals moved in the opposite direction, affirming a stronger thesis of
the social construction of homosexuality that took the form of a radical
politics of difference' (1996: 11).

Dualistic comparator terms, such as 'natural' and 'un-natural', continue to influence discourse. Social and cultural constructs now play a
major role in the theorising of sexuality. This next section will highlight
some of the important thinkers whose work has significantly influenced
discussion and discourse in this area.

Karl Marx (1818–1883)   Marx's work remains influential within social
work (Mullaly, 1997; Jordan, 1990; Ferguson, 2008). Most renowned for
his work critiquing capitalism, Marx's contribution to discourses about
sexuality is linked to his views on the family. He saw the family as an
important organisation in maintaining the means of production via
reproduction of the proletariat to support manufacturing, and in reinforcing the continuation of power, influence and control by the bour-
geoisie via heredity and blood lineage. Engels (1902) expanded these
ideas by linking the patriarchal nature of industrial society to the family
being viewed by the State as a private entity, the members of which
were the property of men and where marriage between men and
women legitimated sexual activity. Women supposedly gained respect-
ability and stability from this arrangement. The family, gender and sexuality are closely linked and this has been commented on extensively by
Marxist feminist scholars. Marxist criticisms of women's position in the
family pointed to the inequality in terms of ownership, reproduction,
sexual activity and the worth given to domestic labour (Wilson, 1977;
Rowbotham, 1972; 1973).

Marxism was a cornerstone of the UK Radical Social Work movement in the 1970s (Bailey and Brake, 1975; Corrigan and Leonard, 1978;
Brake and Bailey, 1980), and these publications contained some of the
first critical pieces about sexuality and social work (Milligan, 1975; Hart,
1980) before the UK publication of Hart and Richardson's book on
homosexuality and social work (Hart and Richardson, 1981). This
period of academic productivity in the area of social work and sexuality
should be seen within the wider social and political context of increased

visibility and activity of lesbians and gay men covered earlier in this chapter.

Sigmund Freud (1856–1939)   One of the major theoretical influences on social work knowledge has been psychoanalysis (Yelloly, 1980; Pearson et al., 1988; Bower, 2005). A comprehensive discussion about and critique of psychoanalysis and homosexuality is beyond the remit of this chapter (see O'Connor and Ryan, 1993; Dean and Lane, 2001; Weeks, 2003). Freud's discussion of pre-Oedipal and Oedipal stages of psychosexual development and the development of individuation and separation from the mother are important in how we understand the role of gender and its development both at a conscious and unconscious level. Freud believed that, 'no self comes into being that is not gendered' (Beasley, 2005: 54). Freud's ideas about infant universal bisexuality at a pre-Oedipal stage are important in terms of explaining desire and pleasure for very young babies as a body experience often concentrated on the mouth and anus. This manifestation of desire and pleasure changes over time to focus on the genitals. Awareness of genitals begins to shape a baby's developing understanding of a sense of 'self' in relation to 'other' (most notably, babies' growing awareness of themselves as separate from their mothers), and in relation to gender. The Oedipal stage is where the role of what Freud termed the 'mother figure and father figure' often, but not necessarily (for Freud) the child's assumed parents, becomes important in terms of how children relate to each of them as separate individuals at unconscious as well as conscious levels (Beasley, 2005: 53). Freud argued that these gender differences of the two primary adult figures were key to the successful developmental processes of children, with children still finding their mother 'desirable' but moving away or rejecting her in order to move towards a sense of self/separateness. Freud argued that this process of separation from the mother is represented by the male or father figure, symbolised by the penis. To not have a penis is to be castrated, that is to be a woman; within a dualistic notion/framework of gender definitions. Being a woman was less powerful and had less status than being a man. The biological sex characteristics of boys and girls then determine the processes children go through in order to understand their gender assignment and how this links to their development accordingly. This is what Freud refers to as 'gendered positioning' (Dean and Lane, 2001; Beasley, 2005). Boys become competitors with their father figure for the attention of their mother, because they also have a penis like their father, whilst girls establish strong links with their father because of desire towards the penis and envy because they do not have one. The process girls go through is more complicated in terms of not only a change of focus of (initially homosexual) desire from mother figure to father figure, but also creating a different body desire and pleasure based around the penis. Freud would say this is an effort of the girl/woman to obtain a penis. Creith comments that:

> Whilst the inconsistencies and ambiguities in Freud's own thinking, as evidenced in his writing, have allowed for pathological interpretations of 'homosexuality', his emphasis on the delicate psychic construction of our sexualities and the role of the unconscious is invaluable. (Creith, 1996: 144)

Beasley suggests that Freud's work is not simply 'modernist' in perspective, in terms of seeking a fundamental 'truth' about the human psyche. There are elements of his ideas which appear 'post-modernist' in terms of how he understands the role of power and the identification of gender within the development of 'self':

> The unconscious keeps leaking into the conscious such that you can never know yourself. Nor can the self ever be fully knowable, as the unconscious is largely lost to us, 'forgotten', repressed. What is post-modern here is Freud's view that there is no set or fixed essence, no original 'true' self. (Beasley, 2005: 63)

However, although noting the considerable influence of psychoanalysis on the ideas of later theorists such as Foucault and Butler, the historical relationship between psychoanalysis and homosexuality is not straightforward. O'Connor and Ryan describe it as:

> one of the most problematic areas of psychoanalysis … [it] has seen all homosexuality as various forms of pathology, perversity or immaturity. It provides no articulated conception within its own terms of an integrated, non-perverse, mature and manifest homosexuality, or of what is required to achieve this. (O'Connor and Ryan, 1993: 9)

The authors argue that as long as psychoanalysis remains within an ontological framework, it cannot allow for 'a theory of separation, of differences' (1993: 266). Within a discussion exploring the meaning of 'desire' and 'identity' which falls outside of the construction of 'normal' (hetero)sexual development, O'Connor and Ryan point towards the development of pluralism within psychoanalysis to reflect the theoretical and social changes within society more generally (1993: 271). Dean and Lane (2001) go on to suggest that this problematic relationship between psychoanalysis and homosexuality does not stem from Freud's original work, but from the work of analysts after Freud, such as Jung and Adler, who:

> helped formalise an institutional split between the Freudians who believed that homosexuality was an unconscious possibility in everyone, and those who accepted Jung and Adler's claims that homosexuality signalled a type of person with a fairly predictable relationship to the world. (Dean and Lane, 2001: 12)

Other more conservative psychoanalysts such as Rado, Bergler and Bieber wrote about an un-natural and pathological homosexuality that could be 'cured' (Dean and Lane, 2001). Llewellyn et al. (2008) argue that such conservative readings of Freud led to, 'a labelling of lesbians and gay men as deviant and historically led to interventions based on "curing people from homosexuality"'(2008: 166). Creith comments that:

> Aware of the complex nature of unconscious desire, Freud's own view of homosexuality was one of non judgementalism as in his letter to the mother of a (male) homosexual: 'homosexuality is assuredly no advantage; but it is nothing to be ashamed of, no vice, no degradation; it cannot be classified as an illness; we consider it to be a variation of the sexual function produced by a certain arrest of development. (1996: 145–6)

Creith goes on to point out that his use of the term 'arrested development' left the floodgates open for others then to pathologise homosexuality.

The relationship between psychoanalysis and homosexuality has also been heavily influenced by social factors, including the gay liberation and feminist movements in the USA and in Europe and by the work of academics from other disciplines. Dean and Lane comment that:

> [I]t is telling that the most innovative recent psychoanalytic work on sexuality derives not from psychoanalytic institutions but from university departments of language and literature. This strange sociological circumstance confirms the persistent tension between psychoanalytic concepts and clinical institutions. (2001: 25)

With regard to sexuality, along with the work of psychoanalyst Jacques Lacan (whose work is also influential outside the field of psychoanalysis), the works of three other theorists are important in this regard: Jacques Derrida, Michel Foucault and Judith Butler.

Jacques Lacan (1901–1981)   Lacan is one of the most significant and influential psychoanalysts since Freud. He reinterpreted Freud's position on sexuality from being largely biologically determined to something located firmly within a social/cultural framework. 'Lacan sees gender difference as a psychosocial construction through positioning in language rather than responses to literal bodily forms' (Beasley, 2005: 55). Lacan's reframing of Freud's work on sexuality is somewhat more palatable for many feminists in terms of his use of symbolism and symbolic order. His comments about the acquisition and meaning of language and his explanations of the development of the unconscious are then used to explain his theories of desire and sexual difference. Lacan saw masculinity and femininity as constructs that could be accessible and apply to both men and women. Sexual difference is understood not through biology but through men and women's relationship to the 'phallus' – a psychosocial concept which represents social power and masculine authority (Beasley, 2005). He distinguished between 'having' and 'being' the phallus; masculinity 'involves the posture or pretence of having the phallus, whilst femininity involves the masquerade of being the phallus' (Homer, 2005: 95). Lacan comments:

> in order to be the phallus, that is to say the signifier of the desire of the Other, [that] a woman will reject an essential part of femininity, namely, all her attributes in the masquerade. It is for that which she is not that she wishes to be desired as well as loved. (Lacan, 1977 [1958]: 289–90)

These are complex and revolutionary ideas in terms of challenging and building on Freud's perceptions of the development of sexuality. Lacan's work in language acquisition and the symbolic moved ideas about gender identification and sexuality away from mainly biological definitions to a process of 'becoming', which also recognised the influences of cultural and social processes. However, despite this identification, Lacan, like Freud, understood the gender hierarchy as inevitable (Beasley, 2005: 67).

Jacques Derrida (1930–2004)   The French philosopher Jacques Derrida's work on deconstruction (describing and transforming) is also influential. Derrida criticises a use of language where 'truth' is seen outside time and change, stressing the 'variety of meanings, interpretations, ranges of reference ...' and '... analyses difference primarily in terms of language functioning' (O'Connor and Ryan, 1993: 19). For example, deconstruction within post-modern thinking (for example, the deconstruction of such dichotomies as: man/woman; good/bad; heterosexual/homosexual; self/other; you/me; us/them; and north/south; east/west; black/white) can highlight and explain the existence of dualistic models and categories where hierarchy and power are also implicitly or explicitly present. Another example of a variety of meanings is the many influential commentators in the area of sexuality studies who have remarked on the problematic use of the term 'sexuality' (Foucault, 1978; Butler, 1990; Weeks, 2003; Hicks, 2005a) regarding definition, identity and power. Deconstruction doesn't necessarily lead to changing this directly but helps as a form of questioning, which can then influence understanding.

Michel Foucault (1926–1984) Michel Foucault's writing on a wide range of topics including the prison service and psychiatry showed how talented and influential this thinker was in his contributions to critical comment and developments in a number of broad and diverse areas. In terms of his views on sexuality, Foucault commented that 'sexuality must not be thought of as a kind of natural given which power tries to hold in check, or as an obscure domain which knowledge tries gradually to uncover. It is the name that can be given to a historical construct' (1978: 105). Foucault's ideas about the relationship between sex and power as a process through which sexual identity is created or constructed within societies transformed debates about sexuality. He believed that minority sexual identities that were marginalised by society were not just victims of power but were actually produced by power and are an intrinsic part of how societies organise themselves (Beasley, 2005: 165). This has ramifications for how we think about identity based politics and will be explored in Chapter 3.

In addition, Beasley comments on the efforts made by Foucault to describe people:

> in terms of their social construction by power relations and hence as having no foundational essence or core … he endorses the political project of remaking the self 'as a work of art' in ways which resist the forms of individuality … hence reassembling the socially formed components in myriad ways. (2005: 109)

Cooper discusses Foucault's use of the concept of power, emphasising:

> the structuring capacity of power rather than focusing solely on 'power over' or power as prohibition … he makes room for people's complex relationship

to power in contrast to models which divide people into those who exercise power and those who have it exercised upon them. (2004: 78)

Cooper also comments that:

> Liberal scholarship that emphasises the importance of formal equality between men and women, for instance, has often ignored the cultural, social and disciplinary factors that not only shape capacity, but also shape the conversion of capacity into action. (Cooper, 2004: 79)

Although hugely influential in the field of sexuality studies, Foucault's analysis of sexuality has been criticised by many feminists as 'gender-blind', although many writers have applied his ideas to gender studies (Beasley, 2005: 165–6).

Judith Butler (1956–)   Judith Butler's work is influenced by Foucault and has been significant in the development of post-modern feminist discourses and studies about sexuality, as well as other areas. Stryker and Whittle comment that, 'Judith Butler's central tenet is that the hegemonic power of heteronormativity produces all forms of the body, sex and gender' (2006: 183). In terms of Butler's work on identity, Beasley states that, '[Butler] replaces the notion of a fixed essential identity with a disclaimer, with a resistance to identity by revealing it to be a fiction' (2005: 105). Butler believes that gender identity is 'performative', a 'fabrication', a 'truth effect', and she highlights the relationship between identity and power in terms of how 'identity is a product of power, not a means of overcoming it (no matter how many identity differences are embraced by identity politics)' (Beasley, 2005: 105). She is sympathetic to psychoanalysis in terms of its ability to explain how and why sexuality falls short of the social and cultural constructs through which it is most commonly understood and played out:

> There is no better theory for grasping the workings of fantasy construed not as a set of projections on an internal screen but as part of human rationality itself. It is on the basis of this insight that we can come to understand how fantasy is essential to an experience of one's own body, or that of another, as gendered. (Butler, 2004: 14–15)

Butler also says that 'psychoanalysis has sometimes been used to shore up the notion of a primary sexual difference that forms the core of an individual's psychic life' (2004: 14). She points out that this is predicated

upon an assumption of heterosexual intercourse, and other psychoanalytic concepts such as the 'primal scene' and the 'oedipal scenario'.

> But if the egg or sperm comes from elsewhere, and is not attached to a per-
> son called 'parent', or if the parents who are making love are not hetero-
> sexual or not reproductive, then it would seem that a new psychic topography
> is required. (Butler, 2004: 14)

Her work has been criticised by feminists writing from other theoretical
perspectives. Liberal feminist Martha Nussbaum accuses Butler of 'playing at abstract rebellious transgression' (Beasley, 2005: 41); and socialist
pro feminist Bob Connell rejects Butler's work because it has not
accounted for the 'material social aspects of gender such as child care,
institutional life and work' (Beasley, 2005: 226). However, in terms of
revolutionising ideas around identity, Butler remains influential.
Featherstone and Green (2009) offer a summary of Butler's ideas and
how they relate to social work.

Sexuality studies: Jeffrey Weeks (1945–) Another critical area contributing to the development of knowledge about sexuality has been sexuality studies. The rise of sexuality studies is related to the political activism
of the 1960s and 1970s and the resulting impact on the academy.
Although historically sexuality studies has been biased towards gay men,
issues for lesbians, transsexuals, transvestites, transgender and intersex
people have also been covered to a lesser extent. Considerable debate
occurs within the field about definitions of sexuality and identities
contained therein, and, as with most areas of academic study there are
a variety of theoretical positions covered within the literature. These
range from liberal and assimilationist positions to more radical forms of
thinking which reject any attempt to define identity, whether it be
sexuality or gender.

One of the well-known academics within sexuality studies is Jeffrey
Weeks. His work is located within a social constructionist position. He
argues that 'the meanings we give to "sexuality" are socially organised,
sustained by a variety of languages, which seek to tell us what sex is,
what it ought to be – and what it could be' (2003: 7). In response to the
'essentialist' (a single, basic, uniform pattern ordained by nature itself)
(Singer, 1973, cited in Weeks, 2003: 7), 'reductionist' (reducing the complexity of something to 'the imagined simplicities of its constituent unit)
(2003: 7) and 'deterministic' (humans are controlled by inner drives –
genes, hormones, instincts or the unconscious) (2003: 7) approach to

sex, Weeks argues for the development of a non-essentialist theory of sexuality. This acknowledges the complexity of sexuality within a framework of 'radical pluralism' (2003: 122) which challenges 'absolutes without falling into the trap of saying no values are possible "anything goes"' (Weeks, 2003: 9), and is based on an appreciation of diversity.

> Moral pluralism begins with a different belief: that sex in itself is neither good nor bad, but is rather a field of possibilities and potentialities, all of which must be judged by the context in which they occur. It opens the way then, to acceptance of diversity as the norm of our culture and the appropriate means of thinking about sexuality. (Weeks, 2003: 122)

Weeks has been critical of Queer theory. His writing supports a qualified use of 'identity' within its 'social fixity', 'he attends to social location, materiality, social structure and stability in identities' (Beasley, 2005: 148) as opposed to its deconstruction, which is the position of queer theorists. This position is not assimilationist nor radically transformative, but instead argues coherently for the middle ground, where advancement in thinking and transformation of people's lives via governmental and legislative processes, are not necessarily at odds with each other.

Weeks' work has also been criticised by feminist writers as not taking gender issues into account in his analysis (Beasley, 2005: 148–9), and this remains a criticism of sexuality studies more generally.

Queer theory

The term 'queer' is an example of how language use can change negative meanings and associations of given words. Until the 1990s, 'queer' was a derogatory term used to describe gay men and to a lesser extent lesbians. This word has been 'reclaimed' by activists, such as Outrage and others, and is now used commonly as a quick-hand way of referring to LGBTI (lesbian, gay, bisexual, transgender and intersex). However, its use is also connected with post-modern perspectives within sexuality studies. Queer theory is associated with more radical positions concerning sexual and any other form of identity, opposing any fixed categorisation of identity whether gender based or based on sexual practice, and instead viewing these categorisations as socially constructed. Queer theory argues for a fluid, constant redefinition of people's sexual/gender choices and argues that this process is continuous, transgressive and also potentially rebellious. Queer theory is heavily influenced by the work of Foucault, Butler – specifically her work *Gender Trouble* (1990), and

Eve Kosofsky Sedgwick, whose work *Epistemology of the Closet* (1990) was considered groundbreaking, and is still read widely.

> *Epistemology of the Closet*, originally published in 1990, is seen as a seminal text in the rise of queer theory alongside another text, Judith Butler's *Gender Trouble*, which was published in the same year. These texts effectively put into discourse questions about a medley of cultural and political epistemes: on identity, on actions, on performance, and on language ... Epistemology is a profound study on how we live our life in culture, and how our actions, identities, and ethics are symptomatic effects of various networks of power at work in society. (Bianco, 2008)

Feminism

The connection between sexuality studies and the second wave of feminism is important to acknowledge, as is the link between Queer theory and the third wave of feminism. Feminism, unlike sexuality studies, has a long history that offers many different perspectives on the emancipation of women and gender/sex constructions, relationships and connections. It is beyond the remit of this book to provide a critical summary and commentary of the history of feminism, including a discussion about how sexuality has been understood and debated within this history. However, the alliances forged between various groups defined through identity have not been easy at times. The politics surrounding identity has played a role within these alliances (or lack of alliances). Some of the issues around the use of the term 'identity' are discussed in Chapter 3.

There are three 'waves' of feminism acknowledged within the literature (Kempe and Squires, 1998; Beasley, 1999; 2005). The first wave refers to nineteenth and early twentieth century activity associated with the suffragette movement and their endeavours to gain the vote for women. There was also political struggle to change other laws of the time which gave men 'ownership' of women and children via marriage. The second wave of feminism refers to women's political activity from the 1960s through to the 1980s, which was intent on ending sex discrimination and creating equality for women. The third wave of feminism brought post-structural interpretations of gender and sexuality to feminism, moving beyond universal and essentialist definitions of women which were considered to favour white middle-class heterosexual women. These new ideas embraced contradictions and conflict, and accommodated diversity as part of the lived experience of women.

The fluidity of our understandings of gender, the power and use of language, and the restrictions of identity labels have all been part of this re-interpretation of feminism.

The categorisation of the different strands of feminism remains contested (Cooper, 1995; Kempe and Squires, 1998; Beasley, 1999; 2005). For the purposes of this publication we identify five main feminist perspectives which illustrate the diversity within the term 'feminism'. Liberal feminism was concerned with inequalities in opportunity between men and women and how change can occur within existing political, social and economic structures. Socialist feminism focused on women's oppression as part of wider social inequalities in a class-based capitalist social structure. Radical feminism was concerned with patriarchy and believed that full equality cannot exist between men and women without a complete change to the patriarchal system. Black feminism focused on the diversity and value of black women's experience, which was by far the majority of the world's female population. Post-modern feminism focused on the cultural and social discourses in society that organise understandings of and constraints placed on both women and men. Judith Butler's work is associated with post-modern feminism.

Relevance to social work   ■ ■ ■ ■ ■ ■

Why is the material we have covered in this chapter relevant to social work with lesbians and gay men? History and ideas are relevant to social work practice today. A common criticism of social workers is that they are sometimes both atheoretical and ahistorical and concerned only with the specificity of their day-to-day practice rather than the development of ideas and knowledge that will improve their practice. This is problematic. Social work, unlike many other professions such as medicine, lacks a distinct and discrete body of knowledge. Social work's relationship with theory and different discourses has at best been tenuous and at worst, in this area of practice, been misapplied to the detriment of lesbians and gay men. Stanley comments:

> Social work's relationship to theory has always been problematic and the
> translation of psychological theory into social work practice has at times
> entailed crude appropriation rather than informed applications of complex
> theoretical models. (Stanley, 1999: 20)

In this chapter, we have covered a number of theorists that we argue have influenced social work with lesbians and gay men. This list is not exhaustive. How their influence has been interpreted and experienced is difficult to quantify. For example, Freudian ideas have become absorbed by society in an implicit rather than an explicit fashion and their use and misuse can be seen in accounts of 1960s social casework (Wilson, 1977). Part of the misapplication of some ideas that we have covered above has been to do with a lack of tenacity on behalf of social work as a profession to understand, apply and develop complex ideas drawn from philosophy, sociology and psychology. For example, Judith Butler's ideas about the construction of gender through language rather than biology challenge how we understand and explain sexuality. This requires a fundamental reappraisal of many of the norms that social work takes for granted about sexuality and relationships. Similarly, Sedgwick's views about the binary homo/hetero sexuality are also helpful in re-evaluating how normative understandings of heterosexuality are insidious within Western culture, and oversimplify complex processes:

> [A] person can never embody an identity, instead, it functions as a container of sorts that is imposed upon the person by society. Thus the implicit sarcasm of Sedgwick's first axiom: 'People are different from each other.' This axiom may seem obvious, but it is fascinating, Sedgwick maintains, how methodologically and linguistically we are unable to account for difference: 'A tiny number of inconceivably coarse axes of categorization have been painstakingly inscribed in current critical and political thought: gender, race, class, nationality, sexual orientation are pretty much the available distinctions. They, with the associated demonstrations of the mechanisms by which they are constructed and reproduced, are indispensable, and they may indeed override all or some other forms of difference and similarity'. (Bianco, 2008)

Effective social work practitioners have to engage with many of these theoretical ideas to better understand how sexuality is viewed, how labels affect people and the consequential social and political positioning of lesbians and gay men. In examining the writings of the theorists above, we have attempted to re-frame or re-interpret some of the perceived truths that permeate social work's unquestioning understandings of sexuality, which are commonly heteronormative.

Not having a distinct knowledge base of its own, social work has absorbed ideas and discourses from other disciplines, including psychology, sociology and philosophy, which have themselves been influenced by their location within particular social, historical and political contexts. This is relevant to historical and contemporary understandings of homosexuality and practices with lesbians and gay men. The challenge for social workers is to remain abreast of debates, ideas and developments within other disciplines, such as the ones discussed in this chapter that can inform our practice. One of the problematic unforeseen consequences of the emphasis on evidence based practice focusing on social work interventions is that we can lose the 'bigger picture', informed by ideas from philosophy, politics, social geography, history, art, and literature. These ideas will in turn benefit our understandings of both the potentiality and fallibility of human beings and the complexity of their interactions with others. We argue that this breadth of knowledge will ultimately improve the quality and effectiveness of social work interventions.

Post-modernism has been influential within theories about gender and sexuality studies. As a profession, social work's engagement with this in terms of how it thinks about sexuality has been limited. Myers and Milner (2007) and Hicks' (2005a) work are examples of the social work academy's acknowledgement of post-modernism's relevance to sexuality. Within social work generally, other social work theorists have looked at post-modernism. For example, Parton and O'Byrne (2000), Parton (2006), Healy (2000; 2005), Garrett (2003) Pease and Fook (1999), Fook (2002) and McCarthy (1999) have been raising and discussing social constructionist and post-modern perspectives for some time, identifying the relevance of these ideas for social work in general. This is exciting in terms of thinking about theoretical approaches which acknowledge the multi-faceted realities of lived experience and relationships and how social work engages with this material. Borrowing from the wealth of material available from other disciplines can also be a strength in terms of using a breadth of critical thinking that can inform sophisticated debate and dialogue. In this book we draw on these ideas when looking at social work practice with lesbians and gay men.

The legal and policy framework for practice

Introduction

This chapter charts the legal developments that saw the UK move from a position of having criminalising and oppressive legislation towards lesbians and gay men, to one where legal protection was afforded through equalities legislation. The Equality Act 2006 protects lesbians and gay men from discrimination in certain areas and the more recent Equality Act 2010 places a duty on public bodies to promote equality for lesbians and gay men. These legal developments have created a very different legal landscape for lesbians and gay men than that which existed in 1885 and 1967 when significant pieces of legislation were passed predominately affecting gay men.

The chapter notes key pieces of legislation and discusses their significance for lesbians and gay men. A comprehensive overview is beyond the remit of this book and can be found in others (Cocks and Houlbrook, 2006; Cook et al., 2007; Jennings, 2007; Brown and Kershaw, 2008). The purpose of this chapter is to inform the reader of the current equalities legislative framework within which social work takes place, and to demonstrate the relationship between social work, the law and wider societal attitudes towards lesbians and gay men.

The past

Authors argue about the significance of different laws related to the history of the social and political position of lesbians and gay men in the

UK. However, all would agree on the significance of the Criminal Law Amendment Act of 1885. Popularly known as Labouchere's amendment, it stated that:

> any male person, who, in public or private, commits … any act of gross indecency with another male person, shall be guilty of misdemeanour punishable by up to two years imprisonment. This was not amended, and then only partially, until the passing of the 1967 Sexual Offences Act following the Wolfenden Report. (Cook et al., 2007: 173)

The Criminal Law Amendment Act 1885 is remembered as an Act that criminalised male homosexuality, despite it being primarily concerned about the regulation of children's sexuality and the limitation of child prostitution. Cook writes:

> Britain's 1885 Criminal Law Amendment Act, which raised the age of consent for girls to sixteen and regulated brothels, was rushed through parliament after a high-profile press campaign supposedly revealing an extensive network of child prostitution in London. (Cook, 2006: 69)

Cook goes on to argue that Section 11 of the Act (the Labouchere amendment) was a last-minute addition which attracted no 'Government comment and was barely mentioned in the press coverage of the Act's passing' (2006: 72). It is therefore interesting that this Act is remembered for its association with the criminalisation of male homosexual acts. It was a powerful tool for the criminalisation of individual men and as a controlling symbolic tool for all gay men, socially as well as psychologically. There were other Acts on the statute book at the time that criminalised male homosexual acts but this is the one that remains in our historical memories and is most often quoted as a reference point for the criminalisation of same-sex sexual activity between men.

For the purposes of this chapter, the next milestone in the history of legal developments relating to lesbians and gay men was the publication of the Wolfenden Report on 4 September 1957. The Wolfenden Committee was established by the Home Office in April 1954 and sat for three years hearing evidence examining laws relating to prostitution and to homosexuality. The Report recommended that consensual homosexual acts between men over the age of 21 should be decriminalised. However, it took ten years for this to be realised, through the passing of the Sexual Offences Act 1967. The climate of the 1960s, with its associated relative affluence compared to the austere 1950s, and the backdrop of demands for increased civil rights both in the USA as well as in Europe, meant that the 1964 Labour Government, under Harold Wilson, tackled a number of matters related to sexuality and the family. These included abortion and divorce as well as homosexuality. The passing of the Sexual Offences Act in 1967 decriminalised sex between consenting men in private above the age of 21. The Act applied only to England and Wales and not to members of the armed forces or the Merchant Navy. Although the Act had a profound impact on many men in that their relationships were no longer illegal, it placed emphasis on 'in private' and was aimed at condoning gay men who lived private domestic lives and did not 'rock the boat' of heterosexual society.

The 1960s and the 1970s saw considerable social unrest. This was associated with resistance to the Vietnam war and the growth of the civil rights and student movements in the UK, Europe and the USA. This period of social upheaval was the backdrop for social and legal change that benefited lesbians and gay men and other groups as well.

As described in the previous chapter, the 1970s saw much 'rocking of the boat' by lesbian and gay male activists, particularly in such organisations as the Gay Liberation Front. Many lesbian and gay activists were not satisfied with being allowed limited acceptance particularly where that acceptance was seen as an imitation of heterosexual conformist domesticity (Cook et al., 2007). Some gay men and lesbians were interested in the deconstruction of notions of heterosexuality as well as homosexuality. The impact of this agitation laid the ground for fundamental legal and social changes for lesbians and gay men, although some of those changes were not recognised by law until the twenty-first century. The 1970s saw the enactment of protective legislation for women through the Sex Discrimination Act of 1975, and Black communities through the Race Relations Act 1976. It took another 20 years for disabled people to be protected from direct discrimination. Such protective legislation for lesbians and gay men had to wait another 30 years.

The period between 1979 to 1997, dominated by the New Right Government of Margaret Thatcher, created a backdrop of conservatism against which economic recession was placed in sharp relief. This significantly affected lesbians and gay men's struggle for equality, particularly in relation to their right to family life. This was articulated through the debates surrounding the passing of various pieces of legislation during this period as well as through Adoption Law Reviews and the passing of Section 28 of the Local Government Act 1988. These impacted on social work practice with children and families. The debates specific to adoption and fostering had implications for social work. Legislation and guidance during this period, where the rights and responsibilities of lesbians and gay men to parent were deliberated, included the Embryology and Fertilisation Act 1990, the Adoption Law Review (DH and Welsh Office, 1992) and the Children Act 1989 Family Placement Guidance (DH, 1991). All these considered: the suitability of single women to parent children either through adoption or fertility treatment; the suitability of lesbians to parent through adoption, fertility treatment or fostering; and the suitability of gay men to parent through fostering or adoption. During these debates the Conservative Government championed a specific model of the nuclear family. However, this 'clashed with increased public awareness and social services recognition of the diversity of family forms. It also coincided with the increased confidence and visibility of lesbian mothers' (Brown, 1998a: 26).

In the debates surrounding the Embryology and Fertilisation Act 1990, the Adoption Law Review (DH and Welsh Office, 1992) and the Children Act 1989 Family Placement Guidance (DH, 1991), the Government failed to limit lesbians and gay men's right to parent in the ways that they had intended. One irony of this period is that inadvertently the New Right Government of Margaret Thatcher became the first Government in UK history to bring the term 'lesbians and gay men' into legislation as well as affording some degree of protection to young lesbians and gay men who were in public care. The Family Placement Guidance in its final form did not limit lesbians and gay men's right to foster and offered some degree of protection for lesbian and gay Looked After Children. Brown and Kershaw comment that:

> it said that the needs and concerns of young lesbians and gay men must be 'recognised and approached sympathetically' (DH, 1991: 97–98) and that 'gay young men and women may require very sympathetic carers to enable them to accept their sexuality and to develop their self-esteem (DH, 1991: 97–98)'. (Brown and Kershaw, 2008: 124)

This protection was in stark contrast to the position taken at the start of the consultation process. The original consultation document stated that:

> It would be wrong arbitrarily to exclude any particular groups of people from consideration. But the chosen way of life of some adults may mean that they would not be able to provide a suitable environment for the care and

nurture of a child. No one has a 'right' to be a foster parent. 'Equal rights' and 'gay rights' policies have no place in fostering services. (DH, 1990: 8)

As a result of pressure from child care organisations the Conservative Government had to drop the last sentence in the final version of the family placement guidance as it was felt that it was there for purely ideological purposes. There was agreement that no adult had the automatic right to foster, but it was argued that each adult should have the right to apply and be assessed.

Section 28 of the Local Government Act 1988 is seen as a significant milestone in the history of lesbian and gay rights. Section 28 prevented Local Authorities using their resources in such a way that might be interpreted as promoting homosexuality as well as forbidding promoting the teaching in any maintained school of homosexuality as a pretended family relationship. Its impact is contested, some seeing it as a significant symbol of the Conservative Government's one success in stigmatising lesbians and gay men. Section 28 'delegitimized lesbian and gay households and those bringing up children' (Cook, et al., 2007: 206). Others argue that the energy, resistance and related organisation that was generated by opposition to the passing of Section 28 strengthened lesbian and gay activism in that it united people through their opposition to it. Carter argues that 'the irony is the aim of brushing issues under the carpet with legislation actually causes them to explode into public debates which can paradoxically strengthen the community' (Carter, 1992: 222).

There were no successful prosecutions under Section 28 in the 15 years before it was removed from the statute books in 2000 in Scotland and 2003 in England. However, its impact was important on two counts. Firstly, people believed it was significant, even if it was not, and it was that belief in itself that acted as a potential negative controlling force. Secondly, it energised and mobilised lesbian and gay men in opposing its enactment. As it relates to social work, Myers and Milner note that it 'impacted on social work practices mainly through creating confusion and anxiety …' (2007: 53) and as such it was highly problematic.

The present

The New Labour Government elected in 1997 heralded major legal changes. These were slow to materialise at first but gained momentum as time progressed. The period between 1979 and 1997 was marked by attempts at legal changes and actual legal developments that were aimed at restricting the rights of lesbians and gay men. The legal changes introduced since 1997 repealed discriminatory legislation towards lesbians and gay men and introduced protective legislation.

The first matter dealt with by the New Labour Government in 1997 was to give the foreign partners of lesbians and gay men immigration rights (Cook et al., 2007). In 2000 the Labour Government lifted the ban on lesbians and gay men serving in the armed forces. Although this was not specifically relevant to social work practice, it indicated the degree of social and attitudinal change occurring in society.

Section 28 of the Local Government Act 1988 was repealed in Scotland in 2000 but not until 2003 in England. Before the 1997 election, the Labour Party had promised that this section of the Local Government Act 1988 would be repealed if they were to be elected. Although in legal terms it had little impact it was symbolically significant.

In 2000 the age of consent for gay men was equalised to 16, the same as for heterosexual men. It had been lowered from 21 to 18 in 1994 by the previous Parliament. This occurred after much stalling in the House of Lords, orchestrated by Baroness Young. Bagilhole describes the degree of parliamentary resistance to these legal changes, particularly within the House of Lords, as 'vociferous opposition' (2009: 114). However, despite Baroness Young's efforts the Sexual Offences (Amendment) Act was passed in 2000 and came into force in 2001; thus amending the 1956 and the 1967 Sexual Offences Act.

For lesbians and gay men who wanted to parent, the Adoption and Children Act 2002 was a watershed as it allowed couples who were unmarried to jointly apply to be assessed as adopters for the first time. All applicants undergo the same rigorous assessment process. The Human Fertilisation and Embryology Act 2008 was also significant in that it recognised same-sex couples as legal parents of children conceived through the use of donated sperm, eggs or embryos (Stonewall, 2009; Cocker and Hafford-Letchfield, 2010). This was a long way from the 1988 pejorative creation of the Conservative Party's 'pretend family' which they had brought into the legal framework in Section 28 of the Local Government Act 1988

Major change has also occurred in the area of sexual offences. Historically the law affected all gay men in that some aspects of their sexual lives could potentially be criminalised. The Sexual Offences Act 2003 abolished the offence of 'gross indecency' and importantly also altered the legal definition of rape to penile penetration without consent of the mouth, anus or vagina. Rape could only, by this definition, be perpetrated by men but could be committed against men or women. This gave men legal protection against being raped. The Sexual Offences Act 2003 also made assault by penetration a separate offence; this related to any part of the body being penetrated by an object if the penetration was sexual and if the person did not consent. These two new areas of protection against sexual assault of different kinds gave legal protection to lesbians and gay men where they did not have that protection before.

In terms of increasing the protection of lesbians and gay men from harassment and assault, Section 146 of the Criminal Justice Act 2003 allowed courts to impose tougher sentences for offences motivated or aggravated by the victim's sexual orientation in England and Wales. However, the perpetrator could only be charged with existing offences such an actual bodily harm. This was different from, for example, racially motivated attacks where there is a specific offence of racially aggravated assault. The Offences Aggravated by Prejudice (Scotland) Act 2009 brought Scotland into line with hate crime legislation in the UK. The Equality and Human Rights Commission published material to further enhance understanding of homophobic hate crimes and hate incidents (Dick, 2009).

In 2003 the Employment Equality (Sexual Orientation) Regulations made discrimination against lesbians, gay men and bisexuals in the workplace illegal. For social workers, and those employed in social care, this was particularly significant. The sackings of Susan Shell in 1981 and Judith Williams in 1982, who were deemed unsuitable to work with young people because they were lesbians, had had a significant impact (Brown; 1998a: 44). Although these events were over 25 years ago they affected the morale of the lesbian and gay social care and social work workforce at the time and have had ramifications since. These ramifications were not entirely negative as the sackings acted as a catalyst for trade union activity to ensure that sexual orientation was included in equal opportunities policies and later in legislation.

Lesbians and gay men are subject to domestic violence as are heterosexuals. The introduction of the Domestic Violence, Crimes and Victims Act 2004 afforded lesbians and gay men more protection from violent domestic partners than previously existed (Brown and Kershaw, 2008). In relation to intimidation, violence and hatred that lesbians and gay men might experience outside the home, the Criminal Justice and Immigration Act 2008 gave protection against incitement to hatred on the grounds of sexual orientation and included major acts of hatred such as assault and murder.

The passing of the Civil Partnership Act 2004 reinforced the changing attitudes to lesbian and gay relationships and their families. This Act allowed lesbians and gay men to register as civil partners and have their relationship legally recognised. With this recognition came rights and responsibilities related to money, tax, benefits and responsibilities related to children that, up to this point, had been associated with marriage.

The Equality Act 2006 and the related Equality Act (Sexual Orientation) Regulations 2007 made discrimination against lesbians and gay men in the provision of goods and services illegal. Brown and Kershaw debate the importance of the Act and its related regulations, arguing that they:

> have particular implications for organisations and individuals who deliver social and other public services … so if social workers are to offer an equitable and effective service to lesbians and gay men, they require knowledge of the legislation that is specifically relevant to their circumstances, as well as being able to apply the law more generally. (2008: 123)

The Equality Act 2010 covers a range of new initiatives, the one most pertinent to this publication is the new 'equality duty' which extends public bodies' duty to consider equality for lesbians and gay men. This means that public bodies will have a duty to:

> have due regard to the need to eliminate unlawful discrimination, advance equality of opportunity and foster good community relations. The new duty will cover race, disability, and gender, as now, but also include age, sexual orientation, religion or belief, pregnancy and maternity explicitly and fully cover gender reassignment: replacing the three existing, separate duties with a single, more effective framework. (Government Equalities Office, 2009: 8)

Whereas the Equality Act 2006 and the related Equality Act (Sexual Orientation) Regulations 2007 made discrimination against lesbians and gay men in the provision of goods and services illegal, the Equality Act 2010 further strengthens the law to place a duty on public bodies to promote equality for lesbians and gay men, amongst others. It is also significant as it places equality for lesbian and gay men on the same footing as other groups who experience prejudice and negative discrimination.

Implications for social work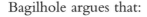

Bagilhole argues that:

> until the 2000s, discrimination on the grounds of sexual orientation mani-
> fested itself in three ways:
>
> - greater restrictions were placed on same-sex sexual activity than on
>   heterosexual sex;
> - there was less respect for the family life of same-sex partners than for
>   heterosexuals;
> - protection against discrimination and harassment in the workplace and
>   other parts of society was non-existent. (2009: 113)

The 1997–2010 Labour Government will be remembered for many
things, both positive and negative. One legacy will be the transformation
of the legislative framework that directly impacts on the lives of lesbians
and gay men. Botcherby and Creegan argue that 'a raft of progressive
legislation in the last decade heralded unprecedented rights and protection under the law for LGB people in Britain' (2009: 5), covering all
three of the areas identified by Bagilhole as having been the focus of
negative discrimination against lesbians and gay men in the past.

As debate has ensued regarding each of these new legal initiatives what
has become apparent is that the pace of legal change has sometimes been
faster than the pace of public attitudinal change. This lack of fit between
legal change and public opinion has been best demonstrated by some press
coverage, for example by the *Daily Mail* (Moir, 2009). In addition, the
content of the debates surrounding the passing of protective legislation
articulated in both Houses of Parliament and particularly in the House of
Lords has demonstrated the range of views that are still held about lesbians
and gay men. Hicks (2005b) notes that some of the legal changes since
2000 provoked powerful feelings during parliamentary debates.

> The parliamentary debates over the Adoption and Children Act 2002
> focused quite a lot of attention on lesbians and gay men. In many ways this
> debate demonstrated that some ideas haven't changed very much: some
> argued that adoption by lesbian and gay couples should be outlawed, some
> that it was supportable only as a last resort, some that the married hetero-
> sexual couple is always best for children, some that lesbians and gay men
> made good carers only in particular circumstances, such as for children with
> disabilities, and some that lesbians and gay men are 'just like' heterosexuals
> and so should not be treated any differently. (2005b: 51)

These arguments that arose within the parliamentary debates identified above by Hicks are the same as those that were expressed in Parliament in the 1980s and early 1990s when the Embryology and Fertilisation Act 1990, the Adoption Law Review (DH and Welsh Office, 1992) and the Children Act 1989 Family Placement Guidance (DH, 1991) were debated. We would agree with Hicks that some things have not changed very much. However, there has been significant legal change since 1997. For those legal changes to have taken place some significant changes in attitudes towards lesbians and gay men must have occurred even if the debates in Parliament gave voice to some established prejudicial views.

What are the implications of these legal changes for social work? It has been argued that in the past social work has been 'historically complicit in the oppression of particular groups of people' (Brown and Kershaw, 2008: 129). However, there is also evidence that social workers were involved in agitating for equal opportunities policies and legal changes that offered protection to lesbians and gay men from the 1970s onwards (Brown, 1998a). Where do we stand now, especially as it appears that the law as it relates to lesbians and gay men is now a 'step ahead' of public opinion and is also a 'step ahead' of social worker practice? Social workers are likely to hold a wide range of views, attitudes and beliefs about lesbians and gay men, some of which will be prejudicial and discriminatory.

> Changing the law is one thing, changing social workers' attitudes is another. It appears that whilst there generally seems to be more tolerance and acceptance of lesbian and gay lifestyles there is no room for complacency, because it seems clear … that despite positive legislative changes, homophobic attitudes, prejudice and discrimination still exist. Legislation does not force people who think homosexuality is immoral and wrong to change their views, however it does require them to be more tolerant and treat people alike. (Brown and Kershaw, 2008: 129)

Whatever the beliefs and attitudes are of social workers today, they have to work within the framework of the GSCC Codes of Practice (GSCC, 2002a), the Equality Act 2006 and the related Sexual Orientation Regulations 2007 and the Equality Act 2010. This should mean that lesbians and gay men receive an equitable and inclusive service from social workers. We explore some of the complexities of this for social work practice in Chapters 6, 7 and 8.

Summary

There have been considerable changes to the legal landscape that sets the context for social work with lesbians and gay men. Social workers have to keep abreast of these legal and policy changes to make sure that their practice is legal, equitable and meets the needs of all clients that they come into contact with, including lesbians and gay men. In areas of social work practice that have been seen to be negatively discriminatory in the past, we argue there is a particular responsibility placed on individual social workers and their social work agencies to make sure that social work and social care practice and resources are accessible, facilitative and effective.

3

Social work values and ethical practice: moving beyond anti-discriminatory or anti-oppressive practice

The persecution of people because of their sexual orientation is every bit as unjust as that crime against humanity, Apartheid. We must all be allowed to love with honour. (Archbishop Desmond Tutu, 2004)

Introduction

One of the key aspects of social work which sets it apart from other professions is its commitment to social justice and its questioning of the dominant power relations present within society. These are heavily influential in determining life chances for those who are poorest, those with complex and entrenched problems, and those who have profound disabilities and consequently require considerable support to live their lives with dignity, choice and respect. For many social workers, this is best summed up in the profession's commitment to anti-discriminatory practice and includes a willingness to acknowledge structural inequalities and to work in a way that does not knowingly disadvantage others. It involves having contact with people whose backgrounds and lived experiences and choices may be very different from a social worker's own experiences. This is clearly expressed in the Social Work Codes of Practice (GSCC, 2002a), and is an expected mandate for practice. However, there are an increasing number of voices critical of the use of anti-discriminatory practice in social work (McLaughlin, 2005; Featherstone and Green, 2009; Millar, 2008; Ferguson, 2008; Ferguson and Woodward, 2009; Hicks, 2009) as an outdated and insufficiently robust paradigm. This chapter will examine the development of anti-discriminatory (ADP) and anti-oppressive practice (AOP), identifying the strengths and weaknesses in its approach, particularly in relation to sexuality, about which the proponents of these theories have been particularly silent. Firstly we define some of the terms used in this area of work, before discussing the historical context of this area of practice, including the legacy of Radical Social Work. We will also examine the 'birth' of the anti-oppressive and anti-discrimination 'industry' in the 1980s and 1990s and discuss its hegemonic dominance in social work practice, including its adoption by the status quo. 'Post-modernism', with its preoccupation with individualism and deconstruction has ironically enabled the binary framework of AOP and ADP with its fixation with identity and categorisation to continue to thrive. However, we will consider how ideas from post-modernism and post-structuralism can assist social work in thinking more critically about difference and diversity and their inherent complexities. It is time for a constructive debate within social work about these issues, to move thinking on from the deficit and reductionist position in which social work practice is currently located.

Definition of terms ■ ■ ■ ■ ■ ■

So what are the differences between anti-discriminatory practice and anti-oppressive practice? What is the difference between equal opportunities and diversity policies? What exactly do these terms mean? Many of the terms associated with equalities are now used interchangeably. It is therefore necessary to explore the meaning behind the terms, because the origins are located in different contexts, and this affects meaning.

Anti-discriminatory practice (ADP)

A term widely used in social and probation work, and in social work training, to describe how workers take account of structural disadvantage and seek to reduce individual and institutional discrimination particularly on the grounds of race, gender, disability, social class and sexual orientation. (Thomas and Pierson, 1995: 16)

Thompson identified a number of key points in anti-discriminatory practice:

- We must develop sensitivity to the existence all around us of discrimination and oppression.
- We must recognise that there is no comfortable middle ground – we are either part of the solution or part of the problem.
- We must address the three key imperatives of justice, equality and participation.
- We must revisit traditional forms of practice and amend them accordingly.
- Non-discriminatory and anti-oppressive assessment is a first step towards the achievement of anti-discriminatory practice. (Thompson, 2008: 109)

The strength of this approach was that it recognised structural disadvantage and the very real effect this can and does have on people's lives. The limitations are numerous and include: the use of identity to create a hierarchy of oppression and of oppressed groups; the proposition that it is possible to 'learn' about someone's oppression and counteract this oppression solely with learnt knowledge; that someone from an oppressed category is then seen as the 'expert' on the life and experiences of that category of people and that problems within families can be attributed just to cultural/gender/class etc. differences rather than recognised for what they are.

Anti-oppressive practice (AOP)

seeks to understand and deal with the structural causes of social problems and address their consequences by altering social relations at all possible levels, from the macro level to the micro level ... [AOP] encompasses all aspects of social life – culture, institutions, legal framework, political system, socioeconomic infrastructure and interpersonal relationships, which both create and are created by social reality. It aims to improve the quality of life or wellbeing of individuals, groups and communities ... [AOP] celebrates diverse identities as being equal to one another, rejects the fragmentation of social like and hierarchies of oppression, with the ensuing isolation of individuals that this endorses, [and] promotes people oriented social environments. (Dominelli, 2009: 53–4)

Dominelli criticises Thompson's PCS model (personal, cultural and structural) as: 'a focus on discrimination emphasises only one element in the web of social relations' (2002: 4) and 'additive approaches rank oppressions in a hierarchy that prioritises one form over another' (2002: 5).

Instead she discusses 'emancipatory' social work where identity is a crucial issue for the development of an empowering social work practice:

> Promoting social justice and human development in an unequal world
> provides the raison d'etre of social work practice, and is a key way of
> discharging society's contract in assisting vulnerable people in its midst.
> (Dominelli, 2002: 4)

Clifford and Burke (2009) continue to use the term 'anti-oppressive'.
They pair it with 'ethics' rather than practice and are critical of its use
in social work. They continue to use it as:

> it does at least make clear that the ethical and political concepts such as
> rights, social justice, empowerment and liberation are fundamental to social
> work ... and believe that the alternative phrases in common parlance, such as
> 'critical' or 'critical best practice' are 'broad term(s)', and like 'empowerment'
> do not necessarily indicate the importance and interconnectedness of struc-
> tural social difference, inequality and ethics. (Clifford and Burke, 2009: 2–3)

Equality

Any definition of equality will refer to 'being equal' or 'having the same
value'. In terms of social work, equality refers to each person being
treated the same as anyone else, regardless of someone's disability, gender,
ethnicity, sexuality and so on. However, this wish for an equal service to
be provided for all doesn't take into account differences in people's circumstances because of discrimination they may experience due to their
age, ethnicity, religion, sexual orientation, gender and disability.

There are substantial economic and social benefits to creating a more
equal society, as inequality creates a myriad of health and social problems
(Wilkinson and Pickett, 2010).

Equal opportunities (EO)

Clifford and Burke state that, '"equal opportunity" issues such as discrimination, harassment and equal access are fundamentally about
respect for individuals and groups from socially diverse backgrounds'
(Clifford and Burke, 2009: 210). Both Clifford and Burke, and Bagilhole
recognise the limitations of the term 'equal opportunities'. Bagilhole
comments that 'the concept of equal opportunities in policy making
was originally based on the now disputed premise of treating everyone

the same. It is both a complex and contested concept' (2009: xiv). It is now more common to see equal opportunities joined with diversity. Bagilhole suggests that this coupling 'emphasises the recognition of difference, the possibility of "multiple disadvantage" and different treatment, which can be legitimate in the pursuit of social equality, fairness and justice' (2009: xiv).

Discrimination

Thompson comments (2003: 10) that, 'at its most basic level, discrimination is simply a matter of identifying differences, and can be positive or negative.' Cocker and Brown state that:

> Parrott, MacIver and Thoburn (2007) make the distinction between two different types of 'discrimination'. Firstly, discrimination which is founded on bigotry, prejudice and intolerance is never justifiable. Secondly they argue that the very act of social work involves making decisions that are discriminatory and that discrimination is in itself a crucial aspect of capable assessment. We argue that this level of discrimination used in assessment – to be able to differentiate between two similar scenarios where variables of a critical nature may be different – is a necessary part of skilled assessment. The reason for this suggested use of language is that 'discrimination' has become one of a number of over-used phrases in social work, where the original meaning has changed significantly over time. (Cocker and Brown, 2010: 20)

In terms of countering negative discrimination – that is, discrimination that is founded on bigotry, prejudice and intolerance – there are a number of distinctions within the law between direct or indirect discrimination, and both are covered by the legislation.

Direct discrimination is when an individual or a group of individuals is treated less favourably. An example is refusing to employ staff or admit potential students based on their disability, gender, race, age, sexual orientation or religion or by dismissing someone because of their sexual orientation, disability, religion/belief, ethnicity, age or gender.

Indirect discrimination is when a criterion, provision, or practice is applied which has the effect of disadvantaging people with a particular disability, gender, race, age, religion, or sexuality.

Harassment and victimisation are also included in discrimination. Harassment is subjecting someone to unwanted conduct that violates that person's dignity or creates an intimidating, hostile, degrading, humiliating, or offensive environment for them. Victimisation, in its legal sense, is retaliation against someone because they have made a complaint or allegation of discrimination (Brammer, 2010).

Diversity

This term is often linked with the word 'difference', and refers to the variation that exists within and between social groups of people. Cooper offers a critique of diversity and difference as political aims, commenting that:

> diversity politics does coalesce around a series of shared concerns, questions and assumptions. First, it goes beyond the conditional liberal promise bestowed upon minorities of toleration, providing their differences are kept from affecting others. As Weeks (1993: 206–7) argues, toleration, with its pragmatic acceptance of unwelcomed difference, is not enough. The space of diversity politics is one in which social diversity is valued and celebrated, not just within the private sphere but within public life and fora as well. In large part this is because diversity is seen as enriching society and making choice possible (e.g., Kymlicka, 1995: 84). In addition, for more radical proponents, diversity is celebrated for its capacity to challenge disciplinary conventions and the status quo. (Cooper, 2004: 7)

Equality strands

In England, there are six identified equality target groups (eight in Scotland), or 'equality strands', that are central to the equality agenda of the Labour Government. All categories are protected under legislation.

These are: race; gender (including transgender); disability; sexual orientation; age; religion and/or belief. The two additional strands in Scotland are: marital status and sex. The Scottish Council of Voluntary Organisations (2003) suggests that there are a number of benefits and barriers to working across the equality strands. The benefits are: identifying people who experience discrimination from multiple sources to create better services that recognise people's individuality; changing the culture within organisations through a recognition of the many ways discrimination can occur; creating a voice for all; influencing policy; learning from each other; learning about each other; savings on resources; and establishing expertise. The barriers include: fear of diluting the message from including many different groups, some with opposing needs; identifying diversity within an equality strand is still important, not just the diversity across the six or eight equality strands; resources; opposition within equality strands, such as religion and homosexuality (see Chapter 5) and unwieldiness of addressing so much at once.

Intersectionality

This term was developed to explain how various types of discrimination interact on multiple and often simultaneous levels. The forms of oppression and discrimination that exist, such as those based on ethnicity, gender, religion, sexual orientation, class, or disability do not act independently of one another. This interrelationship of oppression is referred to as 'intersectionality'. Bagilhole comments:

> Women's different experiences of exclusion help us to understand that there are power relationships based not only on gender, but also on sexual orientation, age, disability, race, and religion or belief. Sex is only one of the many inequalities that construct gender; gender is constructed through and by the distinctions of race and ethnicity, sexuality, disability, religion or belief, and age. These experiences of exclusion and inequality also interact and may conflict with each other. (Bagilhole, 2009: 5)

Oppression

Oppression is the subjugation of an individual or group by a more powerful individual or group. 'Whatever its form, oppression has four essential components: The misuse of power, process of objectification, the silence of witnesses and the entrapment or accommodation of witnesses' (Doyle, 1997: 8).

Historical context   ■ ■ ■ ■ ■ ■

There are a number of key events and movements that, although disparate in nature as well as geographical location, impacted upon the development of Radical Social Work ideas in the 1970s in the UK. These included: the civil rights movements in USA; the Vietnam War; and the 1968 student revolts in USA, UK, France and Germany. These grassroots resistance movements coincided with others, such as the anti-psychiatry movement associated with the work of R.D. Laing. Although this has since been only tangentially linked to the birth of the mental health user movement, it was one of the early manifestations of the user and carer movements in the UK. In many instances the user and carer movement has now become an expected and integral part of mainstream practice, to the extent that colonisation by the status quo is now a concern, which in many ways mirrors the trajectory of the 'anti-discriminatory practice' discourse in social work practice.

To go slightly further back, the decline of the manufacturing industries in the UK after the Second World War and economic and technological developments from the 1950s onwards meant there was a need for a new white-collar service industry and new technologies workforce. This was partially linked to the growth of the university sector to support the new technologies and economic development with the creation of the 1960s New Universities – Kent, East Anglia, Lancaster, Bath, Sussex, York, Keele, Essex and Warwick. This expansion was not the cause of the rise of the academic disciplines of sociology and psychology, as both pre-date this, but it certainly contributed. From the late 1960s onwards, a number of graduates from these universities took up places in the expanding social work workforce created after the Seebohm Report of 1968 and the establishment of the personal Social Services departments under the 1970 Local Authority Social Services Act.

This coincided with post-Second World War continuing migration from commonwealth countries that provided the workforce for rebuilding the UK infrastructure. The 1960s also saw right wing exploitation of racism for political purposes, well illustrated by Enoch Powell's 'rivers of blood' speech on 20 April 1968. This speech and other factors acted as a catalyst for the development of the UK's own civil rights movement. In turn, various black and feminist organisations and individuals began to have an influence on mainstream trade union and Labour party politics during the 1970s and 1980s (Cooper, 1994; Brown, 1998a). This impacted on the pressure for organisations to develop equal opportunities policies offering protection to the workforce as well as clients. These policies emerged from the 1970s and although some of them included groups that were denied protection through law such as lesbians and gay men, these were added to equal opportunities policies from the 1980s (Cooper, 1994). Some councils refused to do this (Brown, 1998a). During the 1980s and 1990s Local Government was the arena for the playing out of these dynamics locally via the development and demise of equalities units and their associated initiatives (Cooper, 1994). This occurred against a backdrop of a Conservative Government infamously passing Section 28 of the Local Government Act 1988, which prohibited Local Authorities from 'promoting' homosexuality or gay 'pretended family relationships', and prevented councils spending money on educational materials and projects perceived to promote a gay lifestyle. It took a further 21 years for the Leader of the Conservative Party to say 'sorry' for his party's role in ensuring this discriminatory section of the Act became law. Trade Unions and Community Activist Groups, as well as individuals within the Labour Party, had an impact on social policy developments and resulting protective legislation such as: the Sex Discrimination Act 1975; the Race Relations Act 1976; the Disability Discrimination Act 1995 and eventually the Equality Act 2006, and the Equality Act 2010.

What did Radical Social Work say in the 1970s? ■ ■ ■ ■ ■ ■

Radical Social Work (RSW) emerged from the application of some of the key ideas in sociological and political discourses of the time to Social Work. Radical Social Work was not a uniform discourse or set of ideas. Rather, Langan and Lee describe it as:

> an internally explosive mixture of activists inspired by Marx, Friere, Alinsky, Illich, Neil, de Beauvoir, Becker, Goffman and Gramsci, among others, made a highly significant impact on the study and practice of social work. (Langan and Lee, 1989b: 1)

Two of the key texts of this period symbolising this breadth of ideas were Bailey and Brake (1975) and Brake and Bailey (1980).

Radical Social Work put forward a critique of existing patterns of social welfare provision:

> This meant relating developments in welfare to the wider social and political context as well as assessing the practical consequences of social work interventions. While RSW has been much criticised for failing to move much beyond a critical mode, there has been a considerable underestimation of how necessary this critique was and of the constructive role it has played. (Langan and Lee, 1989b: 6)

As Clarke also noted, the tensions between social work practitioners and sociological critics of social work created:

> a syndrome in which sociologists have stuck to their task of demystifying social work and attacking its social control functions, whilst social workers, though agreeing with many of these attacks, have failed to find any guidance or solutions to those dilemmas. (Clarke, 1979: 128)

One of the major criticisms of RSW was that it did not move beyond critique and even at the time, writers such as Clarke were aware of this limitation: '… this mode of analysis has failed to move from sociological criticism to political critique, to connect its analysis to action' (Clarke, 1979: 129). Although this critique has some merit, many of the early texts (Corrigan and Leonard, 1978; Brake and Bailey, 1980; Statham, 1978) were closely linked to practice. Since this time individual academics and practitioners have continued to grapple with this tension (de Maria, 1992; Fook, 1993; Pease and Fook, 1999; Fook, 2002; Healy, 2000; 2005; Ferguson and Woodward, 2009). Indeed, Langan and Lee comment, 'For the most part the critics of Radical Social Work have ignored the extent to which radical social workers *are* steeped in practice' (Langan and Lee, 1989b: 7).

A key idea in the 1970s was the possibility of transforming the State from within. One of the best articulations of this position was what is referred to as 'In and against the State' (London/Edinburgh Weekend Return Group, 1980). The new emerging graduate and post-graduate social work workforce that were employed in the generic personal social services departments were believed to hold the mantle for this transformation. However, in reality the workforce wasn't that different and those who held a radical anti-capitalist position remained in the minority. One of the important aspects of this time was the emphasis of working within the trade union movement, and NALGO conference minutes of the 1970s and 1980s evidence the commitment of social work trade unionists to transforming the position of clients as well as securing their own rights.

Although these Radical Social Work activists were few in number, they were prolific and influential within social work education and practice. *Case Con* was a Radical Social Work magazine aimed at practitioners published from 1970 to 1977.

The main tenets of Radical Social Work included: viewing the social work task and role through a political lens; chastising conventional social work for its failure to develop a critical self-awareness and challenging the individualistic explanation of social problems (Langan and Lee, 1989b: 4); encouraging social workers to address the diversity of the client population (Milligan, 1975; Husband, 1980; Hart, 1980); a critical analysis of the professionalisation of social work – seeing it as a mechanism for both the depoliticisation of social work activity as well as divorcing its workforce from the mainstream working class struggle; identifying the role of class as a structural determinant of power and access to resources within society (Corrigan and Leonard, 1978); the extent to which social work exercises its power through the State on behalf of the ruling class (Payne, 2005a), and understanding the impact of this on the individual in terms of the social work role.

> We are supposed to 'help' our 'clients' by making them 'accept responsibility' – in other words, come to terms as individuals with basically unacceptable situations. We must counter pose to this the possibility of changing their situation by collective action. We can only do this by acting collectively our-selves. (Bailey and Brake, 1975: 145)

By the end of the 1970s the political and economic landscape in the UK had changed. Many Local Authorities had to implement cuts in social services budgets in the wider context of a Labour Government experi-encing both industrial and economic downturn. By the time the Conservatives came into power in 1979, embracing a free market econ-omy, the stage was set for a shift in position from radical social workers being critical of the State and its provision to, by necessity, wanting to preserve it. Over time, Margaret Thatcher and her government's New Right ideology, with its emphasis on the individual as opposed to the collective, eroded the Radical Social Work enterprise. The division of the local authority functions of commissioning and providing and the increasing privatisation of some aspects of the welfare state was set within the context of the denationalisation of state-owned industries.

> Although the moment of radical social work has now passed, many of its defining values – community and commitment, equality and empowerment, feminism and anti-racism – have entered the mainstream of social work practice … Is this a post modern paradox: that radical social work has tri-umphed despite the demise of the movement that launched it? Or is it a more familiar irony: that the rhetoric of radical social work has survived the containment of the movement's radical impulse? (Langan, 2002: 209)

From the 1970s feminism and anti-racism had entered mainstream con-sciousness, symbolised by the passing of the Sex Discrimination Act 1975 and the Race Relations Act 1976, and are examples of the bridg-ing that occurred between Radical Social Work and what was to become known as anti-discriminatory practice. For the first time women and Black communities obtained legal protection from dis-crimination in employment and provision of goods and services. Although there was material written on the position of some particular groups within the 1970s (e.g. women, ethnic minority communities, lesbians and gay men), the overall RSW analysis was Marxist and class driven, and understanding social work and the welfare state was from within that paradigm. However, there were also examples of publications within RSW that had a specific focus, for example on women. Weir's (1975) and Wilson's (1977) work are examples of the application of both Marxist and socialist feminist analysis to women, the welfare state and social work.

There was also coverage of issues facing lesbians and gay men in social work practice during the 1970s (Milligan, 1975; Hart 1980; Hart and Richardson, 1981). RSW's discussions about sexuality were politically and socially located. They argued that social work needed to engage with the political position of lesbians and gay men in a heterosexual society and homosexuality was seen as a potential challenge to heterosexual norms, not just as a minority life style which should be tolerated.

Milligan (1975) discussed the psychological and social difficulties of 'coming out' in a heterosexual society that pathologised homosexuality. He argued that helping professions have to have a political understanding of the positioning of lesbians and gay men to be able to be helpful. In addition, the integration of lesbians and gay men meant 'assimilation' and approval by the dominant majority, and that was not necessarily what lesbians and gay men wanted or needed. 'Oppressed people need to define themselves' (1975: 110).

Hart (1980) talked about casework and its location within a dominant heteronormative framework. He commented:

> The purpose of the casework relationship was to redirect behaviour inwards to considerations of the appropriateness of that behaviour to certain ideal forms of family life ... Diverse sexual expression meant physical satisfaction, self-indulgence, and above all a threat to family life. (Hart, 1980: 59)

Hart noted that within social work education there was:

> A certain reluctance to include sexual content on the curriculum involves not just a failure to provide information but rather an avoidance of a discussion of social work values and ideology at a very practical level. (Hart, 1980: 61)

In 1981 Hart and Richardson produced an edited text on homosexuality and social work: the first of its kind in the UK. Contributors included Plummer, Weeks and many other practitioners. This book took a radical, implicitly socialist analysis of the position that lesbians and gay men had in society that did not pathologise homosexuality. It examined different theoretical models and moved towards a view where it wasn't enough to just meet the needs of lesbians and gay men, but rather there was a need to challenge the status quo and the dominance of the heterosexual norm, thus challenging, 'both traditional, sexual and social relationships between the sexes' (1981: 2).

Developments in the 1980s and 1990 and the emergence of ADP/AOP as a dominant discourse ■ ■ ■ ■ ■ ■

After the election of the Conservative Government in 1979 and the defeat of the Labour movement following a number of high profile industrial disputes best illustrated by the miners strike (1984–85), social work's relationship with the working class altered. Commentators at the time observed a distancing of social workers from identification with working class clients, as the influence of radical social work's class analysis started to diminish.

> [T]he tendency to disparage working class people as racist, sexist and, worst of all, lacking in gratitude for state munificence, which Bolger et al. recognised within the Labour Party, became increasingly influential in the world of social work. (Langan, 2002: 213)

The development of a binary analysis ensued with the developments of somewhat simplistic positions of sexism or anti-sexism, and racism or anti-racism. The misuse of the feminist mantra – 'the personal is political' is noted – the role of self-awareness as part of political change became the focus in trying to 'fight' social injustice, so the emphasis changed from political collective action to personal individual change, which mirrored the New Right's emphasis on the importance of the individual.

This coincided with the establishment of Women's Units and Race Units in many Local Authorities (Cooper, 1994). There was a mushrooming/plethora of companies and individuals who offered 'awareness training' during this and later periods. In hindsight, one of the criticisms of some of this training was that it was individualistic, blaming and didn't necessarily facilitate change (Langan, 2002). It also created anxiety. This 'blame' discourse can be seen in some of the anti-discriminatory (ADP) and anti-oppressive (AOP) social work texts published in the 1980s and early 1990, and in the emergence of the notions of 'correct' political and social attitudes which did not enable the complexities of people's lives and situations to be realised or understood. As Langan comments:

> [A]ccording to a book published by BASW in 1993, 'awareness training' had 'a major part to play' in promoting ADP and acted as 'a foundation for other forms and levels of training' (Thompson, 1993: 152). The most significant feature of the concept of race awareness training was how it revealed the shift in attitude of radical social work. A movement which a decade earlier had regarded working class people as the agency of the revolutionary transformation of society now assumed that the same people required professional training to eradicate their prejudices. (Langan, 2002: 214)

We argue that some of the problematic dynamics seen in the 'awareness training' discourses directly influenced some interpretations of ADP leading to poor practice still in evidence today. This was clearly demonstrated through the Wakefield Inquiry, where anxiety about being perceived as discriminatory, and an inability to 'discriminate' appropriately were evidenced in the report.

ADP and AOP are terms that have been in common parlance in social work since the 1980s. These were and are often used interchangeably. Both ADP and AOP were soon absorbed into status quo discourses. This absorption is best demonstrated by their inclusion within the Central Council for the Education and Training of Social Work's regulatory framework for social work education and training (CCETSW, 1989; 1991; 1995). Thus, 'the radical commitment to liberation appeared to have been transformed into a mechanism for regulation' (Langan, 2002: 216). This inclusion provoked the then Conservative Government's disapproval as they were concerned about the seeming politicisation of the roles and functions of social work for specific political ends, such as the eradication of racism. CCETSW had described racism as endemic within British society in Paper 30, which the Government saw as a statement not within social work's remit to make. As a result of this the second DipSW equal opportunities statement only referred to the protection of groups that already had such protection under the law. CCETSW had deliberately excluded a number of groups and areas from their equal opportunities statement: for example, older people, lesbians and gay men and religious belief: 'CCETSW recognises that equal opportunity is something each individual wants for themselves and to which they have a legal right' (CCETSW, 1995: 9).

With the passing of the Equality Act 2006, these hitherto excluded groups and areas are now conveniently covered by the GSCC's equal opportunity statement, which was changed only slightly for the new social work degree (GSCC, 2002b: 10).

We identify three strands of ADP/AOP writing from the 1980s onwards. The first strand includes writers who would not necessarily have described themselves as proponents of ADP/AOP – for example, from the 1980s such authors as: Cheetham (1982); Phillipson (1982); Ahmed, Cheetham and Small (1986); Coombe and Little (1986); Banton, Clifford, Frosh, Lousada and Rosenthall (1985); and from the 1990s – Dalrymple and Burke (1995); Brown (1998a); Lesnik (1998); Barry and Hallett (1998). All of these texts focused on issues related to practice.

The second strand is what we would describe as 'ideologically driven' texts such as Dominelli (1988), Dominelli and McLeod (1989), and Oliver (1990). Such texts provided the momentum for the development of social work's unique perspective on working with diversity in practice and placing social work at the forefront of professional groups in its commitment to tackling discrimination.

The third strand is associated with Thompson's work, further developing these ideas in an accessible way. Because of its simplicity, Thompson's model for practice – P (personal); C (cultural context); S (social/ structural) – was easily understood by students and practitioners (Thompson, 1993; 2003; 2006).

Payne writes:

> Anti-discriminatory and anti-oppressive theories also offer theoretical advantages over other approaches to social work. They develop radical approaches to take into account the range of different bases for oppression of groups and inequalities and divisions in society, and thus provide a more effective account of issues that social work must face. This has also permitted a new and increasingly relevant lease of life for radical approaches within social work. (2005a: 292)

Although we agree about the lease of life this gave social work in tackling discrimination, the colonisation of these ideas by the status quo has meant that they have lacked radicalism and have been linked to problematic dynamics within practice as evidenced within the Wakefield Inquiry (Parrott et al., 2007). Some aspects of the second and third strands, in retrospect, could be considered as being potentially blaming, abstracted, insufficiently related to practice and simplistic models for tacking highly complex human, social and political issues. However, how this material was translated into practice was beyond the control of the authors. We see these developments as having provided important building blocks to take social work from a position of not addressing issues of diversity to making social work consider how it needed to adapt its practice to meet the varied needs of clients from many different groups. It provided an easily digestible model to enable social workers to understand and challenge structural oppression. Through the development of such a model as PCS, which can be applied to the entirety of social work, the necessary complexities, and its relationship to theory, were consequently tenuous (Payne, 2005a; Healey, 2005; Hicks, 2008).

Building on the legacy and moving the debate on within social work

ADP/AOP is an important component of the development of social work in terms of its commitment to working with marginalised and disenfranchised groups (Payne, 2005b). We argue that ADP/AOP is now so embedded within status quo discourses that it no longer offers an alternative perspective on the role of power and difference.

Humphries has issued a wake-up call for the profession in that:

> social work needs to stop pretending that what it calls 'anti-oppressive prac-
> tice' is anything but a gloss to help it feel better about what it is required to
> do, a gloss that is reinforced by a raft of books and articles that are superficial
> and void of a political context for practice. It needs to inform itself of theo-
> ries of power that go beyond individualistic models, and to struggle with the
> challenges that come from engaging with debates within the social sciences.
> (2004: 105)

Since the Dominelli (1988; 2002) and Thompson (1993; 2003; 2006) texts, there have been many other books published about ADP, some of which are not critical of ADP and AOP discourses. A number of these have a social work base (Dalrymple and Burke, 2006; Baines, 2007; Clifford and Burke, 2009), whilst others are written from a different disciplinary background (Bagilhole, 2009). There are critical views about ADP/AOP expressed within other texts, where the author is not exclusively writing about this area (Fawcett and Featherstone, 2000; Humphries, 2004; Healy, 2005; Hicks, 2008; Ferguson, 2008; Featherstone and Green, 2009; Ferguson and Woodward, 2009).

In addition a small number of social work academics have written critical pieces about the ADP/AOP role and influence in social work.

Millar comments that, '"Anti-oppressive" discourse has, arguably, needed precisely the kind of critical, contextualising analysis that it was supposed to espouse' (Millar, 2008: 373). McLaughlin highlights the difficulties that anyone from the left had in offering a critique of ADP or AOP, because the only other voice critiquing these ideas was the political right, and certain parts of the left talked of a right wing 'backlash':

> It is of course correct to point out how the term 'political correctness' was used by the Right as a means of closing down debate, of avoiding criticism or of having to justify opinions or practices, however, the term 'backlash' can serve the same purpose for the Left. Criticism can be dismissed as either part of the 'New Right backlash' or due to inherent racism or sexism. Whether the term used is 'PC' or 'backlash' the same statement is being made; 'I no longer need to justify myself to you, you're part of the a) loony left or b) racist/sexist right' (delete as appropriate depending on which part of your argument you are no longer willing to debate). (McLaughlin, 2005: 296)

Healy also writes about the difficulties of critiquing the ADP/AOP frameworks, and comments:

> that by characterising all those who oppose anti-oppressive practice 'insights' as self-interested or conservative, anti-oppressive theorists insulate their approach from the critical practice reflection required to understand the uses and the limits of the model for promoting critical practice in the diverse institutional contexts of social work activity. (2005: 190)

So where do we go from here? ADP and AOP still has a stranglehold over practice and debate is urgently needed within the profession to consider new ways of understanding diversity and working effectively within our practice to ensure dignity for all in terms of services people receive. What is striking is that in terms of sexuality, the social work academic writing continues to remain largely silent, and the writing that does exist is seen as niche and marginal.

The Government now talks of 'equality strands' within the social policy agendas it sets. However, is this ADP repackaged, with all of the problems of the past still there in terms of the liberal interpretation of oppression? The danger is that this potentially feeds into the problematic nature of identity politics, but with new powers underpinning its implementation (see Chapter 2). McLaughlin asks who it is that is:

> charged with intervening and resolving these ever expanding categories of the oppressed ... it is invariably the state, whether in the guise of the

Government, police or social worker that is likely to be seen as the solution to the problem of oppression. (2005: 294)

This raises a number of issues, including social work's relationship to the State. The care/control paradigm is a powerful one, as social work moves towards gatekeeper for state resources. For McLaughlin, 'AOP views the state as a flawed but ultimately favourable referee, adjudicating between competing identity claims', concentrating on personal rather than structural change as 'the power differences are seen as beyond resolution, so the best we can do is to minimise their impact' (2005: 299). He goes on to comment:

> Taking a stand against oppression in the past brought one into conflict with the state, which stood accused of promoting and benefiting from a society divided along class, race and gender lines. Today, the state and its institutions, increasingly sensitive to charges of discrimination along such lines, publically acknowledge the charge and promise to take steps to eradicate it. (McLaughlin, 2005: 300)

Post-modernism: messages for practice?

In terms of locating the discourses influencing the politics of diversity, Cooper comments:

> Intellectually, diversity politics sits at the confluence of several currents that include liberalism, communitarianism, poststructuralism, post-Marxism, feminism, post-colonialism and queer. Into the twenty-first century, the politics of diversity continue to exert a powerful influence on progressive and radical thinking in the West. (2004: 5)

Healy categorises the ADP/AOP approach to practice as a 'modern critical approach because of its continuing reliance on notions of critical consciousness raising – which imply that there is a singular underlying truth to be exposed' (Healy, 2005: 191).

Healy argues that the four key concepts of 'post theories' are: discourse, subjectivity, power and deconstruction, and it is these concepts that are most helpful in challenging and changing how social work understands diversity in practice. Discourse constructs knowledge in practice. Foucault's view was that 'there is no reality outside of discourse' (1981: 67). Healy (2000; 2005) and Fook (2002) highlight how discourse and language operate in relation to social work practice in different agency settings in powerful and controlling ways.

Subjectivity is concerned with defining self but in a fluid way, thus moving beyond an understanding of 'identity' as rigid and non-changing, which in the area of sexuality is of particular importance. Healy suggests that these identity labels often require us to take on board identifications that are in themselves sources of oppression (Healy, 2005). Butler comments:

> Surely there is caution offered here, that in the very struggle toward enfranchisement and democratization, we might adopt the very models of domination by which we are oppressed, not realizing that one way domination works is through the regulation and production of subjects. (Butler, 1993: 4)

Post theorists have a different understanding of power, and the way in which power manifests within relationships. There is a power connection between discourses that should also not be overlooked. The difference in this understanding is that power is not something to be minimised, rather it is something that is always there and this tension can be productive.

> Foucault's approach to power rests on three axioms:
>
> * Power is exercised rather than possessed.
> * Power is not primarily repressive, but productive.
> * Power is analysed as coming from the bottom up.
>
> Foucault invites us to shift our analysis from a focus on who possesses power to the consideration of how power is exercised from specific social locations and by specific people. (Healy, 2005: 203)

Finally, deconstruction is concerned with 'breaking apart dualisms to show the range of positions that lie within and beyond opposed entities' (Healy, 2005: 205). This may include dualisms such as homosexual/heterosexual; man/woman; black/white; and so on.

In terms of the critique that post-modern approaches can offer social work practice, Healy outlines a number of additional common ideas that underpin all the 'post-theories', as she refers to them. These include: the rejection of a 'truth' and the narrow definitions of 'reason' upon which many dominant discourses in health and social welfare depend, including the 'psy-discourses'; the questioning of 'progress' as defined by an agency in evaluating interventions; the questioning of the humanist ethos of 'helping/rehabilitating/empowering others'; our identities are not fixed, rather they change according to the circumstance and situation we are in: 'postmodernists focus on understanding local details and complexities, such as the diverse experiences of people within a community, rather than trying to construct a single story or narrative about an event or population' (Healy, 2005: 196).

Many of the criticisms that post-modernism can offer social work are important to consider, as they give a different perspective on aspects of practice that we do not necessarily critique – for example, an under-standing of power dynamics within dominant heteronormative discourses. The work undertaken in this area by academics from other disciplines presents social work with an opportunity to critically re-examine some of the aspects of our practice where current frameworks have been found wanting, such as ADP/AOP. The ADP/AOP approach has not suffi-ciently articulated an understanding of the oppressive experiences of lesbians and gay men and as a profession, social work has not sufficiently engaged with these debates. It may well be that a post-modern analysis will assist in helping us understand the complexity behind why this is.

Some of the criticisms levelled at 'post theories' should also be con-sidered to understand their relevance for social work practice. Criticisms include the degree of focus on the individual, to the detriment of any collective or group-based intervention and a concern that deconstruc-tion can lead to fragmentation and an inability to make concepts matter in terms of the effect for the client's experience of service provision. For example, the adult social care transformation agenda's focus on the indi-vidual having control over the services they receive via direct payments and individual budgets could be simplistically construed as a post-modernist approach to welfare, rather than understood as a capitalist market driven initiative with the goal of saving money.

However, we wonder whether the most significant limitation of 'post' theories for social work is closely linked to its strength. As with RSW, 'post' theories have provided social work and other disciplines with alternative discourses to critique much of the knowledge that underpins practice. But does it help us with any more than that?

One of the disputed limitations of the RSW movement was that it did not move beyond a critique of practice. There are potential similarities with evaluating the post-modern contribution. However, ideas and dis-cussion, debate and dialogue that ensue from their expression are impor-tant in and of themselves. As the RSW movement has demonstrated, the power of ideas to question, critique and comment on status quo practices should not be underestimated. The creation of alternative practice paradigms within an environment currently driven by bureaucratic and managerialist practice will not be quick or easy. But it is often during times of significant unrest and political change where opportunities for challenge, radicalism and alternatives are found.

Summary

We have argued elsewhere that we are now in a position where statute is ahead of social work practice in terms of the legislative and policy support for lesbians and gay men in the UK. Many other academic disciplines outside of social work have a complex understanding of the challenges around diversity politics, including Queer theory; cultural studies; sociology (Weeks, 2003); philosophy (Foucault, 1978; Butler, 1990; 2004; 2009); and social, political and cultural theory (Cooper, 2004; Parekh, 2006). If social work is to meet the challenges of working effectively with diversity more generally and with lesbians and gay men in particular, we need to think differently about our practice in terms of whose interests we serve; whether the current knowledge base for social work and the academic disciplines from where this knowledge comes is still relevant; the complexities of relationships between individuals and the many different communities to which they and we belong; and social work's relationship with the mainstream. If social work is truly a political and social activity, then we need to get back in touch with the political and social elements of our work. Despite the changes in the legal system (see Chapter 2), statistical evidence demonstrating disadvantage for particular groups in society is still evident, particularly in terms of ethnicity, class, gender and disability (National Equality Panel, 2010). We need to remind ourselves of the role of social work in countering this, and that countering disadvantage associated with diversity isn't about creating or expecting sameness, or returning to assimilationist practices of the past. Rather there are many ways to live in this world with dignity, honour and grace. The role of social work is not only to value the concept and politics of diversity, but to execute it in our work with others.

4

Family and kinship and their relationship to social work practice

Introduction

Chapter 2 charts the UK's historical and current legal and policy terrain that lesbians and gay men occupy. As discussed in Chapters 1, 2 and 8, the concept of lesbian and gay 'families' elicited considerable ideological, political and social concern during the 1980s and 1990s. Lesbian and gay relationships did not have legal recognition or protection until the first decade of the twenty-first century; recognition and protection that most of the rest of the world still lacks.

Chapter 2 referred to Bagilhole's three areas of discrimination that lesbians and gay men experienced in the UK up until the 2000s:

- greater restrictions were placed on same-sex sexual activity than on heterosexual sex
- there was less respect for the family life of same-sex partners than for heterosexuals
- protection against discrimination and harassment in the workplace and other parts of society was non-existent. (2009: 113)

This chapter is concerned with 'the family' and 'kinship', the second of Bagilhole's areas identified above. It considers the meanings of 'family' and 'kinship' for lesbians and gay men. We then move on to look at lesbian and gay parenting and lastly we address social work practice within the context of lesbian and gay families and networks.

Wilton argued that:

> the family is an important arena of professional intervention both in health care and (perhaps especially) in social care. It is therefore important to have some insights into the origins of 'the family' and into the variety of family structures that exist. In terms of sexuality, too, the family is a crucial concept, since it is a key element in the policing of sexualities. (2000: 109)

This 'policing of sexuality', to which Wilton refers, was demonstrated very clearly by the enactment of Section 28 of the Local Government Act 1988 which defined lesbian and gay families as 'pretend'.

Understandings of what is meant by 'family' and 'kinship' are significant for social workers as families and kinship networks are the sites of most social work practice as well as social work statutory interventions. This chapter does not address the history or structures of the family and kinship but rather considers some of the debates about their meanings as they relate to lesbians and gay men. Excellent histories of the family exist (Stone, 1977; Trumbach, 1978) and are more generally useful in helping social workers understand the changing nature, structures and diversity of the family and kinship over time. Families and kinship networks have been evolving and continue to evolve. Lesbian and gay families and kinship networks are just one component of that continuing evolution, and add to the continuing diversity of family life and structures.

Family and kinship

Cahill and Tobias define the family as:

> a group who love and care for each other and include within this definition of family:
>
> - A same-sex couple living alone, with other family, or with friends;
> - A same-sex couple with children from previous relationships or adopted or conceived during their relationship;
> - A single parent raising a biological child or biological children, an adopted child, or a relative's child;
> - Individuals living with their families of origin or with their 'families of choice' such as close friends who serve essential care giving functions;
> - Multiple parent networks consisting of, for example, two couples or one couple and an individual who are raising children together;
> - Aunts, uncles, or grandparents raising their nephews, nieces, or grandchildren. (2007: 7)

The list is not exhaustive. These various domestic arrangements and relationships identified by Cahill and Tobias as constituting families are different from the stereotypical image of 'the family' composed of a mother, father and two children living alone in one house. Brown noted how 'the family' has been a:

> central building block in most societies and cultures. How the family should be constructed, and who its constituents can and should be, have been key areas of ideological debate (Barrett and McIntosh, 1982; Brosnan, 1996). The 'family' is often taken to mean a two-generational household, made up of a married heterosexual couple and their birth children, the nuclear family. This particular form of 'family' has had tremendous ideological meaning over and above a particular form of parental unit. (1998a: 90)

Definitions of 'family' and 'kinship' have changed over time, are temporal, racially and ethnically specific and are still evolving. Robb argues: 'Of course marriage and families are historical constructs and, as such, have evolved over time, subject to legal developments, economic forces and cultural attitudes' (2006: 87).

Cahill and Tobias' definition of the family, and what human relationship configurations can be included within this category, encapsulates the key variables of bonds of attachment and responsibilities related to care giving towards others, both children and adults. This seems a fairly straightforward state of affairs and one with which social workers should be familiar and could easily engage. However, as has been discussed earlier, lesbian and gay families and kinship networks have existed in an ideological and social policy framework that neither recognised these familial, emotional and social bonds nor supported them. Indeed Weston writes that, 'for years, and in an amazing variety of contexts, claiming a lesbian or gay identity has been portrayed as a rejection of 'the family' and a departure from kinship' (1991: 22). The concomitant assumption was that to be homosexual was to be without love, attachment, commitment, the ability to procreate, care for or nurture children or adults in any meaningful or reliable fashion. Weston goes further to say that: 'it is a short step from positioning lesbians and gay men somewhere beyond the "family" – unencumbered by relations of kinship, responsibility, or affection – to portraying them as a menace to family and society' (1991: 23).

We have seen in Chapters 1 and 2 how the New Right Conservative Government from 1979 tried to limit lesbian and gay men's capacity to gain access to fertility treatment or to foster children or adopt as a means

of limiting their ability to create what that government referred to as
'pretend families' through the enactment of Section 28 of the Local
Government Act 1988. It is therefore of little surprise that in that hostile
context lesbians and gay men claimed that their family and kinship networks, rather than being 'pretend', were as real as their heterosexual
counterparts. This claim was particularly forcefully articulated in the late
1980s when gay men in particular engaged in caring for sick and dying
lovers and friends as HIV and AIDS took a firm grip on gay male communities in Australia, the USA and Europe. Weeks et al. write that:

> the HIV/Aids epidemic dramatised the absence of relational rights for non-
> heterosexuals in a climate of growing prejudice and enhanced need. Same
> sex partners were often ignored or bypassed by medical authorities as their
> lovers lay sick or dying. (2001: 18)

To have those intimate, painful, absorbing commitments relegated to
something lesser than heterosexual caring commitments was both
insulting and inaccurate. At that time the independent social welfare
sector, local authority social services departments and the National
Health Service (NHS) had to respond to the absolute reality of these
homosexual intimate relationships and social connections.

In creating new definitions of family and kinship networks that have
relevance to lesbians and gay men, those writing in this area have drawn
on the work of Butler (2004), Foucault (1978) and Giddens (1992)
amongst others to try to define and re-define the meanings and record
the lived realities of lesbian and gay men's intimate commitments and
responsibilities to others. In doing so, such terms as 'families we choose'
in the USA (Weston, 1991) and 'families of choice' in the UK (Weeks
et al., 2001) were coined. In the attempt to try to define lesbian and gay
intimate attachments, commitments and responsibilities, it could be
argued that in coining this notion of 'choice', those authors positioned
lesbians and gay men in such a way that suggested that they had 'chosen'
the social and familial networks they created whereas heterosexual people had not. We would refute this. Many heterosexual adults' intimate
attachments and domestic arrangements also have an element of choice
attached to them, are not uniform, and are increasingly diverse in structure. We would also posit that lesbians and gay men's familial and social
network and kinship arrangements sometimes lack choice and are as
full of obligation as their heterosexual counterparts; for example, a
grandchild's obligation to visit their grandmother's lesbian partner at

New Year is likely to be as pleasurable and irksome as if their grand-mother had been a heterosexual married woman. The notion of 'choice' is temporally specific and was debated and named in the context of the 1980s and 1990s in the USA and the UK when many of these 'families of choice' involved lesbian and gay men parenting for the first time. We would also argue that these 'life experiments' associated with same-sex intimacies (Weeks et al., 2001) were similar in many respects to the sexual, social and family 'experiments' of the 1920s and 1930s (Nicholson, 2003) and the 1960s and 1970s (Dowrick and Grundberg, 1980). These 1920s, 1930s, 1960s and 1970s 'experiments in living' involved homosexuals, bisexuals and heterosexuals. Weston (1991) was aware that this notion of 'choice' was an adult perspective. She records one of her interviewee's comments when she writes:

> Lesbian and gay parents are part of the 'we' in families we choose, but from a child's perspective, as Jeanne put it; the context is going to be defined by having different parents. And she didn't *choose* it. She just *has* it. (1991: 195)

In problematising this idea of 'choice' we are not suggesting that Weston (1991) and Weeks et al.'s (2001) work on lesbian and gay families and kinship networks is unimportant, as we believe it was significant and still is. As well as it having importance for lesbians and gay men in authen-ticating their lives and day-to-day work and home experiences, their research contributed to debates that have influenced the social policy agenda and impacted on the rapid process of legislative change. Thus their work in the USA and in the UK contributed to debates and the building of knowledge that helped in the recognition, and in the UK context the legislative protection, of lesbians and gay men's intimate and domestic relationships.

Both Weston (1991) and Weeks et al. (2001) provided invaluable information regarding how lesbians and gay men organise and under-stand their intimate domestic, familial and social networks. Weston inter-viewed 80 lesbians and gay men in the San Francisco Bay area from 1985 to 1987 and the Weeks et al. study was conducted in the UK from 1995 to 1996 and involved interviews with 96 lesbians and gay men. Both studies undertook in-depth interviews with their samples and both looked at the interconnections between the interviewees' relationships with their birth families and the families and social networks they had established as adults. Both studies coined the word 'choice' to try to emphasise what might be different about these new lesbian and gay intimate arrangements. Both studies also identified a dynamic of 'assimilation or difference' (Weeks et al., 2001: 191) and 'assimilation or transformation' (Weston, 1991: 197) that has been identified again by Hicks (2011). This dynamic is best articulated by the different positions taken by Butler (2004) and Calhoun (2000) discussed below.

Hicks' (2011) work on queer genealogies offers an excellent commentary on the usefulness or otherwise of the concepts of 'family' and 'kinship' for lesbians and gay men and considers what might take their place as concepts as well as lived forms, spaces and experiences. The major criticism of both the concepts of 'family' and 'kinship' is that they have traditionally been associated with legal and genetic bonds which have excluded lesbians and gay men. Hicks describes two responses, as identified above, to this exclusion of lesbian and gay men; the first being that of Calhoun (2000) who argues that legal recognition of lesbians and gay men's intimate relationships between themselves and their dependent children will provide some degree of remedy for this exclusion. On the other hand, Butler (2004) argues that such legal recognition for lesbians and gay men can in itself be problematic, as it legitimises only certain types of relationships and therefore continues to exclude others. This debate is a continuation of what Weston in 1991 identified as 'assimilation', something that would be achieved for some lesbians and gay men through Calhoun's position of arguing for legal recognition, rather than what Weston described as 'transformation'. However, what 'transformation' would actually entail is less well articulated or developed. Hicks (2011) re-visits this question of what would take the place of family and kinship, describing this as 'queering kinship', and sets out what this might actually look like.

Weeks et al. (2001) identify two important and related 'characteristic elements' in the debates and movements surrounding lesbian and gay equality more generally, and specifically in relation to kinship and family: transgression and citizenship. 'Transgression is necessary in order to face traditional ways of life with their inadequacies, to expose their prejudice and fears. But without the claim to full citizenship, difference can never be fully validated' (2001: 196). Here we have the argument for both difference and transformation but also for assimilation through citizenship, which can only be achieved through legal and policy recognition and protection. With citizenship comes rights as well as responsibilities, and with rights and responsibilities comes the confidence to debate the detail and lived experiences of lesbian and gay family life (Mitchell, 2010).

Lesbian and gay parenting

We have focused on parenting in this chapter as this is the one aspect of lesbian and gay family life that has attracted unprecedented attention. Campion noted that the increasing tolerance of lesbians and gay men did not stretch to increased tolerance of them parenting.

> However, any suggestion of openly gay or lesbian adults as parents seems to produce a huge outcry – somehow, having children brings parents into a public arena where their personal lives can be justifiably criticised. All the age-old arguments come flying forth: homosexuality is sinful, perverted, unnatural. (Campion, 1995: 176)

Although lesbian and gay parenting is now both legally recognised and indeed protected through legislation in the UK, it remains to some degree a contested area. This is not the case for other aspects of lesbian and gay caring roles within families. For example, the care of a mentally ill partner or a chronically sick parent living with their son and his civil partner would attract little public outrage. Such caring relationships would generally pass without comment.

We are reminded of the rapid rate of social change regarding public and legal attitudes to lesbians and gay parenting when we look back at UK publications of the 1980s. Hanscombe and Forster's book was important as a record of conversations with lesbian parents across the UK during 1978. The women they spoke to were living in a variety of different circumstances. Some had conceived children within marriages and had subsequently separated from their husbands, some had conceived children as single parents and others had conceived children within lesbian relationships. The book offers an important historical insight into the lives of lesbian families at that time. Many of these women had experienced custody battles as a result of their lesbianism. At the time of their writing Hanscombe and Forster noted the negativity of the courts towards lesbian mothers.

> The attitude of the courts is exemplified by a House of Lords judgment in 1976: 'Change in public attitudes should not entitle the courts to relax in any degree the vigilance and severity with which they should regard the risk of children at critical ages being exposed or introduced to ways of life which may lead to severance from normal society, to psychological stresses and unhappiness and possibly even to physical experiences which may scar them for life. (1982: 67)

Hanscombe and Forster noted the degree of concern and anxiety that the women they interviewed had about losing custody of their children because of their lesbianism. Given the High Court judgment of 1976 cited above, this is of little surprise.

In the USA and in the UK, during the 1960s and 1970s, lesbians were losing custody of their children because of their sexuality. The idea that children's psychological, educational and emotional development would be impaired if their parents were homosexual was a commonly held belief and held sway within social work agencies as well as within the courts at that time. In 1986 the Rights of Women Lesbian Custody Group wrote the *Lesbian Mothers' Legal Handbook* as an attempt at enabling women to be better prepared when arguing for the custody of their children. They wrote:

> Many lesbian mothers still lose custody of their children solely on the basis of their sexuality, regardless of their parenting abilities and material circumstances. Even if the children wish to stay with their mother and she has looked after them almost exclusively since they were born, the judgment still often goes against her. (1986:1)

In the USA and in the UK during the 1970s child psychologists and psychiatrists became interested in looking at whether or not children's development was impaired through being cared for by lesbian mothers. In the UK the first piece of research to consider this question looked at the outcomes for children of lesbian mothers compared with the children of single heterosexual mothers (Golombok et al., 1983). This study examined the educational, psychological, sexual and social development of the children of these women and found no significant differences in the outcomes between the two groups. In 1990 this early research was further developed into a longitudinal study (Tasker and Golombok, 1995; Golombok and Tasker, 1996) which was the first of its kind in the UK. They concluded that:

> children brought up by a lesbian mother not only showed good adjustment in personal and social development as young children but also continued to function well as adolescents and young adults, experiencing no detrimental long term effects in terms of their mental health, their family relationships, and relationships with peers and partners in comparison with those from heterosexual mother families. (Tasker and Golombok, 1997: 37)

These findings replicated those found in similar studies in the USA (Patterson, 2005).

There has been less research conducted on the outcomes for children brought up by gay men although this is beginning to change (Bailey et al., 1995; Barrett and Tasker, 2001; 2002; Patterson, 2004). These studies indicate similar outcomes for children with gay fathers to those growing up in lesbian families and those who live within heterosexual families.

Since the early research on the development of children growing up in lesbian and gay families started in the 1970s, there have been a significant number of further studies. A number of helpful research reviews evaluate and summarise the main findings (Scott, 2002; Bos et al., 2005; Patterson, 2005; 2006; Tasker, 2005; Tasker and Patterson, 2007; Goldberg, 2010).

In their paper reviewing research on lesbian and gay parenting conducted in Australia, the USA and UK, Tasker and Patterson conclude as follows:

> The main studies examining developmental outcomes report few significant differences between the development of children with lesbian and gay parents and children with heterosexual parents in terms of gender or sexual identity or the many aspects of personal identity development so far considered. However, we know far less about the development of the children of gay fathers than we do about the children of lesbian mothers. Results of research to date suggest that children of lesbian and gay parents have positive relationships with peers and their relationships with adults of both sexes are also satisfactory. The picture of lesbian mothers' children that emerges is one of general engagement in social life with peers, with fathers, with grandparents, and with mothers' adult friends – both male and female and both homosexual and heterosexual. (2007: 27–8)

Goldberg in her review of existing research findings also concludes:

> The research on lesbian and gay parents strongly indicates that they are no less equipped to raise children than their heterosexual counterparts. They possess the skills necessary to be good parents, and they enjoy healthy relationships with their children. (2010: 120)

There have been a number of criticisms levelled at existing research on lesbian and gay parenting. The first criticism concerns the size and demographic characteristics of the samples that have been drawn upon. Goldberg writes, 'We must remember that what we know about lesbian and gay parent families is limited to research that largely references the

experiences of white, middle-class families' (2010: 187). In their consideration of the research findings Mallon and Betts also suggest that 'there
are biases towards surveying white, urban, well-educated and mature
lesbian mothers and gay fathers, and the relatively small samples studied
have been recruited through community networks' (2005: 20). However,
there are important exceptions to this; Golombok et al.'s study (2003)
draws on existing cohort study samples which meant that the sample
they used was demographically diverse and not self-selecting. In addition, Hill's study (1987) looked specifically at Black lesbian mothers and
compared their parenting styles and attitudes to those of Black heterosexual mothers and found no significant differences.

   A second criticism is that most of the research findings relate to
outcomes for the birth children of lesbian and gay parents, rather than
for adopted or fostered children. Although there are a number of
adopted children in some research samples, the overwhelming majority
of the children have been birth children. There have been a small
number of studies comparing the behaviour of adopted children placed
with lesbians and gay men to those placed with heterosexual adopters
and the findings suggest no significant differences between the different
groups of children (Erich, et al., 2005; Averett and Nalavany, 2009).

   Despite the limited nature of this research and the lack of research on
foster children placed with lesbian or gay carers the findings related to
birth children research has often been assumed to apply to adopted and
fostered children where the foster carers or adopters are lesbian or gay.
Both Scott (2002) and Tasker and Bellamy (2007) have raised the question of the probity of applying research findings relating to birth children of lesbian and gay parents to Looked After Children and assuming
that these findings still apply. Scott writes:

> [T]here are also limitations in how far findings of such research on biologi-
> cally related parents and children can be simply 'borrowed' to answer ques-
> tions concerning the impact on children being adopted or fostered by
> lesbians and gay men. (2002: 12)

The *Adoption Quarterly* journal special issue (2009) on adoption by
lesbians and gay men goes some way towards meeting this gap in
research knowledge.

   Thirdly, as noted earlier there has been less research done on the outcomes of children growing up with gay men and the findings from
research on lesbian parenting outcomes have often been assumed to
apply to gay men, without this necessarily being proven. However,

Golombok's general finding regarding parenting and its impact on child and adult development is important to remember here:

> Just because children are conceived in unusual ways, or live in unusual family circumstances, does not necessarily mean that they are more likely to grow up psychologically disturbed. Family structure, in itself, makes little difference to children's psychological development. Instead, what really matters is the quality of family life. (2000: 99)

The impact of research on lesbian and gay parenting, conducted since the 1970s, has had considerable influence on social work, psychiatric and legal opinion as noted by Cahill and Tobias (2007). They point out the impact that such research findings have had on American organisations that influence child welfare.

> The vast majority of children's advocacy organizations recognize that most lesbian and gay parents are good parents and that children can and do thrive in gay and lesbian families. Several leading professional organizations concerned with child welfare have made statements to this effect.
>
> The American Academy of Paediatrics – 'A growing body of scientific literature demonstrates that children who grow up with 1 or 2 gay and/or lesbian parents fare as well in emotional, cognitive, social and sexual functioning as do children whose parents are heterosexual' (Perrin et al., 2002).
>
> The American Psychoanalytic Association – 'Accumulated evidence suggests the best interest of the child requires attachments to committed, nurturing and competent parents. Evaluation of an individual or couple for these parental qualities should be determined without prejudice regarding sexual orientation. Gay and lesbian individuals and couples are capable of meeting the best interest of the child and should be afforded the same rights and should accept the same responsibilities as heterosexual parents' (American Psychoanalytic Association, 2006). (2007: 12–13)

These statements are a long cry from the spirit and content of the UK High Court judgment made in 1976 cited above. Research in this area has had a very real impact on both professional and legal opinion in the past thirty years.

Social work practice within lesbian and gay families and networks

What are the implications of the above for social work practice? Social workers in 2010 are practising within a legal and policy framework in the UK that is very different from that of Weston's, in the USA in the late 1980s, and Weeks et al.'s, in the UK in the late 1990s. Lesbians and gay men have achieved much of Calhoun's envisaged protection of their intimate family relationships involving adults and children, through the impact of research findings and legislative change. Many lesbian and gay men's domestic arrangements, families, kinship and social networks are remarkably ordinary and are a long way from the transformational politics that were envisaged by some. This 'ordinariness' is a considerable achievement in itself. As Weeks writes: '[T]he very ordinariness of recognised same-sex unions in a culture which until recently cast homosexuality into secret corners and dark whispers is surely the most extraordinary achievement of all' (2007: 198).

For social workers, what is important to take from the research conducted by both Weston (1991) and Weeks et al. (2001) and the research on outcomes for children growing up in lesbian and gay families is that the meaning of 'family' and 'kinship' varies over time and in different contexts. Family structures, in and of themselves, are not damaging to children, providing children receive warmth and nurturing care from the adults parenting them (see Chapter 8).

To conclude this chapter we address three areas: social work knowledge; different family structures and conception of children; and the 'coming out' process for lesbians and gay men within the context of the family.

Social work knowledge

Brown considered the problematic nature of social work 'knowledge' in its application to working with lesbian and gay men and their families:

> Social work knowledge is problematic for many reasons. One reason is that social workers' use of aspects of such knowledge may have contributed to the discrimination against lesbians and gay men with whom they came into contact. The relationship between knowledge and values is a complicated one; the use of knowledge is, not surprisingly, subjective. (1998a: 57)

Much 'knowledge' taught on social work courses to inform social workers about both individual and family development and functioning draws on material and research findings that refer, but rarely explicitly, to heterosexual families and individuals. Much of this material will be relevant to social work with lesbian and gay families but some areas might be different and/or need additional knowledge, the research findings above on lesbian and gay parenting being a case in point.

We have also argued the importance of contextualising knowledge historically and socially so ideas are not rejected that might still have significance and value when working with lesbian and gay individuals and families. For example, some aspects of both Erikson's (Bywater and Jones, 2007; Gibson, 1991) and Bowlby's (Riley, 1983) work have been seen as sexist and homophobic. Gibson (1991) points out that Erikson's life cycle approach to human development is explicitly a heterosexual model. He writes in respect of Erikson's sixth stage of development, 'Intimacy versus isolation' (Erikson, 1965), that 'such a definition raises all kinds of issues, not least about the relative importance of orgasm, heterosexual love and procreation'. However, Erikson was writing in 1965 in a context where most people assumed heterosexuality the norm. Knowledge as well as the social and legal position of lesbians and gay men has moved on considerably since that time. To dismiss off hand the work of individuals like Erikson as having no relevance for social work practice with lesbians and gay men would be short sighted.

> To suggest that ideas around intimacy, attachment, mothering and separation are not relevant to lesbians and gay men would be dehumanising. (Brown, 1998a: 67)

When working with lesbian and gay families, whether the focus is on parenting, care of an older person, an adult with a learning disability, or a person with a mental health problem, our interventions need to be informed by relevant knowledge.

> First, all knowledge drawn upon needs to be critically evaluated and contextualised. Second, specific knowledge within a particular area of practice that directly addresses the lives of lesbians and gay men needs to be sought out. This then means that the practitioner can be as well informed as possible before engaging with service users. No knowledge ever allows us to 'know' another's experience, but it does enable the practitioner to engage, in a more informed way. The only way of really 'knowing' another's experience is by asking them. How we ask will be affected by the knowledge we have access to and how we have made use of it. (Brown, 1998a: 71)

There is a close overlap with knowledge and skills. To be able to make use of knowledge to inform practice, social workers need to engage with clients and carers in an effective fashion. To fully engage involves working in such a way as to elicit the actual lived circumstances and experiences of that individual, their family and their kinship and social network. There are a number of publications that put forward a psychological perspective about lesbian and gay family structures and processes that are relevant to social work. Patterson and D'Augelli (1998) is of particular relevance.

Different family structures and conception of children

There is little doubt about the increasing number of children being raised by lesbians and gay men either as their birth children or through fostering or adoption. 'In recent years, the number of children with gay, lesbian, or bisexual parents has increased with more lesbians and gay men having children in the context of a lesbian and gay identity' (Tasker and Patterson, 2007: 11).

Social workers will be in contact with lesbian and gay families for the same variety of reasons that heterosexual families come into contact with social workers. It is therefore important that social workers are aware of and are sensitive to the variety of lesbian and gay family structures. Tasker and Patterson (2007) describe different family structures that lesbians and gay men occupy and the various ways in which, if they have children, those children might have been conceived.

The legal aspects of the interrelationships between the child and the adults will vary according to the conception route and the adults involved with the child. This was discussed by Saffron (1994) and more recently by Stonewall (Stonewall, 2009). The Stonewall publication, which is specifically relevant to lesbians, is particularly helpful for social workers as it has a section within it outlining the legal position of children and adults depending on the family structure and the means of conception.

For social work practitioners it is important to have an understanding of how members of a lesbian or gay family define themselves and what the legal as well as the social and emotional relationships are between all the members. Without this information it would not be possible to make an informed assessment of the family's circumstances and their needs or to make an informed assessment of what social work interventions or resources might be necessary and effective. This is relevant whatever the context of the social worker's involvement whether it be child protection, mental health or supporting a family in caring for a child with cerebral palsy.

The 'coming out' process for lesbians and gay men within the context of the family

A case study

Jeff and Flo are foster carers for a North of England local authority. Jeff is a retired chemistry teacher and Flo has always been a full-time foster carer and mother. They are Scottish, in their early sixties and have been fostering for over 30 years. They married in their early twenties and are devout Christians who attend their local Methodist Chapel regularly. They have two adult children and six grandchildren. Their daughter Julie and her husband Peter are also foster carers for the same local authority. Ten years ago they had a sibling group of three placed with them. The oldest foster daughter has moved on to semi-independent living aged 19. She is now 23 and comes home each Sunday for lunch with her partner Abdul. Their youngest foster daughter is 13 and their foster son Jamie is 17.

Jamie has done well educationally and is now at Sixth Form College studying for his 'A' levels. Jamie wants to be a vet. Peter, Flo and Jeff's son-in-law, is a vet in their local town and for the past three months Jamie has had a work experience placement at his practice every Thursday evening after College.

Despite experiencing severe neglect in their early lives, and after a number of moves between foster placements, the children eventually settled with Jeff and Flo and became attached to them after a difficult first two years. They have no direct contact with their birth parents who did not maintain contact with them after a Care Order was made.

The children's social worker has recently wondered if Jamie might be gay because of his preoccupation with his clothing and personal appearance. He was concerned that Jeff and Flo would not be able to accept this if it were true. At Jamie's most recent children's Looked After Review he raised the possibility of Jamie being gay (Jamie was not present at this point in the review meeting) and asked how Flo and Jeff would cope with this if it were to be the case. He was concerned about Jeff's joking approach to the discussion and recorded in the children's paperwork that he was concerned that Jeff was homophobic. He contacted Jeff and Flo's supervising social worker and said that he thought work should be done around their homophobia. He also informed the supervising social worker that he was exploring other placement options for Jamie that he thought would meet his needs as a young gay man. It then transpired that in the past six months Jamie had started a relationship with a 17-year-old boy who attended the same Sixth Form College. He has confided in Julie, Jeff and Flo's daughter, with whom he has a close bond, about this relationship. She has been supportive and encouraging of Jamie talking with Jeff and Flo.

Comment

This scenario raises a number of questions. Why did the social worker raise the question of Jamie's sexuality in a review meeting? On what basis did the children's social worker make the assumption that Jeff was homophobic, and why did this later extend to both Jeff and Flo needing work done about *their* homophobia? Why would Jamie being gay mean that it would be desirable for him to be moved from his permanent placement with foster carers to whom he is deeply attached and a foster home where he has been successfully placed with his siblings for the past ten years?

For most heterosexual birth, adoptive and foster parents the realisation that a child is gay or lesbian is usually a shock. Strommen (1990) and Lovell (1995) describe the crisis that can be experienced in families when a child's sexuality is revealed to be different from what had been assumed. However, where there is a secure enough attachment, most families manage this crisis:

> The initial feelings of shock and rejection can be worked with in most cases, to facilitate the re-emergence of the more important feelings of attachment that will enable the family to adjust to this new aspect of the young person's identity. (Brown, 1998a: 107)

Strommen writes in a similar vein that:

> [F]amily members undergoing this redefinition and development of new values and roles need factual, unbiased information about homosexuality to help them gain a balanced perspective on the trauma they are experiencing … By providing facilitating, non-pejorative assistance to the family, we can lessen the confusion and uncertainty these families experience as they wrestle with the reconstruction of long held but never-examined beliefs and assumptions, and help them to keep the intimate circle of the family intact and healthy. (1990: 29)

The social worker in this case might be falling into a common trap of over focusing on Jamie's sexuality at the expense of a more holistic understanding of his emotional and developmental needs. We are not suggesting that Jamie's sexuality is not important or that the social worker might not be right in thinking that Jeff and Flo might find caring for a gay young man difficult. However, his attachment to his foster parents is of paramount importance particularly as: he is maintaining his relationships with his siblings; he has been stably placed with them for ten years; he is achieving well educationally; both he and his foster parents have positive aspirations for his future and both he and his foster carers are attached to one another. It is also evident that Flo and Jeff are able to maintain relationships with their foster children into adulthood as has been demonstrated through their continuing relationship with Jamie's oldest sister. Jamie's social worker might himself feel anxious about Jamie's developing sexuality. Rather than working directly with the difficult feelings and responses of Jeff and Flo it might be easier for him to engage in action, for example looking for a new placement. In focusing only on Jamie's sexuality to the exclusion of all else he is in danger of dehumanising Jamie and losing sight of a holistic view of his developmental and emotional needs, and his secure attachment to his foster carers.

In this case Jamie's social worker, who had worked with the children for many years, was helped to work directly with Jamie and his foster carers with their supervising social worker, who knew them well. When Jeff and Flo were talked to in a non-accusatory and facilitative manner, they were able to share that they too had grown to assume that Jamie was probably gay. Flo and Jeff felt that they should not raise the question of 'gayness' with Jamie as this could be too intrusive. However, they were able to hear from the social workers how their joking approach to both gender and sexuality might act as an inhibitor for Jamie talking with them. They considered together how they might introduce conversations that could convey to Jamie that they were open to accepting his sexuality.

Flo and Jeff were able to hold two contradictory positions, as can many parents. The first position was that they did not accept that homosexuality was 'normal'; the second was that they loved Jamie and him being gay would not affect their attachment to him, and indeed they would work hard to make sure he felt secure about his sexuality. When asked if they saw Jamie's sexuality as 'abnormal' they refuted this. As for many parents homosexuality in the abstract was unacceptable but that did not mean that for them their foster child or his sexuality was unacceptable.

The above case study is a composite drawn from other case examples from our social work practice and is an example of how families can enable the bonds of family attachments to be sustained in any manner of circumstances. We have used a positive case example here but by doing so we are not suggesting that all stories have happy endings. What we are suggesting is that when social workers are working with young gay men and lesbians, they do need to actively engage with heterosexual families in an open and sensitive way to help those young people, their carers and parents to sustain their intimate emotional attachments.

> To 'challenge' their 'homophobia' in an angry way will not allow the possibility of the pain, confusion and anxiety lying underneath to be explored sufficiently for them to reconnect with the love they feel for their foster son. This does not mean collusion with homophobia, but enables all parties to engage in real communication and dialogue. (Brown, 1998b: 63)

Even when the outcome is positive, the emotional and social strain of 'coming out' for young lesbians and gay men should not be underestimated.

> Developing a lesbian, gay or bisexual identity is made more complex by the 'assumption of heterosexuality' where people are presumed to be heterosexual unless they state otherwise. A major task therefore facing young lesbians, gay and bisexual people is the process of 'coming out'. It is a continuous one in that it needs to be undertaken in every new situation with new people if the assumption of heterosexuality is going to be challenged. For some young people 'coming out' to family, carers and friends can be a relief and the reactions can be reassuring and supportive. (Bywater and Jones, 2007: 44)

Some young lesbians and gay men do not have such a smooth 'coming out' process within their families. Although conducted many years ago and in a different social context than we have now, the findings of a survey of the experiences of 416 young lesbians and gay men are still relevant today. 'The cumulative effects of a negative self-image, problems at school, the experience of isolation, a lack of the usual support networks, family rejection and so on can lead to a young person feeling quite helpless' (Trenchard and Warren, 1984: 145). The ongoing work of the Albert Kennedy Trust, set up in 1990 to offer supportive lesbian and gay placements for young lesbians and gay men who are unable to live within their own families, is testament to the fact that some heterosexual families do still, in 2011, reject their children on the grounds of their sexuality.

Summary

It is important for social workers not to assume that their own experience and knowledge of family forms and structures will or should apply to everyone. It is necessary to hear from lesbian and gay individual clients or carers how they define the terms 'family' and 'kinship' as meaningful and accurate for themselves. The meaning of family and kinship is not static and will be different for individual clients and carers. As noted earlier in this chapter, it will involve acknowledging the importance of bonds of attachment and responsibilities related to care giving towards others that need to be respected and nurtured by social workers wherever possible.

5

Homosexuality, religion and social work practice

Liberals cannot demand of believers that their beliefs have to conform to some liberal notion of what is right, but neither can religious groups demand that their conscience has a special place in society over and above any other kind of consciousness; the difficulty I think where it arises, is that in defining what constitutes a genuine matter of conscience and how far people should be allowed to pursue their conscience if in so doing they discriminate against others. (Malik, 2009)

Introduction

This chapter will outline and discuss the tensions between homosexuality and religion in social work. This is complex terrain. Not all religions hold a negative view towards lesbians and gay men. However, the influence of many religious leaders and the power of religious teaching are heavily influential in some countries in the world where religion, particularly fundamentalist religious beliefs, are closely associated with significant political and legal influence. We will briefly explore what is meant by fundamentalism before moving on to look at social work's relationship with religion and homosexuality, particularly fundamentalism within Christianity and Islam.

Chapter 3 identified that a major strength of the social work profession is the emphasis that it places on the value base which underpins practice, including a clear professional commitment to diversity and ethical practice. For many marginalised people, prejudice and discrimination are everyday occurrences, whether these acts are based on skin colour, religion, gender, class, age, cultural background, disability, or sexual orientation. The effects of discrimination can be life threatening in their most extreme forms. Discrimination permeates institutional systems and structures (Macpherson, 1999), and affects life chances in terms of employment, housing, and health care (Badgett and Frank, 2007). Given this pervasiveness, there will be times when social workers will also be discriminatory in their behaviour towards others. Whilst the very act of social work involves making decisions that are discriminating in terms of undertaking assessments that will have a role in gatekeeping access to resources and services, the kind of discrimination we are highlighting here concerns a social worker's own prejudices and personal beliefs guiding professional decision-making, where this stands in direct contrast to their professional and legal obligations.

An example of this is social workers' implicit and explicit discrimination aimed specifically at lesbian and gay clients or other social workers who are lesbian or gay (Trotter and Leech, 2002; Trotter and Hafford-Letchfield, 2006; Hicks, 2008). This is not often discussed in social work academia or in practice. In social work education this often, but not always, manifests as a clash in values for students with strong orthodox or fundamentalist religious beliefs. This conflict between individually held religious beliefs and homosexuality and professional expectations and requirements is also witnessed in practice (Sale, 2007). Wilton highlights the links between homophobic attitudes and strong religious beliefs, and states that 'this is as true of clinicians and health and social care professionals as it is of any other group' (Wilton, 2000: 9).

As noted in Chapter 2, in the UK lesbians and gay men now have legal protection in terms of equality in employment law and accessing goods and services; for example: the Sexual Offences (Amendment) Act 2000; the Adoption and Children Act 2002; the Employment Equality (Sexual Orientation) Regulations 2003; the repeal of Section 28 of the Local Government Act 1988 (2003); the Civil Partnership Act 2004; the Equality Act 2006 and the Equality Act (Sexual Orientation) Regulations 2007 (Brown and Kershaw, 2008; Fish, 2007). So where there is irreconcilable conflict between people's personal views and their professional responsibilities, should they be allowed to qualify and practice as a social worker? Is this a legitimate reason to refuse someone access to social work training on the grounds of unsuitability (GSCC, 2002a)? How are the GSCC codes of practice applied when there is a clash between personal belief and professional responsibilities/actions? What is an acceptable solution when problems are identified? How do we get beyond the 'love the sinner, hate the sin' mantra, or the personal values versus professional standards quagmire?

A complicated picture emerges from an examination of the literature as there is limited academic writing that intersects all three areas: social work, religion and homosexuality. Some of the USA and UK based literature looks at the role of religion in social work in terms of issues for service users and how this information is used in assessments and service delivery. This does not include the discussion of where religious views held by social workers pose ethical difficulties in terms of social workers being able to undertake their professional duties or when there is a clash with other values or areas of expression of cultural sensitivity. We will review the UK and USA literature published in this field over the past 10 years.

Laws on homosexuality across the world

There are a number of countries where the death penalty exists for consenting adults taking part in homosexual activities and many other countries where homosexuality is illegal (Ottosson, 2007). Fundamentalist religion is oftentimes embedded in the laws governing the illegality of homosexuality. Iran, Mauritania, Qatar, Saudi Arabia, Sudan, United Arab Emirates, Yemen and Nigeria are the eight countries where the death penalty exists for homosexuality (Amnesty International, 2008). All are nations where Islam is the dominant religion and justify this position under Sharia law. In Nigeria the death penalty exists for consenting sexual acts between adults of the same sex in the twelve Northern provinces with Sharia law. Sharia law is a very strict form of Islamic law, where homosexual behaviour is 'one of the worst possible sins imaginable. A judge may order the execution of any individual believed to be lesbian or gay without a trial' (Wilton, 2000: 43). Amnesty International estimates that there are in excess of seventy countries where homosexuality is illegal (Baird, 2004).

There are also a small number of countries where homosexual partnerships enjoy the same legal position as heterosexual marriage: the Netherlands, Belgium, Canada, Spain and the USA state of Massachusetts. A further number of other countries offer legal protection to lesbian and gay partnerships via civil unions/partnerships: UK, Denmark, Norway, Sweden, Switzerland, Czech Republic, Finland, France, Germany, Greenland, Iceland, Luxembourg, Slovenia, Andorra, New

Zealand, and some parts of Argentina, Australia, Brazil, Canada, Italy, Mexico and the USA (Ottosson, 2007).

Religious fundamentalism   ■ ■ ■ ■ ▪ ▪

Religious fundamentalism involves strict adherence to a literal interpretation of religious texts and sacred writings with very little criticism or debate tolerated. In a number of countries this view is sanctioned by various religious and other institutions such as political and legal structures. This perspective is often understood by believers as promoting a favoured relationship with a divine being. Anyone not meeting these religious requirements is judged unworthy, and can suffer any number of punishments as a result of their lack of demonstrable faith. Wilton defines fundamentalism as:

> [T]he belief that religion and politics are the same thing, that the state should be run according to religious law, and that the judicial system should enforce obedience to a particular creed. Unbelievers or heretics may be excluded from the state, punished or killed, since fundamentalism admits of no debate or religious tolerance. (2000: 39)

Laythe et al. identify three roles within religious fundamentalism: 'a style of belief that is characterised by a militant belief system, a sense of one absolute truth and a sense of a special relationship with God' (2002: 624). Wilton notes that 'an important characteristic of our own post-modern world is the rise of fundamentalist movements, whether Islamic, Christian, Hindu, or Sikh, and such movements may have a dramatic impact on the sexual cultures under their influence' (2000: 37). Religious fundamentalism has been linked to the way in which political power in many countries influences laws and policies impacting negatively on lesbians and gay men (de Jong, 2003; Greenwood, 2007; Ottosson, 2007), and this influence stretches far beyond those countries listed above influenced by Islam. In the USA, the 'religious right' has considerable financial resources and political influence. Within the UK, the 'religious right' has not been as organised in funding campaigns opposing lesbian and gay rights (Wise, 2000).

Laythe et al. (2002) found that religious fundamentalism was a significant positive predictor of prejudice against lesbians and gay men. This study statistically controlled Christian orthodoxy and right-wing authoritarianism and found that prejudice towards lesbians and gay men was present irrespective of this statistical control, whereas it was not present for racism.

Religions and homosexuality   ■ ■ ■ ■ ■ ■

Even though many of the sacred writings of the world's main religions – Judaism, Christianity, Sikhism, Hinduism, Islam and Buddhism – barely mention homosexuality (Wilton, 2000: 9), the tension between homosexuality and religion is longstanding. This chapter will not examine specific pieces of holy writing and examine the various interpretations of sacred texts – this has been done elsewhere (Wilton, 2000: 40–42; Morrow and Tyson, 2006: 386–92; Halstead and Lewicka, 1998). It would, however, be wrong to suggest that each religion had only one perspective on homosexuality. Indeed, Yip notes that theologically, many particularly non-monotheistic religions, such as Buddhism and Hinduism, have a broader tolerance of homosexuality (Yip, 2007: 214). It would also be simplistic to suggest that religious meaning within societies does not change over time. Knowledge about the history and the politics of religion helps us understand how ideas of sexuality within religions have changed (Wilton, 2000).

Within the religious communities in the UK, homosexuality is both divisive and unifying. It is unifying in the opposition directed at it, as most mainstream religions do not embrace homosexuality as a legitimate choice or position equal to that of heterosexuality, even if some Christian denominations are more accepting of their members of congregation who are lesbian or gay than others. From research undertaken in the USA identifying links between religion and public opinion towards homosexuality, there is a high correlation between those who are affiliated to a mainstream religious community and attend services regularly, and opposition to lesbian and gay equality. Those with the most liberal views are Jews, mainstream Protestants (e.g. Presbyterians, Methodists, Church of England), and those with no religious belief or affiliation, whilst those with more conservative views are Catholics and evangelical Protestants (Olson, 2007: 443). In recent years the debates about homosexuality within the world-wide Anglican community have threatened to split the church into fundamentalist/orthodox and liberal/progressive branches.

Homosexuality is enormously contentious within the Muslim community, most often condemned, regarded as an abomination, and rejected as a way of life. This has not often been commented on within social work literature. One exception to this is Ashencaen Crabtree et al. (2008). The authors refer to homosexuality within the Muslim community being seen as an 'unlawful' sexuality, according to religious beliefs. Further, they argue that homosexuality is viewed as a lifestyle choice, and the rejection of homosexuality is cultural, religious/faith based, and influenced by social class and education. The authors do highlight other views present within the Muslim community that suggest a distinction can be made between specific sexual acts of homosexuality, which are problematic, and the 'inclination', which isn't acted upon. This position is shared within other religions (Halstead and Lewicka, 1998: 53), including Christianity. Within Christianity this position has brought about a compromise in the heated debate within the Church of England in terms of embracing homosexuality as an 'orientation' but rejecting the sexual 'practice' (Yip, 2007: 213). The current Church of England view about lesbian or gay clergy is that they must be celibate because of their 'exemplary' role as 'messengers, watchmen and stewards of the Lord' (Church of England, 1991: para 5.14). This discourse is deeply problematic at a theoretical and practical level, because it is a reductionist position that limits sexuality to sexual acts. Yip comments that '"orientation" and "practice" are integrated parts of one's sexual being and identity' (Yip, 2007: 213). Further, it continues to view the dominant discourse of adult sexuality as heterosexual, and expressed within marriage (Yip, 2007; Hicks, 2008). In this regard Christianity is not alone, as this is the position espoused within many other religious teachings, including Islam, with marriage between a man and a woman perceived as divinely ordained.

Within the Muslim community, Yip comments that 'homosexuality is widely perceived as a "Western disease", a natural outcome of what many consider as the West's secularity, excessive individualism and cultural degeneracy' (Yip, 2007: 212). He comments about the lack of 'theological capital' and internal pluralism within the Muslim community as compared to the Christian community, in terms of the growth of theological resources that affirm sexualities other than heterosexual. He also helpfully draws attention to the impact of Islam being a minority religion in the West for believers, in terms of, 'heighten[ing] expectation of adherence and conformity as a form of cultural defence' (Yip, 2007: 212). In this regard it is important to also understand the context in which lesbians and gay men who are Muslim are living in the UK. 'Given that Islamophobia is a problem in general, and that there are indications that this feeds into bullying in schools, a stigmatised sexual identity is likely to add to a deeply troubled dynamic leading to multiple oppression. This victimisation, however, is one which is not likely to be supported through feelings of empathy and solidarity in the immediate community' (Ashencaen Crabtree et al., 2008: 94).

Halstead and Lewicka's article on a Muslim perspective on homosexuality is a useful summary of a conservative position on this topic (1998: 56–62). Their rejection of a secular and liberal approach to homosexuality is based on their view that most religious communities reject homosexuality as a lifestyle choice equal to heterosexuality. They question whether Western societies are indeed supportive of homosexuality as 'an acceptable alternative lifestyle' (1998: 53), and how alternative viewpoints are aired and acknowledged within a developing discourse on this topic. 'Is it possible that their view, though based on a quite different framework of values and presuppositions from the gay and lesbian world view [sic], has nonetheless validity in the modern world as a rationally justifiable alternative cultural perspective on homosexuality?' (1998: 55–6). It is important to consider this viewpoint in terms of understanding the position argued.

Those with orthodox religious beliefs often reject homosexuality as sinful, un-natural, and wicked. Halstead and Lewicka argue that homosexuality is forbidden within orthodox Judaism, it does not have a place within the Sikh way of life, and this is the view held by most other world religions, including Islam (Halstead and Lewicka, 1998: 55–61).

A Church of England Minister, Peter Mullen, wrote in June 2008, 'Let us make it obligatory for homosexuals to have their backsides tattooed with the slogan, "sodomy can seriously damage your health" and their chins with "fellatio kills"' (Butt, 2008). Although publicly apologising after the London *Evening Standard* picked up the story in October 2008, and explaining that his writing was satirical, Mullen said in his apology, 'one might say that what was once a mortal sin is now only a lifestyle choice. And the love that once dare not speak its name now shrieks at us in high camp down every high street ... this situation is what some homosexualist campaigners constantly claim under the doctrine of "rights". It is the reason also that they are so annoyed with me – because I repudiate their "rights" argument' (Greenslade, 2008).

This conflict between personal beliefs and public duties in some circumstances can require the law to mediate. An example of this is the case of Lillian Ladele, a Christian registrar who worked for the London Borough of Islington, who refused to undertake civil partnerships because of her religious beliefs. She eventually took her case to the Employment Tribunal, claiming discrimination, harassment and victimisation because of her religious beliefs, and won (Gammell, 2008). The Local Authority then appealed this ruling and won their case, so her dismissal was lawful (BBC, 2008).

Below are two other examples within England where Christian religious beliefs and homosexuality have clashed in terms of the impact personal beliefs have had on public duties.

Andrew McClintock (a Sheffield Magistrate who is also Christian) said he was forced to resign because he was not prepared to place children for adoption with lesbian and gay couples, and he was refused permission to 'opt out' of hearing such cases by his employer. The Employment Tribunal dismissed his appeal for unfair dismissal. (Fletcher, 2007)

The Catholic Church's Adoption Services were given two years by Tony Blair (the then Prime Minister) in 2007 to conform to the Equality Act (Sexual Orientation) Regulations (2007). Most Catholic Adoption Agencies have now either closed, merged with other voluntary sector adoption agencies which do allow lesbian and gay applicants to be assessed, or have cut their formal ties with the Catholic Church to enable them to meet the legal requirements. Two Catholic Adoption Agencies: St Margaret's Adoption and Child Care Society, a Catholic agency in Glasgow, and the Cornerstone Adoption and Fostering Service, an evangelical agency in the north east of England, have chosen to change their charitable objects to enable them to offer services to married and single applicants only (Caldwell, 2008). The Agency Catholic Care (Diocese of Leeds) appealed to the Charity Commission on the grounds that the organisation had a right to follow church teachings and refuse to consider gay couples (regulation 18 allows charitable agencies to discriminate in certain circumstances and this was the legal loophole that the Diocese of Leeds used to argue their position). However, the Charity Commission has denied the application of other Catholic Adoption Agencies to change the purpose for which they were created in order to avoid dealing with lesbian and gay adoption applicants, and they overturned this legal challenge too on the grounds that this position is unlawful (*Telegraph*, 2009). However in March 2010 the High Court overturned the decision of the Charity Commission, thus allowing the Catholic Care Agency to change its charitable articles to allow it to refuse to assess lesbians and gay men in accordance with its Catholic teachings.

These examples show the strength of negative feeling that exists about homosexuality from a number of religious perspectives. It is plain that there is no easy remedy to resolve such differences in approaches. Within the UK the emerging legal framework now offers lesbians and gay men protection from abuse and blatant homophobia, and religious institutions are expected to comply with this legislation where they offer 'goods and services' to the general public (Fish, 2007; Brown and Kershaw, 2008). The law also protects religious beliefs, but does not allow negative discrimination.

Social work is not immune to these debates either. This next section will summarise some of the debates within the social work literature.

Religion, homosexuality and social work practice: what does the literature say?

There is a growing literature documenting high levels of homophobia amongst social workers (Berkman and Zinberg, 1997; Wisniewski and Toomey, 1987) and social work students (Camilleri and Ryan, 2006; Brownlee et al., 2005; Kohli and Faul, 2005; Trotter and Leech, 2002; Sung Lim and Johnson, 2001; Tirosh, 1998; Trotter and Gilchrist, 1996). This is ironic in a profession that places importance on social justice and anti-discrimination within practice, and presents dilemmas which are not easily resolved.

Van Voorhis and Wagner (2001) reviewed coverage of gay and lesbian subject matter in 12 US social work journals from 1988 to 1997 and found that from a total of 3787 articles published over that period of time, 121 related to lesbians and gay men. The majority of these articles (99%) focused on HIV/AIDS. They surmise about why other articles about lesbians and gay men and social work were published in specialist lesbian and gay journals rather than in the mainstream press.

Since this time there have been some 'think pieces' located in the social work UK and US literature, some of it hotly contested (Hodge, 2005; Jimenez, 2006; Melendez and LaSala, 2006). However, before discussing this, it is important to consider the historical and contemporary role of religion in social work. The term 'spirituality' also requires some explanation.

Religion, spirituality and social work

Within social work literature, the terms 'religion' and 'spirituality' tend to be used to differentiate between beliefs associated with formal institutionalised religions as opposed to a 'spirituality' which affects us all. Although debate exists about what we mean by 'spirituality', Crisp (2008) argues that there is some agreement that spirituality is concerned with how we create narratives which give a sense of meaning and purpose to our lives. Crisp also comments that:

> although religious beliefs … and spiritual values … have been identified as influencing substantial numbers of students to study social work, the social work profession has not, for most of its history, recognised the importance of spirituality in the lives of either service users or the professional workforce. (Crisp, 2008: 366)

Wong and Vinsky (2009) are critical of current theorising about spirituality and religious discourses. They comment:

> [W]e contend that the 'spiritual-but-not-religious' discourse in social work may have inadvertently reproduced the process of colonial othering and further marginalisation of racialized ethnic groups who are more often represented as 'religious'. (Wong and Vinsky, 2009: 1343–4)

Over the last decade there has been a significant rise in the number of published monographs and edited texts about religion and social work (Crompton, 1998; Canda and Furman, 1999; Nash and Stewart, 2002; Canda and Smith, 2003; Moss, 2005; Greenstreet, 2006; Furness and Gilligan, 2009) and academic articles discussing religion and spirituality within social work in the UK and elsewhere (Bowpitt, 1998; 2000; Furman et al., 2004; Gilligan and Furness, 2006; Holloway, 2007; Gray, 2008; Wong and Vinsky, 2009). There is literature available in relation to specific areas in health care, notably nursing (Tanyi, 2002), mental health (Lloyd, 1996; Swinton, 2001; NIMHE, 2003), ageing (Jewell, 1999) and palliative care (Lindgren and Coursey, 1995; Lloyd, 1997).

Prior to this current burgeoning interest, the literature is scant, which is surprising given that modern-day social work has its roots in religious benevolence and philanthropy (Bowpitt, 1998; 2000; Payne, 2005b). Timms commented that it is, 'perhaps in religious belief and practice … a person's values are most clearly apparent … the relationship between religion and casework has received little attention' (Timms (1964) cited in Crompton, 1998).

Bowpitt argued that a re-examination of the religious origins of social work through a lens of 'Evangelical Christianity and its secular humanist transformation' (1998: 675) would show that Christianity still has a role in contemporary social work, although this is now more prevalent within the voluntary sector rather than in statutory social work. He raises some of the conflicts:

> for Christians in statutory social work ... around the ethical issues thrown up around abortion, around certain manifestations of anti-discriminatory practice (e.g. promoting adoption by lesbians and gay men), and around theoretical issues like the nature of ritual child abuse and mental illness (e.g. where spiritual forces are believed to be at work). Social work has become both a land of opportunity and a battleground for Christians. (Bowpitt, 1998: 690)

In the US Journal *Social Work,* a paper by Hodge (2005) that explored the intersection between religion and homosexuality from the perspective of 'people with faith' (2005: 207) elicited two critical responses in the same journal in the following months (Jimenez, 2006; Melendez and LaSala, 2006). These articles helpfully highlight some of the tensions and debates within this area.

Hodge's view is that the differences between Christian beliefs and lesbians and gay men are irreconcilable and that currently lesbians and gay men have more power, more income, more education and more influence within American society and within social work than Christians do. Using a dualistic framework of 'progressive' and 'orthodox' to categorise lesbians and gay men (progressives) and Christians (Orthodox), he suggests that Christians and other orthodox religious people are oppressed within society as a whole and within social work because they are not able to express their views about homosexuality. This is due to fear that these views will be misunderstood as an expression of hatred toward lesbians and gay men, and this is not what is intended, as:

> all human beings have inherent dignity and worth because they reflect the image of God. Gay men and lesbians are no more and no less animated by human turpitude than others. The ethos is egalitarian. All are invited to join the Christian community.(Hodge, 2005: 208)

Hodge also points to the 'transcendent authority' of the Christian faith (2005: 207), and, 'because these values are transcendent, believers do not have the option, at least in principle, of picking and choosing which values they follow' (2005: 208).

Jimenez (2006) and Melendez and LaSala (2006) point out the danger of Hodge's arguments. Melendez and LaSala state: 'to assume that no one can challenge a religious-based position is to expect a privilege that

has no place in an academic setting' (Melendez and LaSala, 2006: 375).
Jimenez comments:

> Are these the dialogues we want, to have to serve the 'gods' of diversity and
> pluralism? Although Hodge does not want the progressive viewpoint
> imposed on him, he does want the freedom to state his views about homo-
> sexuality in the social work classroom. Because the behavior cannot be
> separated from the person (postmodernists argue that our personality is in
> fact a compilation of our behaviors), this discourse would be a condemning
> and destructive one ... But equating respect for religious diversity with the
> right to disparage the actions of our colleagues and our clients is not part of
> the Christian message, although it is part of Hodge's. (2006: 187)

This becomes part of the 'love the sinner, hate the sin' mantra, so often
promulgated by various sections of the Christian religious community
opposed to homosexuality. Melendez and LaSala (2006) locate this
response as a 'double-bind' message and comment: 'At the root of double
bind messages is hostility and aggression that is being masked and denied'
(Melendez and LaSala, 2006: 375). This response is one of the four
Christian ideological responses Canda and Furman (1999) identify.
These four groups are: condemnation; accept the person, condemn the
behaviour; affirmation; and departure from Christianity (Canda and
Furman, 1999).

Empirical studies: homophobia and heterosexism amongst social workers

Wisniewski and Toomey (1987) used the Hudson and Ricketts (1980)
Index of Attitudes towards Homosexuals (IAH) to examine the homophobic attitudes of 77 US social workers, and found that 31 per cent of
social workers were either low grade or high grade homophobic. They
identified that the academic and practice response at that time was to
challenge social workers about how they worked with lesbian and gay
clients in terms of firstly examining their personal beliefs, attitudes and
responses before secondly thinking about their professional response.

> The implied idea was that social workers might view homosexuality as
> pathological, respond effectively to gays and lesbians with fear or disgust, or
> not be sensitive in recognising homophobia in clients. Social workers who
> manifested signs of homophobia were presumed to be less effective, if not
> harmful in the delivery of services. (Wisniewski and Toomey, 1985: 454)

From their examination of previous research in this area undertaken in the USA in the 1970s, Wisniewski and Toomey mentioned a relationship between those with negative attitudes towards homosexuality and more authoritarian behaviour. Their own research supported this finding.

Berkman and Zinberg (1997) also used the Hudson and Ricketts (1980) IAH as well as a number of other scales and measures to examine levels of homophobia and heterosexism within a group of 187 social workers. They found that 10 per cent were homophobic, with the majority of participants heterosexist. They also found that religiosity was associated with higher levels of homophobia and the amount of education and training social workers received related to homosexuality had no correlation to levels of homophobia and heterosexism. This latter finding contradicted earlier research indicating that education had been effective in changing attitudes, and whilst the authors attribute this to differences in methods between their research project and earlier work, they comment that:

> [A]lthough it is possible that our measure of education may not be sensitive to factors that are salient to homophobia and heterosexism, it appears that whatever education is received is of negligible long-range effectiveness. (Berkman and Zinberg, 1997: 327–8)

The relationship between attitudes and religious beliefs is complex. The link in the literature between individuals having conservative religious beliefs, attending church regularly and homophobia is identified by Berkman and Zinberg (1997: 328). They discuss the work of Allport and Ross (1967) and the differentiation made in their work between intrinsic (internal, meaning base) and extrinsic (conventional instrumental approach) orientations to religion. Extrinsic orientations were associated with prejudice whereas intrinsic orientations were more accepting of differences. The work of Herek (1987) 20 years later did not replicate this link and instead found that the degree of orthodoxy associated with belief was the important factor in determining homophobic views, not whether someone's belief was intrinsic or extrinsic.

Berkman and Zinberg's study found no relationship between homophobia and age, but it did find that knowing a colleague or having a friend who was lesbian or gay lessened the prejudicial attitudes held by individuals. This supports other research with similar findings, which has implications for promoting the increased visibility of lesbians and gay men in all areas of social work.

Berkman and Zinberg also questioned whether a correlation could be made between social workers who were homophobic with less effective and harmful services to lesbian and gay clients, given that much of the research supporting this comes from the 1970s and 1980s and since this time there have been a number of changes to the political and social position of lesbians and gay men. They comment, 'Describing the extent of social workers' bias and its correlates is critical to understanding how bias affects clients and to modifying social work education and training to change negative attitudes' (Berkman and Zinberg, 1997: 321).

Professional responsibilities versus personal beliefs

So can social work's professional codes of practice assist with some of the tensions and conflicts that have arisen in the literature? In terms of the US NSAW codes, Pollack states that: 'in the code, discrimination based on sexual orientation and discrimination based on religious beliefs are equally condemned, and respect is equally endorsed. Neither one is "first among equals"' (Pollack, 2007: 179). Pollack acknowledges the incompatibility of some value positions however, but says the following:

> Our job is not to choose between values; it is to provide a safe environment where individual employees, whatever their sexual orientation or religious beliefs, can engage in a meaningful dialogue. Bullying or harassing from either viewpoint should not be condoned. Neither should imperil the other. (Pollack, 2007: 179)

In terms of the UK, Wilton believes that: 'in cases where [faith] comes into conflict with a practitioner's ability to deliver respectful and appropriate care, there is a clear obligation to prioritise professional standards over personal belief or morality' (Wilton, 2000: 10).

Mule (2006) conducted a study examining the relationship between homosexuality and social work ethics and curricula standards in social work qualifying training in Canada, the USA and the UK. He found some consistency between social work codes of ethics and curricula standards in the USA, but less consistency in the UK and Canada. For the UK, Mule used the British Association of Social Work's Code of Ethics (BASW, 2002) and the General Social Care Council's Codes of Conduct (GSCC, 2002a). Although the code of ethics mentions sexual orientation as an area where social workers should not discriminate or 'act out of prejudice' (Mule, 2006: 613), the GSCC (2002a) codes of conduct and practice are less specific, instead using broad terminology that does not name specific groups. This lack of specificity can be linked to the Paper 30 debate which occurred in the 1990s, where the GSCC predecessor, the Central Council for Education and Training in Social Work (CCETSW), described racism as 'endemic' within British society. The Conservative Government of the day reacted to this by pressurising CCETSW to change its equal opportunities statement to only include those groups who had legal protection. At the time lesbians and gay men did not have any legal protection in relation to employment, housing, goods and services, personal and family relationships, so they were not specifically named in the equal opportunities policy (see Chapter 3).

At the time of Mule's research, there were certain requirements for the curriculum covered in the social work degree (Department of Health, 2002a; TOPSS, 2002; QAA, 2000). Whilst the social work standards were revised in 2008 (QAA, 2008), the other two documents have not been updated, and there have been significant legal changes regarding the protection of lesbians and gay men which should be reflected in these documents in terms of information social work students should be taught and have access to on their qualifying programmes. However, Mule comments that these documents and standards are:

> ambiguously written in that they call for social care workers and their employers to address discriminatory behaviour and practice, and to respect diversity, different cultures and values in the absence of any context or definition of these terms ... how they would be implemented remains unexplained. (Mule, 2006: 614)

This ambiguity does not help create structured opportunities for social work students to learn about issues specifically affecting lesbians and gay men, when considering these issues against all the other areas of the curriculum that must be covered. However, many other groups are also not mentioned, and in order to move away from an approach which suggests that one can 'learn' about someone else's oppression, we need to think differently about how these areas are taught in the curriculum.

Complexity in the making

Halstead and Lewicka (1998) are critical of how the liberal values underpinning the education system in the UK and other Western countries are used to influence wider social policy. These values include:

personal autonomy, critical openness, equality of opportunity, rational morality, the celebration of diversity, the avoidance of indoctrination and the
refusal to side with any definitive conception of the good – [these] are clearly
based on the fundamental liberal values of freedom, equality and rationality ...
so too is the notion of rights and, in particular, the rights of minorities in a
liberal democratic society. (Halstead and Lewicka, 1998: 53–4)

They argue that the position of liberal educationalists is that something
is acceptable depending on whether or not it conflicts with 'democratic
principles ... and an acceptance of the gay definition of homosexuality
in terms of orientation rather than behaviour'. They then use survey
material carried out in the USA to show that there is much less support
amongst the general public for homosexuality being viewed and taught
as an acceptable alternative lifestyle:

Undoubtedly the gay and lesbian community will interpret these findings as
evidence of the continuing prevalence of homophobic attitudes, but there is
another possibility – that the underlying presuppositions of the homosexual
perspective, particularly those relating to the notion of sexual orientation,
have not been taken on board by the population at large. (Halstead and
Lewicka, 1998: 54)

However, since this article was published, the social terrain is now different in the UK, with the British Social Attitudes Survey (Park et al., 2010)
reporting that people have become much more tolerant of homosexuality
in the last 30 years, with 64 per cent of the British public now broadly
supporting homosexuality, compared with 1983 where 62 per cent were
of the view that homosexuality was 'always' or 'mostly' wrong.

  Whilst this change in public opinion in the UK is significant and is
to be welcomed, the historical arguments on both sides of the debate
are well rehearsed and are repeated in many of the public debates
which have occurred where homosexuality has arisen as an issue in
public life.

  In terms of understanding the role of religion in the workplace, the
historical roots of the caring professions are religious and this is well
documented (Wilson et al., 2008; Sheldon and Macdonald, 2009).
Greenstreet comments that:

Some individual, contemporary professionals may still see their practice as a
religious vocation and live their faith in the provision of care to those in need
... this intrinsic acting out of religious belief may provide altruistic drive to
individual professional performance, but it is important to differentiate

between practitioner religious fervour and patient/client philosophy to ensure that there is no attempt, either consciously or subconsciously, to pros-elytise. (Greenstreet, 2006: 20–21)

So how does this relate to clashes between homosexuality and profes-sional action? Pollack states that 'as social workers we should be com-fortable in acknowledging that no final conclusion needs to be drawn, no reconciliation needs to be reached' (Pollack, 2007: 180). This state-ment has echoes of the ethnic model of social work 'difference and diversity' perspective which Hicks (2008) criticises as a liberal model highly prevalent in social work that supports the status quo. Tully's (2000) 'empowerment model' for working with LGBT is rigorous in its theoretical underpinning, but relies on a 'strengths based' liberal approach, and whilst this may be a useful tool for practice in some set-tings, it is not easily applicable in cases where considerable conflict and risk are present.

Carr sees the problems within practice as more entrenched and not so 'equi-liberal' in terms of solutions:

> Given that there appear to be difficulties with understanding diversity and the potential conflicts around religion and sexuality at local authority level of service planning and commissioning, it is questionable whether frontline workers are being supported to deal with such complexities at the service delivery level. The extent to which social care practitioners are able to deliver culturally sensitive, innovative and personalised services to a diverse popula-tion without marginalising the needs of LGBT people is also a matter of concern. (Carr, 2008: 116)

We have argued previously that there are dangers in the continued use of ADP as a framework for understanding diversity in practice as it is linked to the politics of a hierarchy of oppression. Carr (2008) argues that one of the unintended consequences of mainstreaming diversity strategies is the creation of a hierarchy of equality that marginalises LGBT interests in order to accommodate faith communities. As we have discussed in previous chapters, the dangers of a simplified use of identity politics and hierarchies of oppression are that they feed into a continua-tion of the status quo in terms of the 'powerful' and the 'powerless' – that is, a society deeply divided and reliant on minority groups fighting amongst themselves to determine whose 'rights' are more 'disenfran-chised' or important at any particular historical moment. This does not drive the agenda forward. We have to feel comfortable in this complexity and move towards a different understanding of its role and purpose. This is where Weeks' social constructionist position, which has a strong ethical base, is useful for social work practice, as is the work of Hicks (2008).

Hicks (2008) uses the work of Lorde to discuss and consider the meaning of 'difference':

> [T]he mere tolerance of difference … is the grossest reformism. It is a total denial of the creative function of difference in our lives. Difference must not be merely tolerated, but seen as a fund of necessary polarities between which our creativity can spark like a dialectic. (Lorde, 1996: 159)

This is not a dualistic situation: not all fundamentalist religious people are anti lesbian and gay men. And some lesbians and gay men are religious. So it is complicated. Judith Butler comments that:

> [P]erhaps there is something more to be considered in the specific forms that ostensible cultural conflicts take, as well as in the way those forms are presupposed by prevalent normative frameworks. The homosexual person at issue may or may not be Muslim, and the Muslim person at issue may or may not be homophobic. But if the framework of cultural conflict (gay versus Muslim) determines how we conceive of those identities, then the Muslim becomes defined by his or her ostensible homophobia, and the homosexual becomes defined, depending on the framework, either as presumptively anti-Muslim or fearful of Muslim homophobia. In other words, both positions get defined in terms of their putatively conflictual relation with one another, at which point we come to know very little about either category or the sites of their sociological convergence. Indeed, the framework of tolerance, even the injunction to tolerance, orders identity according to its requirements and effaces the complex cultural realities of gay and religious lives. (Butler, 2009: 142–3)

Where differences produce conflict is where polarised and simplistic views of both problems and solutions can emerge. These simplify and categorise people, places and positions. This has happened within the religion/homosexuality debate, where the argument has become one of claiming the moral high ground in a bid for creating 'sameness' and creating normative frameworks rather than searching for a meaningful way of understanding the breadth of humanity and experience. All too often this gets lost.

The role of social work, therefore, should move to become one of not only acknowledging the complexities of difference and people's experience of it, but managing across difference in such a way as to proactively search and acknowledge commonalities in human experience, rather than working to a deficit model, which is where the ADP equalities model is located. It is this very notion of 'difference' that is somehow seen as problematic for the client or a block in enabling receipt of appropriate services, rather than a way of being and becoming which is valued for what it is.

Wilton identifies the importance of reflexivity in practice. To look:

> objectively at our own beliefs … may help us respect those of others … it can help us to work out where our own beliefs come from, why we hold them, and to what extent they influence our work. This reflexivity is absolutely central to professionalism in health and social care since, without it, we may be more concerned to 'protect' our sense of what is right than to safeguard the integrity of our client. (Wilton, 2000: 36)

Summary

This chapter has provided a background for exploring the relationship between religion and homosexuality and how this relates to social work. This relationship is not an easy or straightforward one, and there are no simple answers in terms of how the tensions and conflict in the debates between religion and homosexuality in social work can be resolved. If we do not move beyond this current positioning, the argument will always be constructed as one with a lose/win or lose/lose outcome. The significant legal changes introduced over the past ten years in the UK, that now protect lesbians and gay men, will require those individuals with religious beliefs and those religious agencies who offer services to the general community to comply with the legislation. This will create some change in practice. There is, however, some irony in this current situation where legislation and policy are driving through changes in practice in a profession that supposedly aligns itself with a commitment to social justice and social change.

6

Social work practice with lesbians and gay men: working with older adults, adults with learning disabilities and adults with physical disabilities

Introduction

Under the 1997–2010 Labour Government, the modernisation of public sector services has been a priority. Adult social care is no exception, and in recent years a new language of 'transformation' and 'personalisation' has become a feature of the social care landscape, alongside a move to increase the service user voice in the assessment and choice of services via 'direct payments', 'individual' or ' personal budgets'. In conjunction with the introduction of these policy drivers and following the publication of the Gershon report (2004), demographic pressures and the requirement for efficiency savings in the public sector have required the redistribution and reorganisation of available resources in order to meet policy, political and service user led agendas. As the adult social care budget is frequently the largest single budget area of local authorities in England and Wales, the additional scrutiny and pressure on these services has been considerable.

The changing demographic make-up within the UK is an ongoing pressure on services and the significant increase in the numbers of older people living longer will continue to escalate as the post-war baby-boomers reach retirement age. This will invariably place more and different demands on services as expectations change, and will affect the types of services needed by the users who fund themselves as well as those eligible for state funding. In addition, many children and adults with disabilities with more complex needs are now living longer, due to advances in medical care. Increasingly, a higher percentage of people needing adult social care and support services receive them in their own homes rather than having to move into institutions. Support for people to remain as independent as possible, for as long as possible, in their own homes is one of the positive benefits of developments in adult social care over the past decade.

This chapter will provide an overview of some of the major policy agendas within adult social care, examining in particular how the different policy documents address sexuality. Despite some of the positive changes in legislation, lesbians and gay men still face considerable negative discrimination in the provision of adult social care services. This is due to the heteronormative positioning of many of the services, whether consciously or unconsciously, and the invisibility of sexuality generally within social work practice with older adults, adults with physical disabilities and adults with learning disabilities. This chapter will specifically cover these three service areas, whilst the following chapter will address issues of mental health provision. This 'client group' identification in adult social care services has predominated, although there are recent developments which move services away from these definitions. Processes and systems that look at people's aspirations, needs and outcomes, mental capacity and incapacity, risk, enablement and safeguarding are becoming more prominent as transformation and personalisation become more embedded in Adult Social Services.

Adults requiring social services fall into two broad groups. The first group comprises those people with organic and enduring disabilities. This includes adults with either or both physical and learning disabilities, who require continuous services and planning through transitions for lifelong independence or negotiated dependence (i.e. support people to live as independently as possible). Within this area, sexual choices must be respected in the context of a range of decisions about how people want to live their lives. We will look at some of the research being done in this area (e.g. the Tizard Centre at Kent University), and consider how the person-centred planning (DH, 2001) methodology and framework, most often associated with people with learning disabilities, is being used to enable service user choice. This framework has two components: aspirations and needs. We will consider how social workers understand and assess a service user's aspirations and needs in terms of their sexuality, including enabling them to have sexual choice.

Secondly, over time people can develop long term conditions or age related illnesses and disabilities. In these circumstances, most often people have already made decisions regarding their sexuality. Social work practice must therefore consider how to recognise these choices, and meet the needs within available service provision. This includes older people, as age itself is not a criteria for services – it is age related disabilities and illnesses that determines whether someone needs services. Within this group of people, conditions like dementia and mental illness can be relevant. Civil partnerships, pensions and financial information included in the Green Paper published in July 2009 on care options in later life (DH, 2009a) is also significant.

There is a further relevant delineation in the population of people needing adult social care services: those who can afford to fund their own services and access them independently and those who require assistance through statutory organisations and meet eligibility criteria for Local Authority funding of adult social care services. This is discussed below in the context of access to services.

Adult social care: general legislative and policy drivers

Legislation

Following the enactment of the NHS and Community Care Act 1990, there has been little change to the core legislative framework governing adult social care provision. Unlike social work with children and families, the legislative framework is broad and piecemeal, with the National Assistance Act 1948, the Health Services and Public Health Act 1968, the Chronically Sick and Disabled Persons Act 1970, the Mental Health Act 1983 and the NHS and Community Care Act 1990 still determining eligibility for services. However, a number of other pieces of legislation have been passed, including the Disability Discrimination Acts 1995 and 2005, Carers (Recognition and Services) Act 1995, Community Care (Direct Payments) Act 1996, Carers and Disabled Children Act

2000, Carers (Equal Opportunities) Act 2004, Mental Capacity Act 2005, National Health Service Act 2006, Mental Health Act 2007, and the Health and Social Care Act 2008 (Brammer, 2010: 403–6). Some changes to practice have been introduced via case law, especially in relation to eligibility criteria and resources (e.g. R vs Gloucestershire County Council, ex-parte Barry [1997] 2 All ER 1). In addition, the Mental Capacity Act 2005 and the introduction of the Best Interests Assessor (BIA) role for social work has changed the legal framework and protection available for those adults who lack capacity to make decisions for themselves for whatever reason.

The final area that has received considerable attention over the past decade is adult protection and safeguarding. However, this last area is not underpinned through specific legislation, although the 'No Secrets' publication (DH, 2000a) does require Local Authorities to have in place plans to safeguard and protect vulnerable adults from abuse. A recent commitment to pass legislation to put Safeguarding Vulnerable Adults Boards on a statutory footing has been expressed, which will ensure prioritisation across all agencies to deliver appropriate safeguarding (DH, 2009b).

Although much of the legislative developments underpinning the changes within adult social care are to be welcomed, their implementation must also satisfy an expectation of equality and equity for all in access to and provision of services, recognising the complexity of people's lives and the differences in how people choose to live their lives. Stainton comments:

> The idea of equality requires some clarification ... if 'equal' implies simply 'getting the same as everyone else', in essence this means we are ignoring difference that may require either a different way of doing things or additional support ... this complexity makes it impossible to establish general universal provisions that will satisfy all needs. The challenge then for social work and policy is not to find better services, but to create a structure in which individuals can articulate their demands directly and which allow the state to adjudicate and meet legitimate claims. (2009: 352)

For lesbians and gay men, there are a number of factors that might affect any assessment undertaken and any services provided. A decision about whether to 'come out' as gay or lesbian, yet again, and how this is recognised, responded to and included positively in the assessment and service provision process forms part of any lesbian or gay man's experience of the service. As has been covered in Chapter 2, the most significant piece of legislation that ensures legal protection for lesbians and gay men from discrimination in service provision is the Equality Act (Sexual Orientation) Regulations 2007, which prohibits discrimination on the grounds of sexual orientation in providing goods, facilities and services in both the public and private sectors. However, this legal protection is not enough – difficulties are still experienced by lesbians and gay men and we will discuss the reasons for this in the chapter.

Policy

Over the last ten years since the Government launched the White Paper 'Modernising Social Services' (DH, 1998), there have been a number of policy initiatives that shifted the paradigm for adult social care. These arose in response to user led movements, for example from people with disabilities dissatisfied with the way in which care and support have been provided. The establishment of Direct Payments, at first restricted to younger adults with disabilities, provided an initial response. However, the piloting of Individual Budgets aiming to give more choice and control to the service user, through bringing together funding streams to be used flexibly and creatively, has now become mainstreamed through Putting People First (DH, 2007a) and Transforming Social Care (DH, 2008a; 2009a).

The key concept within adult social care is personalisation:

> The direction is clear: to make personalisation, including a strategic shift towards early intervention, the cornerstone of public services. In social care, this means every person across the spectrum of need, having choice and control over the shape of his or her support, in the most appropriate setting. For some, exercising choice and control will require a significant level of assistance either through professionals or through independent advocates. (DH, 2008a: 1)

This is to be achieved through 'transforming adult social care' – the vehicle through which adult social care services change – to be able to provide all adults requiring local authority funded support and care with a personal budget.

'No Secrets' was followed by a number of documents to describe how agencies should work together to deliver the outcomes of protecting vulnerable adults from abuse (ADASS, CSCI, MPS documents). More recently, a process to review 'No Secrets' was undertaken by the Department of Health and the results of extensive consultation published

(DH, 2009d). The proposals in February 2010 to put Adult Safeguarding Boards on a statutory footing can be seen as the first step in taking forward the outcomes of this review.

The recognition and inclusion of lesbians and gay men within the various adult social care policy documents published by the 1997–2010 Labour Government is mixed. Whilst there is recognition of various 'equality strands' and associated agendas within the policy documents themselves, on the whole, the specific needs of lesbians and gay men are not acknowledged. But there are exceptions. Concannon noted that:

> [T]he White Paper 'Better Care, Higher Standards: A Charter for Long Term Care (Department of Health, 1999: 3) addresses the development of non-discriminatory services that treat users with dignity and respect, taking account of sexual orientation. (Concannon, 2009: 403)

The White Paper 'Valuing People – A New Strategy For Learning Disability' (DH, 2001) set out the framework for provision of services for people with learning disabilities, which would promote their rights, inclusion, and choice, enabling them to live 'full and independent lives as part of their local communities', including a comment that:

> Good services will help people with learning disabilities develop opportunities to form relationships, including ones of a physical and sexual nature. It is important that people can receive accessible sex education and information about relationships and contraception. (DH, 2001: 81)

This was the first White Paper on Learning Disability in 30 years, and introduced 'person centred planning' as a methodology for assessing and working with people with learning disabilities. Ambitious targets introduced in this White Paper required the closing of all long-stay hospitals in England by 2004. The final Hospital, Orchard Hill in Sutton, closed in 2009. A follow-up paper, 'Valuing People Now', was published in 2009, which prioritises areas like housing and employment. This paper also looks at sexuality, commenting:

> Like everyone else, people with learning disabilities tell us that relationships are important to them, both friendships and relationships of a personal and sexual nature. Yet the evidence is that people with learning disabilities have very few relationships and limited opportunities to form or sustain them. People are often lonely. One of the reasons for this is their exclusion from

the kinds of places where other people form and maintain relationships, such as work, college, clubs, places of worship, leisure centres, etc., but there are other reasons for this, mostly based on assumptions about people with learning disabilities.

The right to marry or have a civil partnership is both a civil and human right; local systems should enable practice that supports the individual's choice with regard to forming and sustaining relationships. (DH, 2009b: 93)

In 2006 the White Paper 'Our Health, Our Care, Our Say' was published. This built on the 2005 Green Paper 'Independence, Wellbeing and Choice' which was consulted on broadly. The White Paper set out the Government's vision for adult social care services, taking into account the increasing number of older people, the changing nature of communities and the higher expectations within society about what help and support older adults could expect from the Government in their latter years. This White Paper sets out a clear commitment to equality:

In delivering this strategic shift, we are committed to a health and social care system that promotes fairness, inclusion and respect for people from all sections of society, regardless of their age, disability, gender, sexual orientation, race, culture or religion, and in which discrimination will not be tolerated. (DH, 2006: 17)

The 2006 White Paper and other policy papers that followed have focused adult social care on seven desired outcomes that care and support can enable people to achieve. These outcomes are: improving health, quality of life, choice, freedom from discrimination, economic wellbeing and dignity, and helping people make a positive contribution. The 2005 Green Paper (DH, 2005) further extended the role of 'direct payments' and introduced 'personal budgets' to enable service users to have more say, choice and control over the services they wanted and who would provide them. The Green Paper also emphasised expansion of the introduction of 'assistive' technology to enable disabled people of all ages to maximise their independence. Assistive technology ranges from care alarms linked to call centres and call out services, to a variety of equipment that can minimise risks to vulnerable adults or assist them to manage daily living in their own homes. As discussed later, there is some evidence to suggest that lesbians and gay men are more likely to use direct payments and personal budgets to increase their autonomy and control.

Adults and sexuality

The previous section has highlighted that within adult services, the underpinning strategic policy documents all contain a vision of service provision that is modelled on an individualised 'outcomes' focused approach, in order that service users can achieve the aspirations, goals and priorities they identify and set for themselves (Glendinning et al.., 2006). Within mental health, learning disabilities, physical disabilities and older people's services there are a number of system-wide standards for challenging discrimination, promoting dignity and person-centred, individualised care (HM Government et al., 2006; DH, 2007a; 2009a; 2009b), most of which rarely mention sexual orientation and hetero-sexism either implicitly or explicitly. The concern is then, because this is not an area which is specifically addressed in policy, the likelihood of it being seen as an issue for practice is small (Clover 2006; Fannin et al., 2008). The Department of Health established the Sexual Orientation and Gender Identity Advisory Group in the mid-2000s. This was replaced by the Lesbian, Gay, Bisexual and Transgender Advisory Group in 2008 to address this lack of specific focus.

There are small numbers of specialist projects that provide services to the lesbian and gay community, and it is important that the positive work of these projects is acknowledged. We discuss some of this work in the next section. However, as well as the strengths that such specialist services can and do have, there is a need to consider the limitations of relying solely on specialist provision. Enabling lesbians and gay men to access mainstream services must be a priority. Fully utilising mainstream community care and support means services recognising and being sensitive to differences such as class, race, age and other factors, as well as sexuality, because the lesbian and gay 'community' is not homogeneous. Cocker and Hafford-Letchfield (2010) suggest that social work could develop knowledge about local and national networks that might help LGB users 'cohere more effectively' (Cant, 2009: 59), particularly if they are to capitalise on the opportunities afforded by direct payments, individualised budgets, self-directed support and personalisation. There is limited information indicating that lesbians and gay men are more likely to access these kinds of mechanisms to directly purchase services themselves (Commission for Social Care Inspection, 2008).

Assessments commonly used in social work with adults, such as those which determine eligibility for community care services, or assessments determining the needs of carers of vulnerable adults, can and should be used appropriately to assess the needs of adults who are lesbian or gay, or carers who are lesbian or gay, as much work in this arena of social work practice will be the same with lesbians and gay men as with any other client group. However, there is still a need to retain a specific focus on the distinctive experiences of lesbians and gay men. There are occasions when certain types of assessments do need to cover different areas because some experiences are particular to the lives of lesbians and gay men. This would include, for example, the perpetual 'coming out' process required if lesbian or gay service users choose to be out to the assessing social worker and service providers. The experience of homophobia is unique to lesbians and gay men. It is well documented that social care services will assume a service user's heterosexuality unless provided with other information to the contrary. Jeyasingham (2008) suggests that there is a privileging of heterosexuality within social work. The resulting heteronormativity within social work practice and education leads to an exclusion of particular knowledge about sexuality from social work literature, including research. This allows for certain ideas, behaviours and groups of people to be overlooked or ignored at best, or pathologised at worst. The question is whether existing frameworks should be flexible enough to adapt to people's individuality and incorporate differences in a reflexive manner rather than as an 'add on', or not address them at all. Assessment models should be flexible enough to apply to all applicants, regardless of sexual orientation, but unfortunately a model is only ever as good as the service using it.

The introduction of self-assessment frameworks in the new customer journey developed to deliver transforming adult social care could provide opportunities for improvement and empower service users to ensure that their differences are addressed. However, the extent of the impact of these newer processes is yet to be fully evaluated.

Cocker and Hafford-Letchfield (2010) suggest that the issues affecting lesbians and gay men who use adult services are constructed within discourses about sexual orientation as individual pathology, such as the assumption that sexual orientation causes mental health problems (King et al., 2003). However, experiences of heterosexist discrimination have been linked to poor mental health itself (Social Perspectives Network, 2007) and this will be explored in the next chapter.

In terms of work with older adults, people with learning disabilities and people with physical disabilities, a presumption of asexuality is common. However, when sexuality is recognised and acknowledged, it is often within a heteronormative framework. Cocker and Hafford-Letchfield

(2010) suggest that the consequence of this for lesbian or gay adults in institutional care settings is that they are not likely to 'come out' (Commission for Social Care Inspection, 2008). People with learning disabilities are also more likely to experience bullying, harassment, verbal and physical violence because of their sexual orientation, often by their own family members (Abbott and Howarth, 2005). For older lesbians and gay men, hiding one's sexuality because of fear of discrimination and stigma makes it all the more difficult to express intimacy and sexual desire (Fenge, 2008; Hafford-Letchfield, 2008; Concannon, 2009). This is where more lesbian and gay friendly services can be beneficial.

Within caring relationships, similar observations can be made. Manthorpe (2003) suggests that even though care provision is a gendered activity, lesbians caring for their own partners are frequently marginalised and their experience rarely illustrates support being offered in undertaking a caring role. This is made even more difficult by assessments not identifying or acknowledging the different forms that 'family' and family relationships can take – relying instead on a heterosexual relationship model as the basis for identifying and assessing family (see Chapter 4). Lesbians and gay men are more likely to be assessed as individuals outside of this discourse of family (Manthorpe, 2003). Cronin and King's research (2009) suggests that older gay men are more likely to be carers for parents, partners and friends than heterosexual men.

Specific issues for adult social care in relation to sexuality

Older adults

Legally there is no accepted definition of an older person. Local Authorities generally define 'older adults' as people over 65 years because of demographic information, funding formulae and performance management requirements. Using the retirement age is highly problematic due to variations in practice. Changes in policy and discrimination in the different age of retirement for men and women is now unlawful (Marshall v. Southampton and South West Hampshire Area Health Authority [1986] 2 All ER 584; Employment Equality (Age) Regulations 2006). Social workers will therefore be working with people spanning a wide age bracket, with a range of illnesses and disabilities, some age related, others not. However, the diversity of the population of older adults is considerable, and this needs to be kept in mind. Beech and Ray

(2009) suggest that historically policy has not recognised the diversity of the ageing population and many of the problems and issues faced by this population in terms of life changes and physical and emotional transitions. Further they suggest that there are problems for social workers in being able to be as client focused as they would wish:

> Preventative services and strategies continue to be heavily emphasised in policy but remain largely underdeveloped or unavailable. As social work continues to move away from the one-size-fits-all approach to intervention and care planning, it is clear that crucial dilemmas remain in terms of how creative and innovative social work with older people can be ... in the context of increasing managerialist workloads coupled with the lack of adequate preventative services. (Beech and Ray, 2009: 357)

Beech and Ray are not alone in suggesting that assessment is being used as a means to determine eligibility to receive services rather than as a way of understanding an individual and their specific needs (Lloyd and Smith, 1998; Gorman and Postle, 2003; and McDonald et al., 2008). McDonald et al. (2008) have sympathy for social workers caught within bureaucratic systems and structures. However, there are concerns about the effects of such practice in increasing regulation, surveillance and an over-proceduralisation in the search for certainty and avoidance of risk in social work practice. The effect of this is to decrease autonomy and creativity which fails to acknowledge ambiguity and uncertainty in the human experience. Indeed, there is some concern that practice is now so proceduralised that the ideals of social work are now almost unconnected to social workers' actual experience of social work practice (McDonald et al., 2008: 1383). This makes working with the diverse range of individual needs of older people difficult, despite the overarching principles and ideologies inherent in public policy that value this diversity.

There are many stereotypes of older adults – many of them gender specific. This influences the way people are viewed, and research undertaken about the gender stereotypes held about lesbians and gay men suggests that:

> older lesbians and gay men were perceived as similar to older heterosexual women and men with regard to aging stereotypes, such as being judicious. At the same time, sexual minorities were targets of unique stereotypes. Consistent with the implicit inversion theory, lesbians were conceived as similar to heterosexual men, and gay men similar to heterosexual women

with regard to gender stereotypic traits, and regardless of age. These findings suggest the persistence into late adulthood of the belief that lesbians and gay men are inverted females and males. (Wright and Canetto, 2009: 424)

Concannon (2009) suggests that, even with the enormous legal changes and benefits that have occurred for lesbians and gay men within the lifetime of the Labour Government (1997–2010), the impact of these changes on all lesbians and gay men is not the same.

> Men and women over seventy years of age will remember a world in which to be attracted to a person of the same sex was heavily stigmatised and where the only 'choice' was the choice of concealment. When these lesbians, gay men, bisexuals and transgendered people were younger, contact with other gay people was extremely difficult. They reached puberty at a time when homosexuality was considered to be a mental illness, outlawed as a criminal offence and with cures that included electric shock aversion therapy. (Concannon, 2009: 406)

So the current position is complex. It is not as easy as suggesting that because the law has changed, service provision to older lesbians and gay men will have changed as well, and discrimination will no longer exist. The reality of social work practice means that social workers must balance their statutory obligations to service users and employers with their professional obligations. As we have mentioned previously, social workers are required to adhere to the GSCC codes of practice in terms of respecting the uniqueness of the people they work with. However, there are many examples in the professional literature of the homophobia of some social workers in their attitudes toward lesbians and gay men (see Chapters 3 and 4). There is no reason to think that this is any different for social workers working with older people. Indeed service users tell us it is not any different: 'Anecdotal stories within the gay community abound with tales of homophobic instances, and a fear of revealing oneself as gay is endemic ... some feel that attitudes are more entrenched in rural areas than the cities' (Fannin et al., 2008: 41).

Although there is a firm move towards older adults receiving services in their own homes to encourage independent living for as long as is possible, services provided to lesbians and gay men should take into account a number of important factors. In addition to general age-related issues and disabilities that a lesbian or gay man may experience, there are also differences which an assessing social worker should be aware of – notably, the constant process of deciding to either 'come out' to the people providing care services, or stay firmly in the closet. This 'hiding' of oneself because of a fear of a negative reprisal cuts off a core part of someone's identity from assessment or care and support planning. As with members of other minority communities, there is a heightened risk of social and emotional isolation (Lavin, 2008). In addition, Pugh (2005) suggests that every person experiences their sexuality in a unique way, just as they do ageing, and social workers should avoid generalising about what it means to be an older lesbian or gay man. Lavin (2008) explores some of the existing theories of home as a personal, social and physical space, and reflects on why for lesbians and gay men this space is particularly important. This is because, as it is outside the public gaze and expression of political beliefs and views, individuality and intimacy can take place without fear. The challenge for providers of a supported care setting is to provide an environment that can re-create and respect the positive aspects of someone's private home within a much larger institution. There is some research available that examines the type of housing needs and social care that older lesbians and gay men would like to have access to. The overwhelming message is that they would like good quality care that meets their individual needs as a lesbian or gay man, regardless of whether this is specialist provision for lesbians and gay men, or general services (Heaphy et al., 2004; Hubbard and Rossington, 1995; and Places for People, 1999, cited in Lavin, 2008: 57; Gay and Grey in Dorset, 2006; CSCI, 2008; Archibald, 2010). This can either be in 'gay specific' or 'gay friendly' care environments (Lavin, 2008; Knocker, 2006).

There is some evidence that older lesbians and gay men are more likely to live alone, less likely to have family support networks, and more reluctant to access services (Knocker, 2006; DH, 2007a). In this context preventive projects providing outreach and befriending and several national voluntary sector agencies have been active in establishing specialist services for older lesbians and gay men at a local level, specifically Age Concern, the Alzheimer's Association and Stonewall.

People with learning disabilities

There are a number of texts that helpfully provide a history and overview of the oppression of people with learning disabilities and the prominent theoretical models used when working with people with learning disabilities (Ryan and Thomas, 1987; Malin, 1996; McCarthy, 1999; Boxall et al., 2009). Even defining who it is that has a learning disability is contested, moving from definitions relying on individual biological pathology, to definitions relying on intelligence tests that measure intellectual functioning, behavioural attributes and deficits, to 'social models' of disability, which examine the social causes and constructions of disability such as labelling, segregation, stigmatisation, lack of access and denial of citizenship (Stainton, 2009; Oliver, 1990; Boxall et al., 2009).

Stainton (2009) comments that:

> the question of 'what is learning disability?' is neither simple nor without dangers. Being included in the definition has, at different times, meant a total loss of rights, been subject to sterilisation, incarcerated and, in some cases, killed. On the other side, being excluded may mean a lack of access to services or support. Therefore, the critical social worker must be aware of not only what the various definitions are but also, more critically, the implications for the person involved. (Stainton, 2009: 348)

As with older lesbians and gay men, this history portrays a group of people that have been infantilised, deemed unable to make any decisions and unable to have a role in society. Instead they have been hidden away in hospitals and institutions, and cut completely out of any active citizenship, rather than supported to make informed decisions about their own lives. Critiques exist of the medical, psychological and normalisation models that have underpinned service provision in this country and many others over the last century. In summary, a medical model has a pathological viewpoint, and both this approach and the psychological approach argues to control and contain the person with a learning disability, via 'special school and classes, behavioural interventions, medical control, a focus on prevention and institutionalised or specialist provision' (Stainton, 2009: 350).

The move towards 'normalisation' (Wolfensberger, 1972), where people with learning difficulties needed 'normal' opportunities to lead 'ordinary' lives (Boxall et al., 2009) was a welcome shift from the hitherto dominant medical and psychological discourses, towards 'reversing negative roles and images and developing and enhancing more positive social roles for people with learning disabilities' (Stainton, 2009: 350). However, it has also been criticised for reinforcing many of the normative behavioural and cultural standards within our society, and not really giving people with learning disabilities actual choices about their lives (Oliver, 1999; Boxall et al., 2009). This is where discussions about expressions of sexuality, and sexual choice in particular, can become complex and complicated.

The abuse, labelling and stereotyping that people with learning disabilities experience on a day-to-day basis should not be underestimated. If the very living of life is a struggle, how much more difficult is it to enable full participation and choice in the detail of how that life is lived? For people with learning disabilities, sexual expression is filled with socially contrived debate and dispute, and this is without the further complexity of that sexual expression and intimacy being with someone of the same gender.

There is a growing body of research studies that have been undertaken about people with learning disabilities and sexuality (e.g. McCarthy, 1996; 1999; Garbutt, 2008). This includes work about menstruation, pregnancy and contraception (McCarthy, 1999: 178), menopause (McCarthy, 2002; McCarthy and Millard, 2003), sexual health (Cambridge, 1996; Thompson, 1994; McCarthy, 1999;) privacy for sexual intimacy (Cambridge and McCarthy, 1997); the establishment of social spaces for people with learning disabilities to meet other people, good practice in how to provide accessible information about sex and sexual relationships, including sexual health (McCarthy and Thompson, 1994); examining the support that families provide to people with learning disabilities in their relationships (Brown, 1987; Garbutt, 2008) and sexual exploitation (McCarthy, 2003).

A small number of studies have also been undertaken about people with learning disabilities and same-sex relationships (Thompson, 1994; McCarthy and Thompson, 1994; 1998; Partners in Advocacy, 2004). McCarthy and Thompson's work is important in being able to move beyond the normalisation rhetoric of enabling choice for people with learning disabilities in sexual relationships, to the realities of what their experiences were approximately 15–20 years ago.

It is important to remember that a passive, compliant and, on occasion painful experience of sex with men was commonplace among the men with learning disabilities. Their reasons for having sex with men cannot be easily attributed to either sexual preference or sexual pleasure. Although these experiences appear to be negative, many men, most noticeably those who hung around public toilets, were very active in seeking out such encounters. Definitely, these sexual contacts might have offered men incidental sexual pleasure but other incentives have emerged which have nothing to do with sexuality. These include being a way to fill time with few other options, a small financial or material gain, and an exchange for the valued attention of men without learning disabilities. (Thompson, 1994: 262)

McCarthy and Thompson point out that same-sex activity is not neces-sarily an indicator that someone might be gay. Many heterosexual men have at some point been involved in same-sex activities and this may also be the case for men with learning disabilities. They also report that sexual activity between women is the least common form of sexual expression for people with learning disabilities, and they suggest that this may be because it is either not occurring, or it is happening but is not recognised or seen (McCarthy and Thompson, 1998). Many writers also discuss the high number of abusive relationships that people with learning difficulties can become involved in, and the potential adult safeguarding issues that are raised for individuals as well as within group home and residential care settings (Cambridge and McCarthy, 1997; Brown and Stein, 1997a; 1997b; McCarthy and Thompson, 1998).

The growth of advocacy services to support people with learning disabilities (and other vulnerable adults) is important, especially for establishing preferences and achieving choice. The introduction of widespread independent mental capacity advocacy services in the light of the Mental Capacity Act 2005 and the Mental Health Act 2007 has meant that those able to access advocacy has increased, and this is par-ticularly pertinent for enabling the most vulnerable adults to make sig-nificant life decisions. Rapaport et al. suggest that:

> although evaluation of effectiveness is increasingly important in the light of policy change and funding constraints, it is not universally in place and available tools are considered to be inadequate for the task. The explanation of this may lie in the continuing debates over the meaning and purpose of evaluation and fears that it is one-dimensional. Future investment and commitment to advocacy schemes will need to address these issues. (2006: 191)

People with physical disabilities

The social model of disability (Oliver, 1999), 'an approach that examines the social construction of material and attitudinal barriers to disabled people's participation in society' (Sapey, 2009: 89), has been a powerful framework through which disabled people and others have argued for a reframing of the way in which disability is viewed within our society. Within adult social care, the term 'disabled people' is common parlance when referring to adults under 65 who have permanent and substantial disabilities or impairments, such that the disability would affect some-one's ability to carry out ordinary day-to-day activities. Brown comments that the dominant discourse about disability within social work is an 'individual tragedy' model (1998a: 118–19), even though social workers should be aware through various ADP models that the social construction of disability is a powerful force in determining how disabled people are viewed within our society. However, for over 30 years disabled people have been trying to get social workers to use the social model of disability in their practice (Sapey, 2009). Oliver (2004) expresses a sobering view about the success of this for social work:

> The social model of disability has had no real impact on professional practice, and social work has failed to meet disabled people's self-articulated needs. Twenty years ago I predicted that if social work was not prepared to change in terms of its practice towards disabled people it would eventually disappear altogether. Given the proposed changes by the New Labour Government in respect of modernising social services, it seems likely that that forecast is about to come true. We can probably now announce the death of social work, at least in relation to its involvement in the lives of disabled people. (Oliver, 2004: 25)

Given this poor prognosis, there is a high chance that lesbians or gay men who have a physical disability will struggle even more to receive appropriate services within mainstream organisations and specialist disability groups.

> These prejudices and barriers stem from a fundamental lack of knowledge and understanding about issues that relate specifically to sexual orientation and disability and, in particular, a reluctance to talk about issues concerning sexual orientation ... the most significant barriers were a lack of awareness, prejudice, and ignorance about LGBT and/or disability issues and, frequently, homophobia. (Avante Consulting, 2006: 16)

Services that offered 'acceptance, respect, and protection from inappropriate behaviour, language and any form of violence' (Avante Consulting, 2006: 16) are fundamental to enabling lesbians or gay men with disabilities to participate meaningfully and effectively.

In addition, Hasler et al. (1999) illustrate the importance of peer support, maintaining confidentiality and specific measures to consult disabled lesbians and gay men seeking to live independently. Practical issues faced by lesbian and gay users of personal assistants (PA) include discriminatory attitudes by PAs, the difficulties users experience in not knowing when to disclose their sexuality to their PA (Killin, 1993) and finding a gay carer (Gulland, 2009).

What is clear from the literature (Swain et al., 2004; Oliver and Sapey, 2006; Thomas, 2007) is that for many years disabled people have been active in arguing for a revolution in service provision which is not stigmatising, dehumanising and labelling, and allows disabled people the opportunity to take control over their lives, something the majority of us who are not disabled take completely for granted. This struggle has met with some success, but the disabled community is far from homogeneous. For many lesbians and gay men who have physical disabilities, progress towards determining their own identities within the disability community and wider society has been slow and painful. As for the other groups of people we have discussed in this chapter:

> social work, in addressing the individual within their own context, should be able to deliver a non-oppressive and non-patronising service to disabled lesbians and gay men, which both respects individuals' experiences and responses and also can locate them within a broader social and political context. (Brown, 1998a: 119)

Summary

In summary, assessment, care and support services provided for lesbians and gay men continue to be narrowly constructed within a heteronormative framework of social work with adults. In many ways this is no different from any other form of social care and support, as we have outlined in other chapters on mental health provision and work with children and families. Adults should have a direct say in all decisions that are made about their lives. If adults lack mental capacity, there are now specific mechanisms that come into play to formally assess whether an adult has the mental capacity to choose and make decisions in particular circumstances and to ascertain what is in their best interests. What is clear is that some lesbian and gay adults will sometimes require additional support to be able to make decisions about their lives in terms of services and support they may be eligible to receive. Here advocacy has an important role to play.

Lesbians or gay men who need adult social services are not a homogeneous group of people and should not be treated as such. Certainly experience is individual: support needs and appropriate ways to meet these through social care provision will be personal. There may be a positive impact from delivering more personalised services through Transforming Social Care, but it is still too soon to assess its impact.

Further there is evidence of changing attitudes. As noted earlier a government-backed survey (Park et al., 2010) has found that people have become more tolerant of homosexuality in the past 30 years, with 36 per cent of the 4486 adults surveyed being of the view that homosexuality was 'always' or 'mostly' wrong, compared with 62 per cent in 1983. In the latest survey, 39 per cent said that homosexuality was never wrong, while 10 per cent said it was 'rarely wrong'. Whilst this points to an improving social picture, discrimination still exists and this needs to be appropriately challenged when it occurs in lesbians' and gay men's experience of social work and social care provision.

There are, however, many areas of good practice present in this area in the voluntary sector, statutory sector and in service user advocacy led groups. It is not possible to provide a list of all of these, but two examples are: the London Borough of Islington (2008) has published a Lesbian and Gay Charter; and the London Borough of Hounslow, in conjunction with the GMI partnership and Caring with Confidence has launched a programme aimed at supporting lesbian, gay, bisexual and transgendered carers in the London area (2009). In addition, Caring with Confidence also provide support for lesbian and gay carers at the Lesbian and Gay Foundation in Manchester.

7
Social work practice with lesbians and gay men: mental health

Introduction

In this chapter we consider what is known about the mental health of lesbians and gay men and how this knowledge can inform the ways that we work with lesbians, gay men, their families and their social networks when they are affected by mental ill health or substance misuse.

First we consider the prevalence of mental ill health in the lesbian and gay population, and where there are identified problems, some of the reasons that are posited as to why that might be the case. We look next at social work practice and consider how the current legal and policy frameworks and practice initiatives can be used to good effect with lesbians and gay men.

Thompson, discussing the stigmatisation of mental ill health, writes that:

> a clear implication of the critique of mental illness as a valid concept is that the inappropriate application of a stigmatizing label of mental illness can have profoundly oppressive effects, not only in the short term but through a person's life. Mental health is therefore a subject that needs to be handled very carefully and sensitively if we are to avoid such oppressive consequences. (2003: 134)

We argue that this 'carefulness' and 'sensitivity' needs to be the case when working with lesbians and gay men, as they potentially experience double discrimination when they are psychologically distressed: the stigma of mental illness and the stigma of homosexuality. Research undertaken recently in Wales identified this:

> Our research reveals the double stigma experienced by lesbian, gay and bisexual people with mental health issues. This double stigma stems from society's prejudicial attitudes towards both mental health issues and people who identify as lesbian, gay or bisexual. (Stonewall Cymru, 2009: 4)

For lesbians and gay men there is the added complication that homosexuality was considered a mental disorder until relatively recently (Carr, 2005). It was not removed from the American Psychiatric Association's list of mental disorders until 1973 (Wilton, 2000: 104), or the ICD-10 (World Health Organisation Classification of Diseases) until as late as 1992 (Meads et al., 2009: 60), and in the UK 'it wasn't until 1993 that the Government removed homosexuality from its list of psychiatric disorders in England and Wales. In Scotland it was 2000' (Botcherby and Creegan, 2009: 6). Golding (1997) argued that despite homosexuality no longer being formally considered a psychiatric disorder after 1992, 'many mental health professionals still consider homosexuality to be a mental illness or a cause of mental distress per se' (1997: 1). Although we think that this assertion about mental health professionals would need to be tempered in 2010, there is still the need for social work practitioners in the field of mental health to be careful and sensitive when working with lesbians and gay men.

Mental health, suicidal and self-harming behaviours and substance misuse amongst lesbians and gay men ■ ■ ■ ■ ■ ■

When considering the problematic relationship between understandings of homosexuality, mental ill health and research, Cochran and Mays (2005) note that within psychiatry, up to and including the 1970s, homosexuality was psychopathologised. The research undertaken during that period predominately considered lesbians and gay men in psychiatric hospitals and, as the authors note, 'It is not surprising that these researchers found high levels of psychiatric difficulties in their lesbian and gay male participants' (2005: 143). They go on to consider research undertaken since that time and discuss some of the methodological problems within the studies, particularly from the 1970s, when many samples were drawn from bars. Again, not surprisingly, such research found high rates of alcohol consumption amongst their samples. In the past 20 years the question of the prevalence of mental ill health amongst lesbians and gay men has re-emerged. Cochran and Mays again note the methodological limitations of some of this research.

> Sampling bias and absence of heterosexual control groups stand as two of the major difficulties today of interpreting the body of empirical evidence that has accumulated suggesting that lesbians and gay men experience greater than expected rates of depression, alcohol and drug use, and psychiatric help-seeking. (2005: 146)

Cochran and Mays conclude that:

> taken as a whole, results of these studies support concerns that some lesbians and gay men experience somewhat higher rates of stress-sensitive psychiatric disorders than other Americans and may be more likely to use mental health services in the United States. (2005:155)

They go on to say that, because of the small samples and other methodological considerations noted above, 'the results should be viewed as still tentative' (2005: 156).

In the UK context there have been a small number of systematic reviews looking at the prevalence of mental health problems amongst lesbians and gay men. One of these (King et al., 2007), commissioned by the National Institute for Mental Health in England, contributed to the Department of Health's reconsideration of the inclusion of lesbians and gay men in its 2002 National Suicide Prevention Strategy for England (DH, 2002b).

> That is why we will now include LGB people as a specific group who have special needs under Goal Two of the Strategy (to promote the mental well-being of the wider population). This will send out a clear message to organisations working with LGB groups, including health and social care agencies, that actions need to be taken if we are to reduce the risk of suicide in this group. (King et al., 2007: 1)

Three recent regional studies considering the mental health of lesbians and gay men conducted in Brighton and Hove (Brown with Lim, 2008), Wales (Stonewall Cymru, 2009) and in the West Midlands (Meads et al., 2009) have built further on knowledge in this area of practice. Many of the findings of these studies are similar (King et al., 2003; 2007; Meads et al., 2009; Stonewall Cymru, 2009).

King et al., in their systematic review of the research evidence, conclude:

> that LGB people are at significantly higher risk of mental disorder, suicidal ideation, substance misuse, and DSH (deliberate self harm) than heterosexual people. An awareness of the mental health needs of LGB people should become part of the training for health and social work professionals. (2007: 3)

This systematic review considered 28 papers that met their inclusion criteria out of a possible 476. Their main findings were as follows. Regarding drug and alcohol misuse they found that:

> in summary, there was an increased lifetime and 12 month risk of alcohol and drug dependency in all groups compared with heterosexuals with markedly higher risk in lesbian and bisexual women. (2007: 9)

For suicidal ideation they found that:

> there were elevated risks for suicide attempts and ideation in LGB people but quality of studies was limited. Data from higher quality studies showed higher cumulative incidence of suicide in LB school girls, increased lifetime risk of suicide attempts in GB men and increased 12 months risk of suicidal ideation in LB women. (2007: 8)

For depression and anxiety they concluded that:

> in summary, on the basis of studies of relatively good quality, there was an elevated risk of lifetime and 12 month prevalence of depression and anxiety disorders in all LGB groups compared to heterosexual controls. (2007: 8)

They conclude as follows:

> Our findings indicate that LGB people are at higher risk of suicidal behaviour, mental disorder and substance misuse and dependency than heterosexual people. There is currently insufficient evidence to assess risk of completed suicide in LGB people. The results of the meta-analyses demonstrates a twofold excess risk of suicide attempts in the preceding year in men and women, and a fourfold excess in risk in gay and bisexual men in a lifetime. Similarly, depression, anxiety, alcohol and substance misuse were at least 1.5 times more common in LGB people. Findings were similar in men and women but LB women were at particular risk of substance dependence, while lifetime risk of suicide attempts was especially high in GB men. (2007: 9)

King et al.'s research team noted the strengths of their systematic review and its limitations, but still concluded that 'despite these reservations about our review, the consistent direction of our findings suggests that mental health is poorer in LGB people' (2007: 10). In the Cochran and Mays paper, which came to similar conclusions reviewing USA research studies, they wrote, '[W]e do not know or understand the causes of these observed differences' (2005: 156). Both studies note a problem with research being undertaken in this area, as no routine information is kept relating to individuals' sexual orientation. The lack of this data hampers our knowledge but also, as a result, the development of effective preventive interventions. This has also been noted by Botcherby and Creegan on behalf of the Equality and Human Rights Commission. They note that:

> for the first time in British history, the promotion of equality on the grounds of sexual orientation will be required under the forthcoming Equality Act, which is due to become law in 2010. It will require all publicly-funded bodies to promote equality for all and remove barriers to fair service provision under a single equality duty. (2009: 5)

They go on to identify the difficulties for public bodies, which include the NHS and Adults Social Services Departments, of realising this requirement and evidencing how they have realised it for sexual orientation. Because there is patchy information available to public bodies regarding the numbers of lesbians and gay men, and who those lesbians and gay men are, it is difficult to plan a service that meets their mental health needs.

> The absence of reliable statistical data is a major obstacle to measuring progress on equality for lesbians and gay men ... In addition, without this data, public authorities cannot deliver services that (fully) meet the needs of LGB people in key areas such as education, health and criminal justice. (2009: 6)

Without this information it is difficult for mental health services to be able to plan the utilisation of their resources in such a way that will meet the needs of lesbians and gay men that seem, from the above research findings, to be a particularly vulnerable group. King et al. argue that 'in order to identify this high risk group, sexual orientation should be included in routine demographic data collection at assessment' (2007: 11).

How do we understand the poorer mental health of the lesbian and gay population? King et al. surmise that it is:

> likely that the social hostility, stigma and discrimination that most LGB experience is likely to be at least part of the reason for the higher rates of psychological morbidity observed. Prejudice against homosexuality is unlike other intolerance in that it can reach into families; rejection from parents of their own children because of their sexual orientation is likely to have a severe emotional impact. This social exclusion of LGB people encourages social contacts in specific LGB venues such as pubs, clubs and bars. Thus mental distress may be aggravated by easy access to alcohol and drugs in gay venues that LGB people frequent both to find the company of others who will accept them less critically and to meet potential partners. (2007: 10)

In Ellison and Gunstone's online survey of over 5000 respondents they indeed found that many lesbians and gay men still experience 'social hostility, stigma and discrimination'. They recorded that 43 per cent of the lesbians and gay men in their study reported stress related to discrimination they experienced as a result of their sexual orientation. They also found that 42 per cent of the lesbians and gay men reported that they suffered from low self-esteem, and 37 per cent said that they had been bullied as a result of their sexuality (Ellison and Gunstone, 2009). The negative impact of such discrimination on lesbians and gay men's mental health is further re-iterated in the Stonewall Cymru study which involved an online survey undertaken by 116 lesbians, gay men and bisexual people and 30 who attended a focus group or were interviewed. The age range of this sample ranged between 15 and 73 years of age. When asked if the respondents thought there was a link between their sexuality and their mental health the authors write that:

> it was the view of the vast majority that sexual orientation is not the cause of mental health issues. To the contrary respondents argued that the enduring pressures and experiences of discrimination from family, friends, services, and society more generally throughout the life course impact on LGB mental health and wellbeing. (Stonewall Cymru, 2009: 12)

King et al. also commented on some problems within psychiatry itself:

> Unfortunately, despite considerable change for the better in the attitudes of psychiatric professionals towards LGB people, in parts of the developed world gay men and lesbians continue to be encouraged to seek to change

their sexual orientation, an attitude that can only prolong the impression of disapproval and social exclusion. (2007: 11)

Drescher (2002) makes a similar point and questions the ethics of allowing such interventions to continue without a sound evidence base. This point is developed further in a research study by Bartlett et al. who found that a:

> significant minority of mental health professionals are attempting to help lesbian, gay and bisexual clients become heterosexual. Given lack of evidence for the efficacy of such treatments, this is likely to be unwise or even harmful. (2009: 3)

The findings of a systematic review of lesbian, gay, bisexual and transgender health in the West Midlands (Meads et al., 2009) were in line with those of King et al. (2007) in that they noted higher rates of mental health problems in the lesbian and gay population compared with the general population. These problems related to depression, anxiety, suicide attempts, eating disorders, self-harm and illegal drug use. 'The West Midlands survey results suggest a general level of poor mental health in the LGBT population' (Meads et al., 2009: 22). However, they note one interesting exception to this:

> The systematic review by Bos et al. (2005) found that the overall mental health of lesbian mothers (for lesbians with children born in a previous heterosexual relationship and for planned lesbian families) was no different to heterosexual mothers. (Meads et al., 2009: 22)

This is of interest to social workers and other mental health professionals because it is as important to identify what the protective factors are for lesbians and gay men's mental health as it is to identify risk factors relating to their mental ill health. Cochran and Mays argue that:

> it is also important that we explore those things that keep people safe and highly functioning despite negative views of homosexuality ... There is much that we can learn from this population about how people cope well with social inequality. (2005: 158)

Writing about the interrelationship between sexual orientation, racism, poverty and mental health, Diaz et al. (2006) note the importance of resilience for individuals' mental health. They identified, from their research sample, the protective factors that enhance resilience for lesbians and gay men's psychological and emotional well-being. These included 'family acceptance, supportive social networks, and participation in social activism' (2006: 219). Brauner also considers the relationship between race, culture and sexuality, and makes an important point that white lesbians and gay men have often equated 'being out' with political solidarity as well as mental well-being. She argues that this is a Eurocentric view and that for her Black clients that she sees in therapy, 'the concept of "coming out" as an individual does not necessarily fit into the value system of themselves, their families and communities' (2000: 16). On the same theme Brown writes:

> Lesbian and gay culture, writing, politics and organisation have been dominated by white people. Black lesbians and gay men have sometimes felt marginalised, talked for and about, but rarely with, stereotyped and overerotised. The state of play is changing, but only slowly. These factors mean that some lesbians and gay men, who feel they cannot rely on the lesbian and gay community for support, may decide that dealing with racism and homophobia simultaneously is, understandably, too much and decide to focus on managing the racism and not coming out in certain settings. (1998a: 50)

We have referred to the 'double stigma' that lesbians and gay men with mental health problems may face. It is important to remember the added complexity that Black lesbians and gay men with mental health problems might face. Diaz et al. in their study, looking at the interrelationship between racism, homophobia and mental health, write: 'Our analysis suggest that the three measured oppression factors – experiences of poverty, racism, and homophobia – all contribute independently and negatively to the mental health of those who are most affected' (2006: 222).

Professional and social work responses in the current legal, policy and practice frameworks

Barriers to effective mental health care

Carr argues that:

> the challenges to mainstream services is to creatively engage marginalised peoples, the concerns of whom often extend beyond service provision to creating positive social and political identities in the face of discrimination. (2004: 21)

Golding articulates some of the specific difficulties that lesbians and gay men can experience in accessing mainstream mental health services when she writes:

> There is plenty of anecdotal evidence to suggest that lesbians, gay men and bisexuals face specific problems accessing and using mental health services, and that prevention strategies and primary care often fail to reach this group. Mind hears frequently of people whose therapists or doctors see their sexuality as the problem; who suffer discrimination within mental health services; and who would not consider using 'mainstream' services because they consider such services to be anti-gay, anti-lesbian and anti-bisexual. (Golding, 1997: 1)

Meads et al.'s (2009) study looks in detail at what some of these difficulties might relate to, and identifies specific barriers to health care for lesbians and gay men. Their study focuses primarily on medical staff but is also relevant to social workers.

> Although LGB individuals may be a vulnerable group, experiencing poor mental health and influenced by a social 'scene' that advocates high consumption of drugs and alcohol, the qualitative literature reviewed suggested strongly that there was inadequate health care support. (2009: 58)

There are a number of barriers that are relevant to social work in the field of mental health: relationship barriers including homophobia; heterosexist assumptions; lack of a professional approach; lack of knowledge and misunderstandings. Homophobia was identified in their systematic review as both internalised by lesbians and gay men and conferred by practitioners. In relation to homophobia they note that, 'In the studies of the current review, LGB respondents frequently cited examples of homophobia they experienced in the healthcare setting' (Meads et al., 2009: 59). Scourfield et al. note psychological and emotional difficulties for lesbians and gay men in developing a healthy sense of their own homosexual identity: 'developing a positive LGB or T identity requires them to construct themselves against the overwhelming pressure of the heterosexual norm' (Scourfield et al., 2008: 332). This 'overwhelming pressure' can paradoxically lead some lesbians and gay men to identify with homophobia, which as a result has a negative impact on their self-esteem and psychological and emotional well-being.

    When looking at heterosexist practice that created barriers to health care, Meads at al. also identified good practice.

In these studies there was evidence of heterosexism in the attitudes of some medical staff although some may try to avoid these assumptions. In one study a doctor describes how he strived to put questions across in a way that did not assume heterosexuality … Although this may not be the norm, using open questions, that do not assume that people are heterosexual, may be an important step in negating barriers to communication. (Meads et al., 2009: 64)

In Meads et al.'s consideration of professionalism they raise important points that are relevant to both health and social work professionals. They argue that the evidence from their systematic review strongly suggests that it is possible for some professionals to hold personal views that are negative towards homosexuality but that such views are able to be contained by some professionals and that their negative views therefore do not impact on their professional practice. This is a contentious point. However, they argue that: 'Although not ideal, a recognition of homophobic feelings and an attempt to facilitate communication may be the most positive approach for some doctors and may lead to adequate patient care' (2009: 65). They go on to argue that mental health professionals' homophobia can also be linked to 'a lack of professionalism' that 'may lead to rudeness but, of more concern, may result in improper treatment, discrimination and breaking the law' (2009: 65). In both the Meads et al. systematic review (2009) and the Stonewall Cymru (2009) study, a lack of knowledge was identified as a barrier to effective mental health care. 'For some respondents … there was a sense of not being treated and supported adequately because the practitioner was ill-equipped to address LGB issues' (Stonewall Cymru, 2009: 11). Meads et al. note that although lack of knowledge might act as a barrier, this does not necessarily have to be the case.

A lack of knowledge however may not necessarily act as a barrier where an interested, polite approach is taken … A lack of knowledge … may not always limit effective treatment or inhibit good patient–professional relationships where sensitivity and openness are used. (2009: 66)

Meads et al. also noted that misunderstandings between clients and professionals can act as a barrier to effective care.

Misunderstandings between patient and health care workers may inhibit forming positive relationships. In the current review, factors that appeared to be sources of misunderstanding were: preconceptions of homophobia by LGB patients, differences in terminology used and embarrassment of health professionals. (2009: 67)

Although Meads et al. primarily focused on health care workers, we believe that their findings are also relevant to social work practitioners, particularly where they have identified barriers to effective working and mental health care.

The legal and policy framework

We have covered the legal and policy framework relevant to social work with lesbians and gay men in Chapter 2 and that which is relevant to community care in Chapter 6. It is clear that in the field of mental health, and more generally, there are no longer any legal or policy barriers that prevent social workers working effectively with lesbians and gay men. The Mental Health Act 1983 and the Mental Health Act 2007, as well as the Mental Capacity Act 2005, provide a legal framework for working with lesbians and gay men that should mean their needs are met as well as those of their heterosexual counterparts. We have seen above how it is the quality of direct practice that can create barriers for lesbians and gay men in need of mental health interventions; the law is not a barrier in this regard. Indeed, the Code of Practice for the Mental Health Act 1983 (DH, 2008b) and the Mental Capacity Act (DH, 2007b) both require mental health practitioners to work equitably and in line with the Equality Act 2006.

One of the guiding principles that should underpin mental health interventions is the 'respect principle'. This includes the following:

> People taking decisions under the Act must recognise and respect the diverse needs, values and circumstances of each patient, including their race, religion, culture, gender, age, sexual orientation and any disability... There must be no unlawful discrimination. (DH, 2008b: 5)

Therefore in the field of mental health lesbians and gay men are protected by the Equality Act 2006 and the Mental Health Act 1983's Code of Practice (2008b). Although the Code of Practice for the Mental Capacity Act 2005 (DH, 2007b) does not address sexual orientation directly, it does make reference to the importance of 'social inclusion, equality and social justice' (DH, 2007b: 259). Guidance on the Care Programme Approach considers equitable practice and service delivery in more depth and makes explicit reference to sexual orientation (DH, 2008c). This is partly as a result of the DH now being required to address equality as a necessary dimension when developing policy guidance.

As part of its statutory obligations, the Department of Health (DH) is required to assess the impact of any policy proposals on different groups in the community in terms of equality of access and impact on the rights and needs of those groups. It is also DH's policy to extend such an assessment to consideration of impact on equality in terms of religion or belief and sexual orientation. In producing this guidance we have undertaken a Single Equality Impact Assessment (SEIA) to help ensure that this guidance takes account of the diverse individual needs of service users, paying proper attention to issues of age, disability, gender, sexual orientation, race and ethnicity and religious beliefs. (2008c: 5)

The document goes on to note the:

DH would also urge services to adopt good practice when addressing any adverse impact due to inequalities in terms of age, religion or belief and sexual orientation of the service user and carers. (DH, 2008c: 9)

Later in the document they write that: 'assessments, care plans and reviews should take account of the needs of individuals in respect of age, disability, gender, sexual orientation, race and ethnicity and religious belief' (2008c: 21). In their statement of values and principles they set out their vision of effective assessment and planning in mental health:

Care assessment and planning views the person 'in the round' seeing and supporting them in their individual diverse roles and the needs they have, including: family, parenting; relationships; housing; employment; leisure; education; creativity; spirituality; self-management and self-nurture; with the aim of optimising mental and physical health well-being. (2008c: 7)

This is a practice framework that is as applicable to lesbians and gay men as to the rest of the population.

Practice

So, what does social work practice in the field of mental health that 'takes account of the diverse individual needs of service users, paying proper attention to issues of age, disability, gender, sexual orientation' (DH, 2008c: 5), look like?

Whether a social work practitioner is: an Approved Mental Health Practitioner undertaking an assessment looking at a lesbian or gay person's need to be admitted to psychiatric hospital; someone undertaking a best interest assessment under the Mental Capacity Act 2005 of an older lesbian or gay man in a residential setting; a social worker working with a lesbian mother with mental health difficulties where there are child protection issues; or a social worker working with a distressed Looked After young gay man, all need to be aware of the research findings noted above that look at the particular mental health vulnerabilities of lesbians and gay men. Webber puts together a coherent argument for the importance of mental health practitioners being evidence based (2008). This knowledge should be supplemented by further knowledge, also noted above, about what practitioners need to be mindful of when working with lesbians and gay men.

One of the key messages from the research is the importance, as for all people who are substance dependent or mentally ill, of building on their resilience and protective factors. Diaz et al. noted the primacy of 'family acceptance, supportive social networks, and participation in social activism' (2006: 219) for building resilience and lessening social isolations and low self-esteem for lesbians and gay men. When working with lesbians and gay men social workers have to consider these factors. In Chapter 4 we discussed family and kinship and the importance of the social worker understanding the diverse forms of lesbian and gay men's family and kinship. Recognition of lesbian and gay men's significant relationships is a necessary prerequisite in enabling social workers to engage with lesbians and gay men in a meaningful way.

Given that marginalisation and discrimination seem to have a negative impact on mental health, social work organisations should be careful to make sure that their organisations and their workforce are welcoming to and affirming of lesbians and gay men. The Stonewell Cymru research noted lesbians and gay men's reluctance to use mainstream services because of the discrimination they thought they would experience.

> Of those who were 'out' about their sexual orientation and perceived that they were discriminated against in their treatment, 57% indicated their experiences impacted or were likely to impact on their level of openness about their sexual orientation when accessing mental health services. 55% also indicated that it impacted on their willingness to access mental health services. (Stonewell Cymru, 2009: 11)

This is a serious indictment of our mental health services if this is the case, and it also contravenes the spirit of the legislation cited above. It is therefore of no surprise that King et al. argue that 'an awareness of mental health needs of LGB people should become a standard part of training for health and social work professionals' (2007: 3) and that in

Stonewall Cymru's recommendations to the Welsh Assembly they ask that:

> LGB specific and mental health specific training and awareness raising should form a compulsory element of key professional qualification for professions such as health workers, social work and social care, education, youth work, housing, criminal justice and the police. (2009: 5)

They also recommended to the Welsh Assembly that in addition to lesbians and gay men being offered quality mainstream services and being able to access lesbian and gay specific projects, agencies need to take on an active health promotion role in relation to mental health.

> Services should target health promotion around (1) drug and alcohol use and (2) mental health and wellbeing to LGB people through harm reduction strategies, promotional materials at key venues, funding targeted at LGB specific mental health wellbeing activities. (2009: 5)

We argue that the Care Programme Approach (DH, 2008c) and the recovery model (Shepherd et al., 2008; Watkins, 2007), both of which embrace the notion of 'personalisation' and require a person-centred approach, are conducive to good mental health social work practice with lesbians and gay men. This is because they embrace a holistic approach to assessment, care planning and review which should enable social workers to work with the diverse needs and the full complexity of each individual, within their own familial, cultural and social context. For lesbians and gay men, the recovery model has the additional strength of emphasising the importance of social inclusion, which is cited above as a factor that is likely to lessen lesbian and gay men's psychological vulnerability (Repper and Perkins, 2003). Smail writes that:

> social inclusion and full citizenship can have a greater positive impact on recovery than any other factor and should therefore be at the top of the agenda for mental health workers seeking to work in a recovery-orientated way. (2007: 99)

All mental health and substance misuse mainstream services have to meet the needs of all their clients and we are suggesting that the current legal, policy and practice frameworks in the UK can facilitate social workers engaging in a helpful way with lesbians and gay men. However, we are also aware that some research, cited above, indicates that mainstream services are not always working well with lesbians and gay men. Smail,

discussing psychiatry, social inclusion and mental health services' inability
to fully engage with the equality and citizenship agenda, writes:

> I find it hard to understand how psychiatry can remain so apolitical. How
> can we continue to treat the casualties of a society that is damaging to men-
> tal health without challenging social policy and working for social change?
> Could it be that somewhere in that dark paranoid vision of psychiatry as an
> agency of the state lays a kernel of truth that the unspoken role of psychiatry
> is to pathologise and pacify the distressed so as to mollify social malcontent!
> (2007: 109)

When working with lesbians and gay men in the field of mental health,
social workers cannot be apolitical. To work effectively requires the
ability to understand and seek to ameliorate lesbians and gay men's
continuing social marginalisation, which continues despite their current
legal recognition and protection. A sharp reminder of lesbian and gay
men's continuing marginalisation comes from Stonewall's reports on
homophobic bullying in schools (Hunt and Jensen, 2007). The study
involved 1145 young people at secondary schools in the UK, and it
found that 65 per cent of young lesbians, gay and bisexual respondents
experienced homophobic bullying in school (2007: 3). This has serious
implications for young people as this gives them a clear message early
in their lives that being lesbian or gay is likely to have negative consequences. Such bullying is also likely to impact on their self-esteem and
overall well-being.

> Although the long term effects bullying can have are yet to be established
> fully, it is now believed that repeated exposure to violence or harassment can
> have detrimental effects upon psychological wellbeing. (Rivers, 2000: 147)

This finding is particularly important for social workers working with
Looked After young lesbians and gay men in public care. This group of
young people have a higher rate of mental health difficulties than the
general population (Cocker and Allain, 2008: 123), and the added marginalisation due to their sexuality, if they are lesbian or gay, might add to their
potential mental health vulnerabilities. For these young people, social
workers have a responsibility to engage actively with schools to make sure
that they are protected from potential bullying or marginalisation.

We referred earlier to Cochran and Mays' (2005) call for the need to
consider why many lesbians and gay men are psychologically and emotionally well despite being subject to discrimination and marginalisation.

Given the long history of stereotyping gay men and lesbians as mentally defective, it is also important that we explore those things that keep people safe and highly functional despite negative views of homosexuality. (2005: 158)

We also need to learn from the effective mental health practices of specific mental health projects designed to meet the mental health needs of the lesbian and gay community such as the Metro Centre in South London and Mind Out. Mind has done a considerable amount of work in this area and has a fact sheet on lesbians, gay men and bisexuals' mental health that is a helpful summary for social workers (Mind, 2010). In addition SCIE's Social Care T.V. has a short video about lesbian, gay and transgendered people's mental health needs (SCIE, 2010) which is designed for social workers and social care workers.

Summary

It is important to remember that most lesbians and gay men neither experience mental health problems nor are substance dependent. However, we have seen from the research findings above that lesbians and gay men do seem to be more vulnerable to mental ill health than the heterosexual population. To reiterate King et al.'s conclusion, 'LGB people are at significantly higher risk of mental disorder, suicidal ideation, substance misuse, and DSH than heterosexual people' (King et al., 2007: 3). However, we have also noted that homosexuality isn't the cause of lesbian and gay men's psychological vulnerability but rather it is the discrimination that they experience that becomes an added vulnerability factor for some lesbians and gay men.

Lesbians and gay men are individuals with their own genetic makeup, family histories and their own psychological and emotional protective factors as well as vulnerability factors. Discrimination and marginalisation may, for some lesbians and gay men, add additional vulnerability that leads them towards serious psychological and emotional difficulties.

This might make them wary of mainstream social work and mental health services. This places the onus on mainstream services to be mindful of the legal and policy context to make sure that they work in an inclusive way that works with the complexity of individuals' lives and is truly inclusive.

8

Social work practice with lesbians and gay men: working with children and families

Introduction

Social work with children and families is the area of practice with lesbians and gay men that has attracted most political and media interest. As discussed previously in Chapters 2 and 4, this attention has been to the extent of the various governments of the time trying to intervene to either limit lesbians' or gay men's right to parent, or more recently to introduce legislation to affirm the social and emotional relationships within lesbian and gay families, including between children and adults. Considerable media attention has been given to these debates.

In this chapter we will explore how sexuality still has a powerful effect on social work practice with lesbians and gay men and their children. We will look at how services have developed in the areas of family support and prevention; child protection; Looked After Children; residential care and fostering and adoption.

Background

In the 1960s and 1970s discussions within the public arena about lesbian and gay men's parenting focused on lesbian mothers and custody issues.

At this time courts tended to award custody of children to fathers. The Rights of Women Custody Group wrote:

> Divorce law regards lesbianism in itself as unreasonable behaviour and the burden shifts to the lesbian, particularly in custody disputes, to prove otherwise. Many lesbian mothers still lose custody of their children solely on the basis of their sexuality, regardless of their parenting abilities and material circumstances. Even if the children wish to stay with their mother and she has looked after them almost exclusively since they were born, the judgement still often goes against her. (Rights of Women Lesbian Custody Group, 1986: 1)

Richardson highlighted three concerns that abounded at that time about the suitability of lesbians to care for their children, as follows:

> that the child would grow up to be homosexual and/or develop an atypical gender-role orientation; that the child is in 'moral danger'; that the child will suffer social isolation from her or his peers and significant others as a result of the stigmatisation of lesbian relationships in society. (Richardson, 1981: 149)

Richardson argued that these were essentially moral concerns. She commented that:

> singling out lesbian mothers in this way is in itself highly significant, given that the majority of women who become mothers do so without any questions being asked. The complex culturally and socially determined hierarchy of beliefs about what constitutes the ideal family unit is particularly relevant here. (Richardson, 1981:150)

Within lesbian custody cases the sexual orientation of the mothers was the primary concern, not the level of care afforded the child and the attachments the child had with his or her parents. Practice has now moved on considerably and we examine some of the specific ways in which social and legal changes have impacted on the experiences of lesbians and gay men and their families. However, a sense of taboo still permeates some of these discussions, especially about problematic parenting. A considerable number of lesbian mothers lost their children due to the political and moral pressure and pervading social belief systems of that time, so this taboo is partially understandable. However, parenting and safeguarding issues exist in lesbian and gay families as with any other family. Although in the 1980s there were increasing pressures from some quarters to expand and officially sanction fostering and adoption by lesbians and gay men (Skeats and Jabri, 1988), child protection concerns within lesbian and gay families remained hidden and not mentioned in child protection practice.

Family support and prevention   ■ ■ ■ ■ ■ ■

Brown noted over ten years ago that there was a scarcity of literature about working with lesbians and gay men to support their children and families (1998a: 96). Since that time little else has been written, and what material does exist is predominately from the USA. However, Strega (2007) makes a helpful contribution with her considerations of AOP in support services for children and their families. This reflects the different UK and USA structures in place for the delivery of social services.

In the UK the Local Authority and Social Services Act 1970 has meant that social work provision supporting families comes under the umbrella of social services departments. The original social services departments, as envisaged in the Seebohm Report (1968), included the idea of local universal services that would build social capital in communities and families that in turn would mean a reduction in the need for statutory interventions. However, the recession of the 1970s and the related cuts in state funding for social services meant that over the last 30 years there has been a reduction in family support and preventive work undertaken by social services departments other than that which is defined under the Children Act 1989. This trajectory of diminishing family support work was interrupted by the 'building social capital' agenda of the 1997 New Labour Government, with such initiatives as Sure Start (Home Office, 1998) and Think Family (Cabinet Office, 2008). Although these initiatives were laudable they meant that additional state funding was siphoned to such initiatives rather than into mainstream social services provision.

'Family support is an umbrella term covering a wide range of activities at different levels of individual, family, neighbourhood and community' (Adams, 2009: 311). Family support and prevention initiatives within social care are designed to provide community based interventions to children and families via a range of generic and specific service providers. Unlike universal services, such as education and health, or interventions such as child protection, family support is offered on a voluntary basis to families and their children as a way of building family cohesion and preventing family breakdown. The New Labour Government's social policy agenda in this area was underpinned by the document 'Every Child Matters' (DFES, 2004), with its five outcomes for all children. These are: staying safe, being healthy, enjoying and achieving, making a positive contribution and achieving economic wellbeing. Adams articulates the complexities within child welfare policies in terms of the State's relationship with families.

> Government policies reflect ambivalence towards parents rather than unconditionally supporting them. Policy and social work with children and parents tend to be built around the twin objectives of supporting families, and imposing punitive sanctions on parents who fall short and are held responsible for perceived shortcomings in their children's behaviour. In the post-welfare state era, good citizenship is held by government to be conditional upon the parent socialising the child adequately. (Adams, 2009: 311)

The underlying agenda is to ensure that families are able to raise children who can contribute to society. Good citizenship has become the responsibility of parents. Therefore it could be argued that because lesbian and gay families have for many years been located outside society's norms they are sidelined, and could be seen as subversive because of their sexuality and their alternative family structures which are perceived as threatening and in opposition to the State's agenda. The recent inclusion and protection of lesbian and gay families within the legislative framework is significant as there is now a duty placed on Local Authorities to provide equitable services to lesbians and gay men, and their children including family support.

Brown comments that lesbian and gay families are not a homogeneous group and some families may need family support and prevention services for the same reasons as their heterosexual counterparts.

> However, as an oppressed group there has been a tendency not to wash the dirty linen in public for fear that every day upset, or more fundamental crisis, difficulties or real disturbance will be attributed solely to sexual orientation, that the stereotypes will take precedence over the specific, unique individual in their own context. This shying away from the admission that 'sometimes things really do go wrong', however understandable, perpetuates oppression because it contributes to lesbian and gay individuals and families not receiving the support they may need. (1998a: 96)

The current policy framework for the delivery of support services to children and their families in England is referred to as Every Child Matters (DFES, 2004). These are universally available services delivered via extended school provision, through children and family centres and multidisciplinary teamwork led by a lead professional. For this support structure to work there needs to be effective multi-professional working. A significant number of support and preventive resources operate within a multi-disciplinary context and this is an environment in which social work has often been a part. Social work can play a key role here when it embraces criticality and reflexively in facilitating complex understandings of lesbian and gay families, thus enabling effective multi-professional preventive interventions.

Joined-up services include education, health and social services. The UK assessment tools for the assessment of children and their families, when considering support services and preventive interventions, are underpinned by systemic and psychodynamic ideas. The ecological model (Jack, 1997) is used explicitly in both the Framework for the Assessment of Children in Need and their Families (DH, 2000b) and the Common Assessment Framework (DfES, 2006). They are both frameworks that assess families within their social and environmental systems and describe strengths as well as identifying weaknesses of families and their members. The child's developmental needs, parenting capacity and family and environmental factors are all considered. This framework should work as effectively for lesbian and gay families as with any other family because one of the key principles that runs through these frameworks is equality of opportunity and an acceptance of diversity.

> Ensuring equality of opportunity does not mean that all children are treated the same. It does mean understanding and working sensitively and knowledgeably with diversity to identify the particular issues for a child and his/her family, taking account of experiences and family context. (DH, 2000b:12)

We argue that the tools themselves are potentially helpful in facilitating a holistic and complex assessment. However, we know that a tool is only effective in capable hands. Such capability means that the social work focus with lesbians and gay clients needs to take account of their total experience and work with each person's unique individuality.

Child protection

At the time of writing the Children Act 1989, The Adoption and Children Act 2002, the Children Act 2004 and the Children and Young Persons Act 2008 were the significant pieces of legislation for statutory interventions with children and families. Parton reminds us that the Department of Health's publication Messages from Research (DH, 1995) 'recommended adopting a broad perspective on needs and that child protection should be seen in the wider context of child and family support' (Parton, 2006: 76). There has been very little written about either child and family support or child protection work with lesbian and gay families although this work does occur. Some lesbians and gay men do harm their children, just as some heterosexuals do.

> People abuse their children for a whole range of highly complex reasons and there is a huge body of literature which debates the many different arguments addressing the question of 'why'. Although there is scant material that specifically addresses lesbian and gay parents who abuse their children, there is little reason to assume that lesbians and gay men are not subject to the same degree of complexity in relation to causation. (Brown, 1998a: 98)

In 2007 the publication of the Inquiry Report into the Circumstances of Child Sexual Abuse by Two Foster Carers in Wakefield (Parrott et al., 2007) was helpful as, although it looked at foster carers who had abused children, its findings were relevant to child protection work with lesbians and gay men more broadly. The resulting Inquiry Report noted that social workers involved with the case had demonstrated anxiety about being perceived as discriminatory, and demonstrated an inability to discriminate appropriately:

> alongside anxieties on their part about being or being seen as prejudiced against gay people. The fear of being discriminatory led them to fail to discriminate between the appropriate and the abusive. Discrimination based on prejudice is not acceptable, especially not in social work or any public service. Discrimination founded on a professional judgement on a presenting issue, based on knowledge, assessed evidence and interpretation, is at the heart of good social work practice. These anxieties about discrimination have deep roots, we argue – in social work training, professional identity and organisational culture. (Parrott, et al., 2007: 4)

This report was a sharp reminder for social workers that alongside the need to make sure that practice and service delivery should never negatively discriminate against people on the grounds of gender, sexuality, age, race, religion and disability (as indeed is required by law in the UK under the Equality Act 2006), social workers also have a professional duty not to lose sight of the need to analyse and synthesise material to form professional judgements. Discrimination in its correct non-prejudicial form is an essential ingredient in this analysis and synthesis in social work practice.

The Assessment Framework Triangle

In recognition of what *Messages from Research* (DH, 1995) was conveying about the importance of locating child protection work within the wider context of child and family support and trying to be more specific about what Parrott et al. describe as 'good social work practice' (2007: 4), we have re-examined the Assessment Framework Triangle (DH, 2000b: 17) to consider what might need to be held in mind when working with lesbians and gay men. To remind the reader, the Assessment Framework Triangle has three areas that have to be considered in a core assessment of a child in terms of safeguarding and promoting welfare. This work with children and their families relates to work that is undertaken with 'children in need' as defined by Section 17 of the Children Act 1989 and when undertaking child protection investigations under Section 47 of the same Act.

We have argued above that much work in this arena of social work practice will be the same with lesbians and gay men as with any other client group. However, having said that, social workers do have to be sufficiently self-aware and be able to critically apply knowledge to be effective. They have to be able to describe, analyse and synthesise the material that they gather from observations, interviews and working inter-professionally. This work is highly complex as well as being emotionally demanding and often involves the management of fear for the worker which is an area not sufficiently addressed in the literature (Cooper, 2005). If we add anxiety about working with perceived 'difference' and anxiety about homosexuality to this cocktail, the importance of skilled supervision and management is clear.

Child's developmental needs

On this side of the Assessment Framework Triangle, the area that needs to be specifically considered with lesbians and gay men is 'social and family relationships'. Lesbians and gay men who are subject to state involvement with their families because of concerns relating to their parenting might be more reticent about revealing the detail of their family and social relationships. These relationships are likely to be different in some ways from those within heterosexual families. Eliciting information to facilitate a thorough assessment needs skill and sensitivity; for example, lesbians conceive children in a range of different ways from donor insemination undertaken at an NHS or private fertility clinic, to donor insemination with a known donor, through to having sex with a man. Similarly, ongoing relationships with putative fathers range from no contact to a high level of involvement with a child or children and equal child care responsibilities. Of course, child care arrangements and family relationships are varied within heterosexual families as well. However, lesbian and gay clients might be more tentative about being open with social workers, assuming a censorial response.

Accessing health and educational provision can be complicated for lesbians and gay men because of their own reticence to engage with services based on their assumption that such services will have negative views about lesbian and gay families. Some education and health professionals continue to demonstrate negativity, a lack of familiarity and anxiety towards lesbians and gay men. This will need to be unpicked in the core assessment process.

The identity of children of lesbians and gay men is something that has been explored. As discussed in Chapter 4 research has shown that there are very few differences between children who grow up in homosexual and heterosexual families. Golombok states that, 'family structure, in itself, is not a major determinant of children's psychological adjustment ... It is what happens within families, not the way families are composed, that seems to matter most' (Golombok, 2000: 101). She also comments that, 'Among children of lesbian mothers the outcomes are worst for those children whose mothers are insensitive to the difficulties they face as a result of prejudice from the outside world' (Golombok, 2000: 101).

Parenting capacity

The capacity of parents to meet the needs of their children is no different for homosexual parents than it is for heterosexual parents. The important point here is to consider parenting capacity in the context of the family's structure and functioning (DH, 2000b: 20). These factors will be different for every family. What is different for lesbian and gay families is the effect of implicit and explicit discrimination related to homophobia on the parent(s) and their ability to try to protect children from the worst aspects of this and to try to build resilience.

We argue that the quality of the relationship established between the worker and the client is essential to good outcomes. However, this must come with a health warning attached – the correct checks and balances within the system should support adequate reflection and thinking time for the worker to avoid collusion with the adults within a family, or to avoid positive stereotyping:

> Child care inquiries repeatedly indicate we are sometimes better at forming relationships with adults than protecting the children. This may be exacerbated when the worker understands the additional pressures and difficulties some lesbian and gay parents may experience, living in a homophobic society. The interests of the child are paramount, however understandable the adults' predicament, and this should constantly be reinforced in the supervisory process. (Brown, 1998a: 101)

In the assessment framework, factors related to the parenting capacity domain are premised on the ability of parents to offer those factors (or not), for example, emotional warmth. What isn't explicitly named in this domain is that the adults' ability to offer 'good enough' parenting is dependent on the psychological and emotional health of the parent(s). One of the indicators that might be considered relevant to psychological health is a secure sense of identity for the adult. However, many people's sexual identities are quite fluid and some people who have sex with people of the same gender might not necessarily identify as lesbian or gay, as the terms themselves denote a fixed sexuality. This lack of a named fixed sexual identity is not in itself indicative of poor psychological or emotional health.

Social and environmental factors

In assessing the factors within this side of the triangle, four areas in particular raise different issues for lesbian and gay families than for heterosexual families, although all factors are significant.

In terms of 'family history and functioning', there are a number of areas pertinent to an investigation. Firstly, it is important not to make assumptions about adults and children living in a family setting but to ask sensitively about family composition. The family's narrative about their relationships, significant life events and the meanings associated with these for the child(ren) and parents will be helpful in identifying significant relationships for the child and the impact of any potential stressful events or situations for the family (e.g. coming out experiences or family's experience of homophobia). Of course, many ordinary events that families may find stressful might also apply and it is important not to view these events solely through a sexuality lens, although for some complex situations someone's sexuality might be an added factor which can complicate responses from professionals and the adults involved through their perceptions and assumptions being made.

The wider family networks should be explored and questions asked to establish who is significant for the child. Social aunts and uncles (as opposed to biological ones) may be significant here. Who are the significant other adults for the child? Who are the significant supports for the adults? Careful questioning about the potential stressors (if any) in the extended family network for the adults is important. Do not assume that the wider family is supportive or not supportive. You may consider asking the family to draw an ecogram as part of the assessment, which would enable the family to talk about their support network and community contacts.

The family's social integration is important in establishing whether they are well supported within the community or whether the family are isolated or insular in any way. How 'out' is the family within these networks? What networks does the family have and use within their immediate locale? These are the sorts of things to be held in mind whilst being open to hearing the narrative that the family reveals, which might be entirely different; for example, in drug and alcohol using families where there might be a highly supportive (if dysfunctional) network of other users, these networks may act to give some psychological and practical support. If these networks are going to be removed, then what will be put in its place to offer new functional support? We know isolation is a major vulnerability factor in relation to child protection, and skilled engagement with the client will enable the meaning of the isolation and the underpinning causes to be identified. Again, experiences of homophobia might be a compounding factor here.

How families access community resources is important. This can cover universal services such as education and health as well as local services and include both informal and formal relationships; for example, the child in a family may have formed a positive bond with their classroom assistant or the lollipop lady/man. The family's experience of acceptance by their wider family and community is important. Financial resources also play a part in enabling families to form positive links within their communities. 'Poverty, and the social disadvantages that accompany it, is one of the most detrimental and pernicious influences faced by children today' (Golombok, 2000: 102). The experience of living within a potentially non-inclusive or accepting environment can exacerbate all these factors for lesbian and gay families.

Sometimes there can be an assumption that sameness between worker and client in terms of sexuality is helpful. Of course it can be, however differences in class, culture and lifestyle in particular have a powerful effect on lived experience, which go far beyond one's choice of sexual partner. Brown (1998a) noted in her discussion of working with five lesbian families through child protection issues, 'The work with these families illuminated a "culture" gap at that time, between the discourses of the predominantly working class lesbians involved and the agencies' adoption of predominantly middle class lesbian or gay "professional-speak"' (Brown 1998a: 99). It is the capability of the worker to work across cultural and class differences which will contribute to a positive working relationship, not whether the client and worker are both lesbian or gay.

> The assumption that is sometimes voiced in anti-discriminatory practice literature, that if the social worker is from the same oppressed group as the service user/client, then the quality of service provision is improved, was not borne out in this sample … the intervention outcomes were not affected by the sexual orientation of the workers, but by their abilities. (Brown 1998a: 99)

In the Department of Health's guidance to staff completing the assessment framework, inclusive practice is stressed. There are a number of pitfalls staff are asked to avoid, and these include:

> Using one set of cultural assumptions and stereotypes to understand the child and family's circumstances; insensitivity to racial and cultural variations within groups and between individuals; making unreasoned assumptions without evidence; failing to take account of experiences of any discrimination in an individual's response to public services; failing to take account of the barriers which prevent the social integration of families with disabled members; attaching meaning to information without confirming the interpretation with the child and family members. (DH, 2000b: 27)

These points are pertinent to lesbian and gay families and their children.

Looked After Children

There is a significant literature about Looked After Children and social work practice. In this section we focus on young lesbians and gay men and consider how the Looked After Children system facilitates their development.

Looked After Children are not a homogeneous group and within the population of children who are in public care, a small number of lesbian, gay or bisexual young people will be included. The family placement guidance recognises this and makes the following statement: 'the needs and concerns of gay young men and women must also be recognised and approached sympathetically' (DH 1991: 97) and 'gay young men and women may require very sympathetic carers to enable them to accept their sexuality and to develop their own self esteem' (DH, 1991: 98).

Adolescence is a time of intense and immense physical and emotional change for young people. Erikson (1965) in his life cycle approach identifies the potential conflicts and powerful feelings that abound at this point in a young person's life, naming it as 'identity vs role confusion'. This period is often the time where young people will become aware of their sexuality and begin to grapple with feelings of difference. Tully provides a helpful framework for social workers to consider their work with young lesbians and gay men. By the use of what she refers to as an empowerment approach she looks at work related to the micro, mezzo and macro levels of intervention (2000: 127–42).

Tharinger and Wells argue that young lesbians and gay men develop their sexuality in a 'context and ecology of cultural denial, distorted stereotypes, rejection, neglect, harassment, and sometimes outright victimization and abuse' (Tharinger and Wells, 2000: 159). Similar findings are reiterated in the UK context by Coyle (1998), emphasising the complexity of the coming out process for young lesbians and gay men within their families. One of the major events with which a young person has to grapple is the 'coming out' process and this marks out lesbian, gay and bisexual young people's experiences as different from their heterosexual peers. Often (but not always) this experience can be compounded by a lack of social support available via families, friends and surrounding networks. For lesbian and gay young people who are not living with their birth families, this can create any number of additional tensions, difficulties, pressures and experiences that will affect their development during this time. In applying Erikson's life cycle development model, this process of 'coming out' for the individual adolescent is an additional complication to the crisis of the fifth stage of the life cycle (identity vs role confusion). As noted in Chapter 4, Strommen considers the 'crisis' a family experiences when a young person comes out. He argues that social workers 'by providing facilitating, non pejorative assistance to the family ... can lessen the confusion and uncertainty these families experience as they wrestle with the reconstruction of long-held but never-examined beliefs and assumptions, and help them to keep the intimate circle of the family intact and healthy' (1990: 29).

This work with families also needs to take place within a fostering context where the gay or lesbian young person may have been placed for a considerable period of time. It is particularly important that the foster family do not reject the young person during this time and that work is done to facilitate the process of the family, the aim being to facilitate the foster carer meeting the young person's needs. Indeed, the Children's Workforce Development Council's Training, Support and Development Standards for Foster Care require foster carers to 'understand the different types of prejudice and discrimination which can affect children and young people' (CWDC, 2007: 5). This will include the impact of homophobia on lesbian and gay young people. With regard to family protective factors for young lesbians and gay men, Morrow argues that:

> a positive and supportive family relationships can be central ... a validating family system can be crucial for youth who, on a daily basis, encounter shame and ridicule from the broader society because of their sexual orientation. (2006: 187)

Foster families have to be able to act as a buffer for young people's experiences of adversity and have the ability to help that young person make positive links with other organisations and people. Within this process it is also important to ensure that a split does not occur between the supervising social worker for the foster carer and the social worker for the child.

In addition, social workers have a responsibility to young people who are looked after who are lesbian or gay in identifying suitable placements. Local Authorities need to have foster carers available who can meet their needs. These placements won't necessarily be with lesbian or gay carers. Historically, Local Authorities haven't robustly met the needs of young lesbians and gay men for whom they are responsible. The Albert Kennedy Trust (AKT) was established in Manchester in 1989 by a heterosexual foster carer and the lesbian and gay community following the death of Albert Kennedy at age 16 who, at the time of his death, was looked after and had experienced homophobic bullying. The purpose of the Trust was to recruit lesbian and gay carers for homeless lesbian and gay young people. Their work often involves joint work with social services departments in finding suitable carers for specific young people who are lesbian or gay.

Albert Kennedy's experience of homophobic bullying is not unique. The organisation Stonewall has noted that 'research shows that homophobic bullying in schools increases truancy, self harm and suicide rates by young people, damages self esteem and lowers educational attainment' (Bywater and Jones, 2007: 45). The authors note that schools are under a legal obligation to prevent bullying of pupils because of their sexual orientation (DfEE, 2000). Stonewall, in conjunction with the Mayor of London, has developed helpful materials to enable schools to tackle homophobic bullying effectively. An example of this is the *Spell It Out: Tackling Homophobia in Our Schools* teacher's guide DVD (Stonewall, 2006).

For Looked After Children and young people there are a range of mechanisms through which young people can have a say about issues that affect them. The structural markers include Personal Education Plans (PEPs – these should be reviewed regularly), Looked After Children Reviews (these should happen every six months), and care plans. This is not to detract from the importance of ongoing work being completed with the young person in terms of understanding their everyday experiences of school, friendships, personal relationships, and developing sense of self including their sexuality. Work done within the context of their placement setting should include, as with any adolescent, helping them think through forming appropriate and safe sexual relationships, safer sex practices, information on sexually transmitted diseases, risky sexual behaviours (such as prostitution) and the adults should remain mindful that the development of a young person's sexuality is not just about risk, sorrow and awfulness. It is also about pleasure, self-awareness and discovery.

We know that: 'Young people in care are four times more likely than their peers to smoke, use alcohol and misuse drugs' (DfES, 2007: 90). Lesbian and gay young people will be represented in these statistics. We also know that young lesbians and gay men in particular have higher rates of suicide than heterosexual young people (D'Augelli and Hershberger, 1993; Warner et al., 2004). The professional network engaged in working with the young person should keep in mind potentiality of risk.

In many ways the needs of Looked After Children are the same as those of every other child. They do have additional needs which relate specifically to their experiences of harm, abuse or separation from their families. However, often both their basic and additional needs can get forgotten or go unacknowledged, as they are not 'held in mind' by individuals and the various systems they work within, which are complex and bureaucratic … making a difference to the lives of Looked After Children involves recognising and responding to the uniqueness of each child. (Cocker and Allain, 2008: 192–3)

The child's uniqueness includes their sexuality and sexual orientation, but this is not the only factor which may be relevant for a young person who is lesbian or gay. Stewart and Ray (2001) noted that disabled young people are less likely to receive effective relationship and sex education, either at home or at school. A young person who is disabled may also be lesbian or gay, which adds a potential further complication to their experiences of being supported. Similarly the interrelationship of race and racism for a young lesbian or gay man is complex. Mason-John and Khanbatta (1993) talked about the complexity of the interrelationship between racism and homophobia. Some young Black lesbians and gay men, may be reticent about coming out as they might not want to have to deal with racism and homophobia. Managing both might feel too much at that stage in their lives. The assumption that being 'out' equates to psychological health is not always the case. People can and do manage to live with complexity in their lives.

Residential care for Looked After Children   ■ ■ ■ ■ ▪ ▪

Much of what we have discussed above about foster carers' roles in meeting the needs of young lesbians and gay men also applies to residential social workers. These settings need to be inclusive and enabling so that young lesbians and gay men can feel safe and secure where they live. Mallon (1999) identifies a number of themes emerging from the experiences of lesbian and gay young people in residential settings: 'invisibility and hiding; stress and isolation; multiple placements and feelings or rejections; verbal harassment and physical violence' (1999: 115–18). He then develops recommendations for developing an environment in which all young people can be safe.

Cocker and Allain comment that 'residential care often deals with young people who are in crisis, have a variety of complex needs, and have often experienced several placement moves' (2008: 43). This is acknowledged by a number of authors who also emphasise the potential mental health vulnerabilities for these young people (Clough et al., 2006; Scottish Institute for Residential Child Care, 2006; Ward, 2006). Briggs (2002) notes how for all adolescents this period of time involves loss and change which can be difficult to manage emotionally and psychologically. Linked with these feelings is anxiety and this can be associated with risky and self-harming behaviour. We argue that the cumulative potential impact of the combination of adolescence, being in public care, being lesbian or gay and being placed in residential care for some individuals means that they are particularly vulnerable. However having said this, we also agree with Golombok when she says: 'Not all children are crushed by adversity. Some can overcome even the most extreme difficulties to lead successful and fulfilling lives' (2000: 102).

For lesbian and gay young people who are placed in residential settings there are additional stresses associated with their sexuality and perceptions of their difference. Cocker and Allain commenting on all Looked After Children write that 'the issue of "fitting in" with peer groups is likely to be central' (2008: 67). It is therefore particularly important that residential social workers are able to manage complex relationships between the young people who they are caring for to enable young lesbians and gay men to feel part of the group and not to be marginalised (Smith, 2009).

Fostering and adoption

There has been more written about this area of social work practice with lesbians and gay men than the above areas. This is partly explicable because this writing built on existing research and publications about lesbian and gay parenting stimulated by the lesbian custody cases of the 1960s–1980s. The research about lesbian and gay families and child development has been covered in Chapter 4. Chapter 1 covered the political, social and policy context in which lesbians and gay men came forward to be assessed as foster carers and as adopters. In this section we are addressing matters related to practice as follows: the assessment process for prospective carers; matching children to adoption and fostering placements; safer care and post-placement support.

Hicks (2005b) outlines the history of lesbian and gay fostering and adoption and has contributed to this area of practice more widely (Hicks, 2000; 2008; 2009; 2011; Hicks and McDermot, 1999). There are two key reasons why fostering and adoption by lesbians and gay men has developed in the ways that it has in the UK. Firstly, research looking at the development of children in lesbian families stimulated by lesbian custody cases both in the UK (Tasker and Golombok, 1997) and in the USA (Patterson, 2005) evidenced that children were not damaged as a result of being raised in lesbian families. Secondly, lesbian and gay men themselves placed pressure on fostering and adoption agencies from the 1970s to have the right to be assessed as foster carers and as adopters. The combination of these two factors has meant that there have been an increasing number of lesbians and gay men coming forward to care for Looked After Children either through adoption of those children or by fostering. The degree of change in this area has been symbolised by the legal recognition of these changes through the Adoption and Children Act 2002 as noted in Chapter 2.

There is less research on outcomes for children growing up with gay fathers (Tasker, 2005) than there is about children's development in lesbian families. There is also a distinct lack of research findings addressing outcomes for children in the UK growing up in lesbian and gay adoptive families and with foster families. For our practice to be properly evidence based there needs to be longitudinal studies of these adopted as well as fostered children. Tasker and Bellamy comment:

> Leaving aside the objections some would make on religious grounds, placing children with same-sex couples is likely to remain vulnerable to criticism when evidence on developmental outcomes for children adopted or fostered by lesbians or gay men rests on generalising results from the wider literature on lesbian and gay parenting. The case for further research in this area is compelling. (Tasker and Bellamy, 2007: 529)

As noted in Chapter 4, there is some US research available examining outcomes for adopted children growing up within lesbian and gay families.

Assessment processes for prospective carers

We have argued elsewhere the importance of the assessment process for prospective lesbian and gay adopters and foster carers (Brown and Cocker, 2008; Cocker and Brown, 2010). The assessment process needs to be rigorous at the same time as being an arena for the development of applicants through the process. This is only possible when the assessment itself takes account of the importance of the relationship between the assessor and the applicants to enable trust to develop. It is through the telling of the applicant's life story and the social worker's ability with the applicant to reflect upon, analyse and synthesise the related material that an assessment of their suitability to become carers for children is realised. 'While the quality of the information is of paramount importance, it is the analysis of this information by the applicant and the social worker that is the kernel of sound assessment' (Brown and Cocker, 2008: 25).

The Wakefield Inquiry (Parrott et al., 2007) was a timely reminder of the need for social workers to remain objective and critically questioning during assessments, and take account of the dynamics of the relationship that is formed between the social work assessor and the applicant. In addition, we note the importance of observation as part of the assessment. 'Reflexive observation also forms a key part of the arsenal of skills a social worker deploys in this process' (Cocker and Brown, 2010: 25).

Brown (1991) was the first person in the UK to consider the detail of what needed to be addressed in the assessment of lesbian and gay adoptive and foster care applicants in addition to what was covered in the assessment of all applicants. This work has been further developed by Mallon and Betts (2005), Manchester City Council, Children, Families and Social Care (2007), Brown and Cocker (2008) and Cocker and Brown (2010). In this chapter we have reproduced in full the areas from Brown and Cocker (2008) that we consider necessary to address in the assessment of lesbians and gay men. Brown (1991) argued that in addition to a thorough assessment, the following five points were relevant when assessing lesbian and gay applicants:

Firstly, the individual's experience of their homosexuality (their own and their families' response historically)   It is essential to have an understanding of applicants' histories including their experience of 'coming out' as lesbians or gay men. This is necessary so that both parties consider any implications of this regarding the applicants' ability to care for Looked After Children. For example, if they have had a severed relationship with their birth families as a result of 'coming out', what might be the implications of this on how they will be able to facilitate contact between a child placed with them and that child's birth family? It will be important not to assume that this will be problematic for a potential carer but to work with them about how they might experience this and how they would manage their own feelings about their own birth family and not project those feelings onto either the Looked After Child or that child's birth family.

Secondly, how confident they feel in relation to their sexuality and how comfortable they are as lesbians and gay men   To care for Looked After Children successfully, carers need to have a secure sense of themselves because children have a powerful ability to identify areas of vulnerability in their carers, and to play on those areas. In relation to sexuality, potential carers need to feel sufficiently secure as lesbians and gay men as part of their overall sense of themselves as emotionally robust and resilient adults.

Thirdly, how homophobia and heterosexism has impinged on their lives and how they feel they dealt with this and what coping devices they use It is important to explore applicants' experience of heterosexism and homophobia in terms of how they have responded to these in their lives. This is important because as carers they will have to manage difficulties they encounter confidently and in such a way that is in the interests of the children they are caring for.

Fourthly, what are their present relationships: sexual, emotional, supportive, family, etc.? How do they negotiate homophobia within close relationships (e.g. siblings)? Assessors can be reluctant to talk with lesbian and gay applicants about the intimate details of their relationships because of shyness or a perceived lack of knowledge about lesbian and gay men's lives or a fear of being seen as homophobic by the applicants; however, this fourth point is critical.

Fifthly, transition to parenthood – making links with the local community regarding child care resources, and contact arrangements with birth family members of fostered/adopted children Caring for Looked After Children transports carers into the public domain. Some lesbians and gay men may be used to occupying an exclusively lesbian and gay environment. Applicants have to show sufficient flexibility to move beyond what feels comfortable and into new situations, dictated by the child's needs.

In addition, the assessment should explore with the prospective carer how they would support a child who experienced prejudice because of the sexual orientation of their carer. There are real issues about lesbians and gay men being confident enough to manage the integration of vulnerable children into their community given potential homophobia within the wider community. This has to be an explicit part of the assessment.

One of the areas of assessment that paradoxically is not often commented upon in the literature or in practice is the importance of applicants' attitudes to sex and sexual relationships. The paradox is that to ignore this aspect of human beings stands in stark contrast to the prurient fascination often focused upon lesbian and gay sex. The issue is that sex is a powerful form of communication and pleasure within adult relationships and the meaning of both of these for the applicants needs to be made explicit. This is an important area for children being placed in the home because:

Firstly, children will grow to understand sex in terms of their own relationships through what they observe in families.

Secondly, children who bring particular histories that impact on their own behaviour and feelings require carers who have a level of insight to understand the impact this might have on themselves and the dynamics within the family. The placement of any child into a family will change the rhythms of family experience of everyday life, including expression of sexual feelings and affection by adults. If the adults are secure in their sexual relationships they will be able to adjust and adapt to these new constraints in a comfortable enough way without their relationship being undermined.

Thirdly, some relationships are sexually inactive – and the meaning of this needs to be explored with both the individuals concerned. This is not necessarily a contra-indication for suitability for fostering or adoption.

Fourthly, assessors need to be able to predict the longevity of the couple's relationship. This is not always possible. However, an exploration of people's sexual partner histories and patterns that might emerge, as well as assessing the history and quality of the current relationship in depth, should be explored within the assessment. People's motivation to foster and adopt are many and varied and sometimes their motivation might be partly driven by a desire to cement or rescue their relationship. In-depth and critically analytic assessments comprise: what is said, what is observed, what is not said and patterns that emerge through the exploration of people's histories and current relationship (Brown and Cocker, 2008: 25–7).

Matching children to adoption and fostering placements

The process involved in matching a child to a carer is one of the most important variables in ensuring successful placements (Sellick et al., 2004). At this point it is the skills, ability and aptitude of the carers which are most important in terms of their ability to meet the particular needs of individual children, not the sexuality of the carer. However, this is arguably the point at which most prejudice is apparent. Brown and Cocker argue that 'children and family social workers, birth families, permanency panel members and previous foster carers can all object to such placements, expressing fears that are often founded on beliefs that children cannot develop "normally" in lesbian and gay households' (2008: 27). The Fostering Services National Minimum Standards state:

> In matching children with carers, responsible authorities take into account the child's care plan and recent written assessments of the child and their family and the carers. Matches are achieved by means of information sharing and consideration involving all relevant professionals, the child and her/his family and potential carers, their families and other children in placement. (DH, 2002c: 12–13)

Whilst the matching of children for adoption is governed by different standards, the role of the adoption or fostering social worker in these circumstances is twofold. Not only are they identifying appropriate families for children for whom they are family finding, they are also in a position of often having to persuade other professionals of the individual family's strengths and attributes rather than allow stereotypes to be made about families based solely on their sexuality.

There have been some highly publicised cases where birth families have objected to their children being placed with lesbian and gay carers (Weale, 1993), although the numbers of cases hitting the headlines has lessened over the last ten years. The change in law may have helped; however, the placement of children with lesbian or gay carers can still be fraught with tensions. For example, the child's social worker has the power to veto a potential placement, deeming it unsuitable because of a child's perceived need to have a mother and father, in effect creating a hierarchy of preferred family forms and structures. Information presented by BAAF at a conference on lesbian and gay adoption (Stott, 2009) on the adoption register showed that in terms of families on the register waiting to be matched with children, heterosexual two parent families waited the least amount of time, lesbian two parent carers came next, and single carers waited the longest to be matched with a child, often after other potential families had said 'no' to the child. There are not enough approved gay men currently to know how social workers are matching children with gay families. This is not to say that there aren't very good reasons why individual children's needs on occasion may mean that they should be placed with a particular gendered carer or heterosexual couple. Matching should never be an ideologically driven decision.

Safer care

Safer care practices were developed in the 1980s and 1990s in response to allegations being made against adopters and foster carers. Writing in 2000, Nixon stated that it was difficult to measure the extent of allegations being made. However, it is generally accepted that the rate of allegations increased throughout the 1980s. Rather than this being a reflection of an increase in abusive incidents, it is likely to be related to an increased climate of adults being more likely to listen to what children were saying.

In the UK context, helpful practice guidance is available for practitioners and foster carers (Slade, 2006) on safer care. Particularly in foster care, safer care is now embedded into practice. Safer care policies are usually developed at placement agreement meetings at the start of each foster placement and an individualised safer care policy devised for each child in placement and updated when necessary or at least once a year. For adopters, like foster carers, this will be an area that is explored during their assessment, but unlike foster carers it won't necessarily be followed up post-adoption.

For lesbian and gay carers there will be additional areas that need to be addressed. For example they might be slightly more vulnerable to allegations being made about them from people associated with the child who might not agree with the placement of a particular child with lesbian and gay carers.

It is important that lesbian and gay adopters as well as foster carers are helped to consider what they might need to adapt about their lifestyles to make sure that they are as prepared as possible for caring safely for a child. This preparatory thinking can helpfully be done in the assessment process by asking applicants to think through the everyday detail of their lives; to think about what they take for granted as 'ordinary' and how the 'ordinary' might be open to misinterpretation by others.

One of the authors developed the following model as a way of helping applicants understand allegations that are made against both adopters and foster carers.

- Actual: the event described happened
- False: the event described didn't happen
- Perception of the child/young person: resulting from past experience and other factors, the child/young person misinterprets the behaviour of the carer
- Behaviour of the carer: resulting from the impact of the child/young person's behaviour and the dynamics between the carer (or members of the carer's household) and the young person, the behaviour of the carer is affected.

> Many allegations fall into the last two categories and often overlap … Placing children with troubled pasts in new families inevitably stirs up complex and difficult feelings for both the child and family. (Brown, 2009: 267)

It might be that a child is unfamiliar with lesbians and gay men and because of this unfamiliarity their placement adds to the stirring up of such complex and difficult feelings. These dynamics are manageable and can be anticipated but lesbians and gay men who are adopters or foster carers do need to be sufficiently prepared and supported.

Post-placement support

Post-placement support involves different structures and processes for adoption and fostering. In fostering, the carers' supervising social worker will continue working with the foster carers throughout each placement. The foster carers will also be reviewed annually as to their suitability to continue to be registered as foster carers and to make sure that their terms of approval are still appropriate (DH, 2002c). Parrott et al. (2007) identified the importance of the review process in identifying patterns that might be significant to address, and the importance of triangulation of evidence in the review process regarding the foster carers' continuing suitability.

The quality of the working relationship between the supervising social worker and the foster carer is of paramount importance as it is the vehicle through which ongoing work with foster carers happens. The supervising social worker needs to be comfortable with the sexuality of the foster carer where the foster carer is lesbian or gay as well as properly equipped to support all foster carers irrespective of their sexualities who have lesbian and gay young people placed with them.

With regard to adoption, the post-placement support needs of lesbian and gay adopters are the same as for any other adopter. The child's placing agency should provide access to necessary support for the adoptive placement for three years post-placement. If the child has significant additional needs at the point of placement then adoption allowances and additional support can be negotiated at the point of matching and this support will be reviewed annually.

Problems for lesbian and gay adopters emerge when accessing support from external agencies where heterosexuality is assumed until otherwise stated. Brown and Cocker note that:

Lesbians and gay men who are approved as carers continue to face dilemmas. Their approving agency has assessed them as having the abilities to care for vulnerable children but they encounter conflicts through being expected to care for children in a society that is still deeply ambivalent about their competence and suitability. (2008: 28–9)

Once again, sexuality can then become the lens through which all difficulties are then viewed, which is unhelpful. Wilton (2000) comments that in respect of health and social care provision more broadly, the interface between the private family and the public service arena may dictate a very different experience for the lesbian and gay family and child than their heterosexual counterparts. Lesbians and gay men have had to become more visible as parents in terms of accessing public services associated with parenting such as schools, health and mental health services, play groups, after school clubs and so on. However, this visibility and involvement should not be read as increased acceptance by wider society – but it will hopefully have a positive effect over time.

Summary   ■ ■ ▪ ▪ ▫ ▫

In all aspects of decision-making about children, the child is paramount. This is a guiding principle of the Children Act 1989 (Section 1) and it is important to always hold on to this principle, especially in this area of practice, where ideological dogma has sometimes taken precedence over sound professional judgement in decision-making.

Conclusion

In the introduction we argued for 'a new radicalism: a radicalism that challenges the status quo and social work theory and practice to enable lesbian and gay social work clients and carers to realise their individual and collective potential'. This radicalism needs to build social work knowledge and practice with lesbians and gay men. We conclude the book by reiterating some thoughts about five areas as follows: knowledge, legislation, difference, the unsaid and relationships.

Knowledge

Gray and Webb argue that:

> social work knowledge is in a constant state of flux and might be best described as a continuing activity that is formed and re-formed over time. Old wisdom is constantly tested against new ideas and conceptual formulations. (Gray and Webb, 2009:2)

We have considered the problematic nature of some 'old wisdom' as it relates to lesbians and gay men and have argued that social work knowledge, which includes theory and research, needs to be deconstructed to examine its applicability to lesbians and gay men. However, this 'deconstruction' does not equate to 'destruction'. Some ideas drawn on by social workers have been seen as oppressive to lesbians and gay men as well as women, for example John Bowlby's work on attachment. We believe such work, when considered within its historical and social context, still has much to offer. As well as the deconstruction of knowledge social workers have to seek out new knowledge that is specific to lesbians and gay men to better inform their understanding and their practice. However, because lesbians and gay men have been a marginalised group, there is a distinct paucity of knowledge in this area of social work practice. Therefore there is a need for knowledge to be built that informs social work practice with lesbians and gay men. Higher Education Institutions have two crucial parts to play in this process. Firstly, research about social work practice should include and make visible lesbians and gay men's experiences. In addition specific research is also needed about the lived experiences of lesbians and gay men and the effect of social work interventions. Secondly, when students undertake their qualifying and post-qualifying courses, Higher Education Institutions should ensure they are equipped to work effectively with lesbians and gay men.

Knowledge from outside the discipline of social work contributes to thinking and practice. We need to spread our net wide to benefit from ideas that are relevant to lesbians and gay men from such disciplines as sociology, philosophy, the humanities, history, law, cultural studies and social geography.

Legislation

The rate of legislative change impacting on the lives of lesbians and gay men in the UK in the last ten years has been beyond what was imaginable in 1967, the year of the Sexual Offences Act which made sex between men in private legal. Even after the passing of that Act lesbians and gay men had no legal protection in any area of their lives and many aspects of gay male sex were still criminalised. By 2011 all criminalising laws had been repealed. Lesbians and gay men now have the benefit of protection through legislation.

This legal protection and equitable treatment under the law represents years of gay and lesbian political activism that secured protective legislation as well as the repeal of that which was discriminatory. Legislative change also reflects changing public opinion and increased public acceptance of lesbians and gay men. However, there is still a long way to go as demonstrated by research in schools that showed that homophobic bullying is still common place (Hunt and Jensen, 2007).

The relationship between homosexuality, the law and social work practice is a complex one and legal changes do not necessarily equate with social workers' attitudes. We argue that social work's professionalisation has led to its distancing from political activism. As discussed in

Chapters 1 and 2, social work was a profession at the forefront of arguing for Local Authority and national protective policies for lesbians and
gay men. In the 1980s in many Labour controlled Local Authorities,
social workers' practice was ahead of legislation. Social workers' practice
adhered to equal opportunities policies that included lesbians and gay
men at a time when there was no national protective legislation.
However, times have changed. Social work practice now lags behind
legislation and if lesbians and gay men are going to have equitable treatment, as dictated by the Sexual Orientation Regulations 2007, then
social work needs to address its knowledge base and its practice.

Difference

Theoretical expositions about difference have been profitably informed
by post-modern thinking, particularly by the work of Judith Butler.
Fawcett and Featherstone comment that, 'a relational understanding
treats the notion of difference itself as problematic, and allows us to
explore how differences are reproduced and maintained in ongoing
psychic and material practices' (2000: 15–16). Social work's relationship
with 'difference' does not demonstrate 'relational understanding' as it has
been primarily informed by discourses taken from 'anti-discriminatory
practice' and reflects a deficit model. This ultimately supports the continuation of the status quo, and normative understandings of human
performance and relationships.

   In practice, 'difference' often invokes anxiety. Difference becomes the
focus of intervention, and a holistic appraisal of other dimensions of the
client are lost. In the effort to be 'anti-discriminatory' and value difference, the social worker inadvertently dehumanises 'the other' and can
over focus on a particular aspect of difference, or ignore it. Both
responses are fuelled by anxiety and are problematic. For example, for
young people who are looked after and gay, there can be an over-
concentration on their sexuality at the expense of other developmental
needs.

The unsaid

Social work engages with the interface between the intimate personal
worlds of men, women and children and the public sphere. It is therefore, by its very nature, a profession where discretion, discernment,

clarity and sensitivity are essential. Avoidance has no place in social work practice. We have noted a number of unspoken areas that we believe to be counterproductive for social work with lesbians and gay men, particularly: child protection; the relationship between sexuality, religion and social work practice; social workers fears about being accused of homophobia and other acts of negative discrimination. In some circumstances, not speaking about these areas can be positively dangerous.

We have noted that virtually nothing has been written addressing child protection in lesbian and gay families. Child abuse does occur in lesbian and gay families, as it does in heterosexual families. We have argued the protection needs of children are the same whatever their family circumstances, and that the current child welfare frameworks can be used effectively with all families. However, social workers should hold in mind the specific meanings of 'family' and 'kinship networks' for lesbians and gay men and their families.

Social workers' fear of being accused of homophobia was noted in the Wakefield Inquiry (Parrott et al., 2007) and the results of this fear were serious. When social work engages with groups that are discriminated against, this raises levels of anxiety for practitioners. Social workers can fear that they will be perceived as further adding to the negative discrimination that someone experiences.

We have argued that 'anti-discriminatory practice' has contributed to this fear of being accused of homophobia. Social work has to break free of such prescriptive and blaming discourses. Practitioners need to engage in the realities of lesbians and gay men's lives which sometimes go wrong in the same ways that heterosexual people's lives do. This engagement will include statutory interventions in people's lives that are against the wishes of the individuals involved, either to secure their welfare or the welfare of those to whom they have caring responsibilities.

Polarisation of views concerning religious beliefs and practice and their relationship with homosexuality is another area of social work practice that has garnered little sophisticated debate. Too often this is spoken of as one group's rights over another's, and which prevails. This is unhelpful as it will always result in a rigid prescribed positioning.

Relationships

The radicalism that we are arguing for includes aspects of social work practice that have been described as 'liberal'. However, we argue that in the current climate of managerialism and the bureaucratisation of social work, emphasising the importance of the direct working relationship between a client and their social worker is indeed 'radical'. When engaging with groups that have been marginalised by social work, the skills of engagement, integrity, warmth, reliability and clarity are particularly important. We are in agreement with Wilson et al. when they write:

> Relationships are at the heart of effective social work ... As a social worker you have to be capable of thinking simultaneously about:
>
> - The uniqueness of each individual service user
> - The relationship of service users to their social circumstances
> - Your relationship with individual service users
> - Your relationship with the socio-political context in which you practise. (2008: 3)

We argue that these 'capabilities' are fundamental to all practice and are particularly pertinent when working with lesbians and gay men. Social work is about facilitating change, whether it is with an individual, group or community. We have noted the importance of social workers appreciating and respecting lesbians and gay men's relationships, families and networks and the importance of building on the strengths of these relationships. By doing such work, social work becomes a political as well as a social activity that is rooted in the complexity of the human psyche, experience and relationships.

References

Abbott, D. and Howarth, J. (2005) *Secret Loves, Hidden Lives*. London: Policy Press.

Adams, R. (2009) 'Working with children, young people and families', in R. Adams, L. Dominelli and M. Payne (eds), *Social Work: Themes, Issues and Critical Debates* (3rd edn). Basingstoke: Palgrave Macmillan. pp. 301–19.

Adoption Quarterly (2009) Special Issues on lesbian and gay adoption, 12 (3 and 4).

Ahmed, S., Cheetham, J. and Small, J. (1986) *Social Work with Black Children and their Families*. London: B.T. Batsford.

Allport, G.W. and Ross, J.M. (1967) 'Personal Religious Orientation and Prejudice', *Journal of Personality and Social Psychology*, 5: 432–43.

American Psychoanalytic Association (2006) *Position Statement on Gay and Lesbian Parenting*. New York: American Psychoanalytic Association.

Amnesty International (2008) *Love, Hate and the Law: Decriminalising Homosexuality*. London: Amnesty International. www.amnesty.org/en/library/asset/POL30/003/2008/en/d77d0d58-4cd3-11dd-bca2-bb9d43f3e059/pol300032008eng.html (Accessed 27.05.2009).

Archibald, C. (2010) 'A path less travelled: hearing the voices of older lesbians: a pilot study researching residential care and other needs', in R.L. Jones and R. Ward (eds), *LGBT Issues: Looking Beyond Categories*. Edinburgh: Dunedin Academic Press.

Ashencaen Crabtree, S., Husain, F. and Spalek, B. (2008) *Islam and Social Work: Debating Values, Transforming Practice*. Bristol: Policy Press/BASW.

Avante Consulting (2006) *On Safe Ground – LGBT Disabled People and Community Groups*. Edinburgh: Avante Consulting.

Averett, P. and Nalavany, B. (2009) 'An evaluation of gay/lesbian and heterosexual adoption', *Adoption Quarterly*, 12: 129–51.

Badgett, M.V.L. and Frank, J. (2007) *Sexual Orientation Discrimination: An International Perspective*. London: Routledge.

Bagilhole, B. (2009) *Understanding Equal Opportunities and Diversity: The Social Differentiations and Intersections of Inequality*. Bristol: The Policy Press.

Bailey, J.M., Bobrow, D., Wolfe, M. and Mikach, S. (1995) 'Sexual orientation of adult sons of gay fathers', *Developmental Psychology*, 31: 124–9.

Bailey, R. and Brake, M. (eds) (1975) *Radical Social Work*. London: Edward Arnold.

Baines, D. (ed.) (2007) *Doing Anti-Oppressive Practice: Building Transformative Politicized Social Work*. Black Point, Nova Scotia: Fernwood Publishing.

Baird, V. (2004) *Sex, Love and Homophobia: Lesbian, Gay, Bisexual and Transgender Lives*. London: Amnesty International.

Banton, R., Clifford, P., Frosh, S., Lousada, J. and Rosenthall, J. (1985) *The Politics of Mental Health*. London: Macmillan.

Barrett, H. and Tasker, F. (2001) 'Growing up with a gay parent: views of 101 gay fathers on their sons' and daughters' experiences', *Educational and Child Psychology*, 18: 62–77.

Barrett, H. and Tasker, F. (2002) 'Gay fathers and their children: what we know and what we need to know', *Lesbian & Gay Psychology Review*, 3: 3–10.

Barrett, M. and McIntosh, M. (1982) *The Anti-Social Family*. London: Verso.

Barry, M. and Hallett, C. (1998) *Issues of Theory, Policy and Practice*. Lyme Regis: Russell House Publishing.

Bartlett, A., Smith, G. and King, M. (2009) 'The response of mental health professionals to clients seeking help to change or redirect same-sex sexual orientation', *BMC Psychiatry*. www.biomedcentral.com/1471-244X (Accessed 12.01.2010).

Beasley, C. (1999) *What is Feminism? An Introduction to Feminist Thought*. London: Sage.

Beasley, C. (2005) *Gender and Sexuality: Critical Theories, Critical Thinkers*. London: Sage.

Beech, C. and Ray, M. (2009) 'Older people', in R. Adams, L. Dominelli and R. Payne (eds), *Critical Practice in Social Work* (2nd edn). Basingstoke: Palgrave/Macmillan. pp. 356–67.

Berkman, C.S. and Zinberg, G. (1997) 'Homophobia and heterosexism in social workers', *Social Work,* 42: 319–32.

Bianco, M. (2008) 'Book review: *Epistemology of the Closet* by Eve Kosofsky Sedgwick', *Feminist Review* (21 February). http://feministreview.blogspot.com/2008/02/epistemology-of-closet.html (Accessed 28.02.10).

Blasius, M. and Phelan, S. (eds) (1997) *We are Everywhere: A Historical Sourcebook of Gay and Lesbian Politics*. London: Routledge.

Bos, H.M., Van Balen, F. and Van den Boom, D.C. (2005) 'Lesbian families and family functioning', *Patient Education and Counseling,* 59(3): 263–75.

Botcherby, S. and Creegan, C. (2009) *Moving Forward: Putting Sexual Orientation in the Public Domain*. Manchester: Equality and Human Rights Commission, Research Summary 40.

Bower, M. (ed.) (2005) *Psychoanalytic Theory for Social Work Practice: Thinking Under Fire*. London: Routledge.

Bowpitt, G. (1998) 'Evangelical Christianity, secular humanism, and the genesis of British social work', *British Journal of Social Work*, 28: 675–93.

Bowpitt, G. (2000) 'Working with creative creatures: towards a Christian paradigm for social work theory, with some practical implications', *British Journal of Social Work*, 30: 349–64.

Boxall, K., Speakup Self Advocacy and Eastwood Action Group (2009) 'Learning disability', in P. Higham (ed.), *Post-Qualifying Social Work Practice*. London: Sage. pp. 103–21.

Brake, M. and Bailey, R. (eds) (1980) *Radical Social Work and Practice*. London: Edward Arnold.

Brammer, A. (2010) *Social Work Law* (3rd edn). Harlow: Pearson Longman.

Brauner, R. (2000) 'Embracing difference: addressing race, culture and sexuality', in C. Neal, and D. Davies (eds), *Issues in Therapy with Lesbian, Gay, Bisexual and Transgender Clients*. Maidenhead: Open University Press. pp. 7–21.

Briggs, S. (2002) *Working with Adolescence: A Contemporary Psychodynamic Approach*. Basingstoke: Palgrave Macmillan.

British Association of Social Work (2002) 'The code of ethics for social workers'. www.basw.co.uk/pages/info/ethics.htm

British Broadcasting Corporation (2008) 'Council in registrar appeal win' at BBC News Online 19 December. http://news.bbc.co.uk/1/hi/england/london/7791660.stm (Accessed 27.5.2009).

Brosnan, J. (1996) *Lesbians Talk: Detonating the Nuclear Family*. London: Scarlett Press.

Brown, H. (1987) 'Working with parents', in A. Craft (ed.), *Mental Handicap and Sexuality: Issues and Perspectives*. Tunbridge Wells: Costello. pp.158-76.

Brown, H. and Stein, J. (eds) (1997a) *But Now They've Got a Voice: A Tape About Sexual Abuse for Service Users made by Service Users*. Brighton: Pavilion Publishing.

Brown, H. and Stein, J. (eds) (1997b) *A Nightmare That I Thought Would Never End: A Tape About Sexual Abuse for Staff Made by Service Users*. Brighton: Pavilion Publishing.

Brown H. C. (1991) 'Competent child-focused practice: working with lesbian and gay carers', *Adoption and Fostering*, 15(2): 11–17.

Brown, H.C. (1992) 'Lesbians, the state and social work practice', in M. Langan and L. Day (eds), *Women, Oppression and Social Work: Issues in Anti-Discriminatory Practice*. London: Routledge. pp. 201–19.

Brown, H.C. (1998a) *Social Work and Sexuality: Working with Lesbians and Gay Men*. Basingstoke: Macmillan.

Brown, H.C. (1998b) 'Working with lesbians and gay men: sexuality and practice teaching', in H. Lawson (ed.), *Practice Teaching – Changing Social Work*. London: Jessica Kingsley Publishers. pp. 49–65.

Brown, H.C. (2009) 'Fostering and adoption', in R. Adams, L. Dominelli and M. Payne (eds), *Critical Practice in Social Work* (2nd edn). Basingstoke: Palgrave Macmillan.

Brown, H.C. and Cocker, C. (2008) 'Lesbian and gay fostering and adoption: out of the closet and into the mainstream?', *Adoption and Fostering*, 32(4): 19–30.

Brown, H.C. and Kershaw, S. (2008) 'The legal context for social work with lesbians and gay men in the UK: updating the educational context', *Social Work Education*, 27(2): 122–30.

Brown, K. with Lim, J. (2008) *Mental Health Additional Findings Report. Count Me in Too: LGBT Lives in Brighton and Hove*. Brighton: University of Brighton/ Spectrum.

Brownlee, K. Sprakes, A., Saini, M., O'Hare, R., Kortes-Miller, K. and Graham, J. (2005) 'Heterosexism among social work students', *Social Work Education*, 24(5): 485–94.

Burke, B. and Harrison, P. (2009) 'Anti-oppressive approaches', in R. Adams, L. Dominelli and M Payne (eds), *Critical Practice in Social Work* (2nd edn). Basingstoke: Palgrave Macmillan. pp. 209–19.

Butler, J. (1990) *Gender Trouble: Feminism and the Subversion of Identity*. New York: Routledge.

Butler, J. (1993) *Bodies that Matter: On the Discursive Limits of 'Sex'*. New York: Routledge.

Butler, J. (2004) *Undoing Gender*. New York: Routledge.

Butler, J. (2009) *Frames of War: When is Life Grievable?* New York: Verso.

Butt, R. (2008) 'Vicar could be disciplined for blog slurs against gays and muslims', *The Guardian*, 6 October. www.guardian.co.uk/world/2008/oct/06/religion/ (Accessed 14.10.2008).

Bywater, J. and Jones, R. (2007) *Sexuality and Social Work*. Exeter: Learning Matters.

Cabinet Office (2008) *Think Family: Improving the Life Chances of Families at Risk*. London: Cabinet Office.

Cahill, S and Tobias, S. (2007) *Policy Issues Affecting Lesbian, Gay, Bisexual and Transgender Families*. Michigan: University of Michigan Press.

Caldwell, S. (2008) 'Loophole offers hope to adoption agencies', *The Catholic Herald*, 21 November. www.catholicherald.co.uk/articles/a0000419.shtml (Accessed 27.05.2009).

Calhoun, C. (2000) *Feminism, the Family and the Politics of the Closet: Lesbian and Gay Displacement*. Oxford: Oxford University Press.

Cambridge, P. (1996) 'Men with learning disabilities who have sex with men in public places: mapping the needs of services and service users in South East London', *Journal of Intellectual Disability Research*, 40: 241–51.

Cambridge, P. and McCarthy, M. (1997) 'Developing and implementing sexuality policy for a learning disability provider service', *Health and Social Care in the Community*, 5(4): 227–36.

Camilleri, P. and Ryan, M. (2006) 'Social work students' attitudes towards homosexuality and their knowledge and attitudes towards homosexual parenting as an alternative family unit: an Australian study', *Social Work Education*, 25(3): 288–304.

Campion, M.J. (1995) *Who's Fit to be a Parent?* London: Routledge.

Canda, E. and Furman, L. (1999) *Spiritual Diversity in Social Work Practice: The Heart of Helping*. New York: The Free Press.

Canda, E. and Smith, E. (eds) (2003) *Transpersonal Perspectives on Spirituality in Social Work*. New York: The Howarth Press.

Cant, B. (2009) 'Legal outcomes: reflections on the implications of LGBT legal reforms in the UK for health and social care providers', *Diversity in Health and Social Care*, 6: 55–62.

Carr, S. (2004) *Has Service User Participation Made a Difference to Social Care Services?* Position Paper 3. London: SCIE.

Carr, S. (2005) 'The sickness label infected everything we said: lesbian and gay perspectives on mental distress', in J. Tew (ed.), *Social Perspectives in Mental Health: Developing Social Models to Understand and Work with Mental Distress*. London: Jessica Kingsley Publishers.

Carr, S. (2008) 'Sexuality and religion: a challenge for diversity strategies in UK social care service development and delivery', *Diversity in Health and Social Care*, 5: 113–22.

Carter, V. (1992) 'Abseil makes the heart grow fonder: lesbian and gay campaigning tactics and Section 28', in K. Plummer (ed.), *Modern Homosexualities*. London: Rouledge. pp. 217–26.

CCETSW (1989) *Improving Standards in Practice Learning*. London: CCETSW.

CCETSW (1991) *DipSW: Rules and Requirements for the Diploma in Social Work*, Paper 30 (2nd edn). London: CCETSW.

CCETSW (1995) *Assuring Quality in the Diploma in Social Work −1*. London: CCETSW.

Cheetham, J. (ed.) (1982) *Social Work and Ethnicity*. London: George Allen and Unwin.

Children's Workforce Development Council (2007) *Training, Support and Development Standards for Foster Care*. London: CWDC.

Church of England (1991) *Issues in Human Sexuality*. London: Church House Publishing.

Clarke, J. (1979) 'Critical sociology and radical social work: problems of theory and practice', in *Social Work, Welfare and the State*. London: Edward Arnold. pp. 125–39.

Clifford, D. and Burke, B. (2009) *Anti-oppressive Ethics and Values in Social Work*. Basingstoke: Palgrave Macmillan.

Clough, R., Bullock, R. and Ward, A. (2006) *What Works in Residential Child Care. A Review of Research Evidence and the Practical Considerations*. London: National Centre for Excellence in Residential Child Care/National Children's Bureau.

Clover, D. (2006) 'Overcoming barriers for older gay men in their use of health services: a qualitative study of growing older, sexuality and health', *Health Education Journal*, 65: 41–52.

Cochran, S.D. and Mays, V.M. (2005) 'Estimating prevalence of mental and substance-using disorders among lesbians and gay men from existing National Health data', in A.M. Omoto and H.S. Kurtzman (eds), *Sexual Orientation and Mental Health: Examining Identity and Development in Lesbian, Gay and Bisexual People*. Washington: American Psychological Association. pp. 143–65.

Cocker, C. and Allain, L. (2008) *Social Work with Looked After Children*. Exeter: Learning Matters.

Cocker, C. and Brown, H.C. (2010) 'Sex, sexuality and relationships: developing confidence and discernment when assessing lesbian and gay prospective adopters', *Adoption and Fostering*, 34(1): 20–32.

Cocker, C. and Hafford-Letchfield, T. (2010) 'Critical commentary: out and proud? Social work's relationship with lesbian and gay equality', *British Journal of Social Work*, 40. http://BJSW.oxfordjournals.org/cgi/content/abstract/bcp158 (Accessed 10.03.2010).

Cocks, H.G. and Houlbrook, M. (2006) *The Modern History of Sexuality*. Basingstoke: Palgrave Macmillan.

Commission for Social Care Inspection (2008) *Putting People First: Equality and Diversity Matters. Providing Appropriate Services for Lesbian, Gay and Bisexual and Transgender People*, Issue 7. London: Commission for Social Care Inspection.

Concannon, L. (2009) 'Developing inclusive health and social care policies for older LGBT citizens', *British Journal of Social Work*, 39(3): 403–17.

Cook, M. (2006) 'Law', in H.G. Cocks and M. Houlbrook (eds), *The Modern History of Sexuality*. Basingstoke: Palgrave Macmillan. pp. 64–86.

Cook, M., Mills, R., Trumbach, R. and Cocks, H.G. (2007) *A Gay History of Britain: Love and Sex Between Men Since the Middle Ages*. Oxford: Greenwood World Publishing.

Coombe, V. and Little, A. (eds) (1986) *Race and Social Work: A Guide to Training*. London: Tavistock Publications.

Cooper, A. (2005) 'Surface and depth in the Victoria Climbié Inquiry Report', *Children and Family Social Work*, 10(1): 1–9.

Cooper, D. (1994) *Sexing the City: Lesbian and Gay Politics within an Activist State*. London: Rivers Oram Press.

Cooper, D. (1995) *Power in Struggle: Feminism, Sexuality and the State*. Buckingham: Open University Press.

Cooper, D. (2004) *Challenging Diversity: Rethinking Equality and the Value of Difference*. Cambridge: Cambridge University Press.

Corrigan, P. and Leonard, P. (1978) *Social Work Practice under Capitalism – A Marxist Approach*. London: Macmillan.

Coyle, A. (1998) 'Developing lesbian and gay identity in adolescence', in J. Coleman and D. Roker (eds), *Teenage Sexuality: Health, Risk and Education*. London: Harwood Academic Press.

Creith, E. (1996) *Undressing Lesbian Sex: Popular Images, Private Acts and Public Consequences*. London: Cassell.

Crisp, B. (2008) 'Social work and spirituality in a secular society', *Journal of Social Work*, 8(4): 363–72.

Crompton, M. (1998) *Children, Spirituality, Religion and Social Work*. Aldershot: Ashgate.

Cronin, A. and King, A. (2009) 'A queer kind of care: some preliminary notes and observations', in R.L. Jones and R. Ward (eds), *LGBT Issues: Looking Beyond Categories*. Edinburgh: Dunedin Academic Press..

Dalrymple, J. and Burke, B. (1995) *Anti-Oppressive Practice: Social Care and the Law*. Buckingham: Open University Press.

Dalrymple, J. and Burke, B. (2006) *Anti-Oppressive Practice: Social Care and the Law* (2nd edn). Maidenhead: Open University Press.

D'Augelli, R.R. and Hershberger, S.L. (1993) 'Lesbian, gay and bisexual youth in community settings: personal challenges and mental health problems', in *American Journal of Community Psychology*, 211: 421–48.

Dean, T. and Lane, C. (eds) (2001) *Homosexuality and Psychoanalysis*. Chicago: Chicago University Press.

de Jong, A. (2003) 'Attacks against lesbian, gay and bisexual people: warning signs of fundamentalism?' www.wluml.org/english/pubs/pdf/wsf/02.pdf (Accessed 3.12.2008).

de Maria, W. (1992) 'On the trail of a radical pedagogy for social work education', *British Journal of Social Work*, 22(3):231–52.

Department for Education and Employment (2000) *Guidance of Sex and Relationship Education*. London: HMSO.

Department of Families, Education and Skills (2004) *Every Child Matters: Change for Children*. London: TSO.

Department for Education and Skills (2006) *Common Assessment Framework for Children and Young People*. London: DfES

Department for Education and Skills (2007) *Care Matters: Time for Change*. London: TSO.

Department of Health (1990) *Foster Placement: Guidance and Regulation*, Consultation Paper No. 16. London: Department of Health.

Department of Health (1991) *The Children Act 1989: Guidance and Regulations*: Vol. 3 – Family Placements. London: HMSO.

Department of Health (1995) *Child Protection: Messages from Research*. London: HMSO.

Department of Health (1998) *Modernising Social Services: Promoting Independence, Improving Protection, Raising Standards*. London: TSO.

Department of Health (2000a) *No Secrets: Guidance on Developing and Implementing Multi-Agency Policies and Procedures to Protect Vulnerable Adults from Abuse*. London: Department of Health.

Department of Health (2000b) *The Framework of Assessment for Children in Need and their Families*. London: HMSO.

Department of Health (2001) *Valuing People: A New Strategy for Learning Disability for the 21st Century*. London, HMSO.

Department of Health (2002a) *Requirements for Social Work Training*. London: HMSO.

Department of Health (2002b) *The National Suicide Prevention Strategy*. London: Department of Health.

Department of Health (2002c) *Fostering Services National Minimum Standard. Fostering Services Regulations*. London: TSO.

Department of Health (2003) *Adoption National Minimum Standards. Services Regulations*. London: TSO.

Department of Health (2005) *Independence, Wellbeing and Choice: Our Vision for the Future of Social Care for Adults in England*. London: HMSO.

Department of Health (2006) *Our Health Our Care Our Say: A New Direction for Community Services*. London: HMSO.

Department of Health (2007a) *Putting People First: A Shared Vision and Commitment to the Transformation of Adult Social Care*. London: HMSO.

Department of Health (2007b) *Code of Practice, Mental Capacity Act 2005*. London: TSO.

Department of Health (2008a) *Transforming Social Care LAC (DH) (2008) 1*. London: Crown Copyright. www.cpa.org.uk/cpa/Transforming%20social%20care%20DH.pdf (Accessed 06.02.2010).

Department of Health (2008b) *Code of Practice, Mental Health Act 1983*. London: TSO.

Department of Health (2008c) *Refocusing the Care Programme Approach: Policy and Positive Practice Guidance*. London: DH.

Department of Health (2009a) *Transforming Adult Social Care LAC (DH) (2009)*. London: Crown Copyright. www.dh.gov.uk/dr_consum_dh/groups/dh_digital assets/documents/digitalasset/dh_095813.pdf (Accessed 06.02.2010).

Department of Health (2009b) *Valuing People Now: A New Three Year Strategy with People with Learning Disabilities.* London: Crown Copyright.

Department of Health (2009d) 'Written Ministerial Statement. Government Response to the Consultation on Safeguarding Adults: the Review of the "No Secrets" Guidance', Tuesday, 19 January. London: Crown Copyright. www.dh.gov.uk/en/Consultations/Responsestoconsultations/DH_111286 (Accessed 06.02.2010).

Department of Health and Welsh Office (1992) *Review of Adoption Law: Report to Ministers of an Interdepartmental Working Group,* Consultation Document. London: HMSO.

Diaz, R.M., Bein, E. and Ayala, G. (2006) 'Homophobia, poverty, and racism: triple oppression and mental health outcomes in Latino gay men', in A.M. Omoto and H.S. Kurtzman (eds), *Sexual Orientation and Mental Health: Examining Identity and Development in Lesbian, Gay and Bisexual People.* Washington: American Psychological Association. pp. 207–24.

Dick, S. (2009) *Homophobic Hate Crimes and Hate Incidents.* Manchester: Equality and Human Rights Commission.

Dominelli, L. (1988) *Anti-racist Social Work* (2nd edn). Basingstoke: Macmillan.

Dominelli, L. (2002) *Anti-Oppressive Social Work Theory and Practice.* Basingstoke: Palgrave.

Dominelli, L. (2009) 'Anti-oppressive practice: the challenges of the twenty-first century', in R. Adams, L. Dominelli and M. Payne (eds), *Social Work: Themes, Issues and Critical Debates* (3rd edn). Basingstoke: Palgrave Macmillan. pp. 49–64.

Dominelli, L. and McLeod, E. (1989) *Feminist Social Work.* Basingstoke: Macmillan.

Dowrick, S. and Grundberg, S. (1980) *Why Children?* London: The Women's Press.

Doyle, C. (1997) 'Protection studies: challenging oppression and discrimination', *Social Work Education,* 16(2): 8–19.

Drescher, J. (2002) 'Sexual conversion ("reparative") therapies: history and update', in B.E. Jones and M.J. Hill (eds), *Mental Health Issues in Lesbian, Gay, Bisexual, and Transgender Communities.* Washington: American Psychiatric Publishing Review of Psychiatry, 21: 71–91.

Ellison, G. and Gunstone, B. (2009) *Sexual Orientation Explored: A Study of Identity, Attraction, Behaviour and Attitudes in 2009.* Manchester: Equality and Human Rights Commission.

Engels, F. (1902) *The Origin of the Family: Private Property and the State.* Chicago: Charles H. Kerr and Company.

Erich, S., Leung, P. and Kindle, P. (2005) 'A comparative analysis of adoptive family functioning with gay, lesbian and heterosexual parents and their children', *Journal of GLBT Family Studies,* 1: 43–60.

Erikson, E. (1965) *Childhood and Society.* Harmondsworth: Penguin.

Fannin, A., Fenge, L., Hicks, C., Lavin, N. and Brown, K. (2008) *Social Work Practice with Lesbians and Gay Men.* Exeter: Learning Matters.

Fawcett, B. and Featherstone, B. (2000) 'Setting the scene: an appraisal of notions of postmodernism, postmodernity and postmodern feminism', in B. Fawcett, B. Featherstone, J. Fook, and A. Rossiter (eds), *Practice and Research in Social Work: Postmodern Feminist Perspectives*. London: Routledge.

Featherstone, B. and Green, L. (2009) 'Judith Butler', in M. Gray and S.A. Webb (eds), *Social Work Theories and Methods*. London: Sage. pp. 53–62.

Fenge, L.A. (2008) 'Striving towards inclusive research: an example of participatory action research with older lesbians and gay men', *British Journal of Social Work*, 40: 878–94.

Ferguson, I. (2007) 'Increasing user choice or privatising risk? The antinomies of personalisation', *British Journal of Social Work*, 37: 387–403.

Ferguson, I. (2008) *Reclaiming Social Work: Challenging Neo-liberalism and Promoting Social Justice*. London: Sage.

Ferguson, I. and Woodward, R. (2009) *Radical Social Work in Practice: Making a Difference*. Bristol: Policy Press.

Fish, J. (2006) *Heterosexism in Health and Social Care*. Basingstoke: Palgrave Macmillan.

Fish, J. (2007) 'Getting equal: the implications of new regulations to prohibit sexual orientation discrimination for health and social care', *Diversity in Health & Social Care*, 4(3): 221–8.

Fletcher, H. (2007) 'Christian JP refused to rule on adoption', *Times Online*, 23 October. www.timesonline.co.uk/tol/news/uk/article2719462.ece (Accessed 27.05.2009).

Fook, J. (1993) *Radical Casework: A Theory of Practice*. St Leonards, New South Wales: Allen and Unwin.

Fook, J. (2002) *Social Work: Critical Theory and Practice*. London: Sage.

Foucault, M. (1978) *The History of Sexuality, Volume 1: An Introduction*. New York: Random House.

Foucault, M. (1981) 'The order of discourse', in R. Young (ed.), *Untying the Text: A Post-Structuralist Reader*. London: Routledge and Kegan Paul.

Furman, L.D., Benson, P.W., Grimwood, C. and Canda, E. (2004) 'Religion and spirituality in social work education and direct practice at the millennium: a survey of UK social workers', *British Journal of Social Work*, 34: 767–92.

Furness, S. and Gilligan, P. (2009) *Religion, Belief and Social Work: Making a Difference: Developing Cultural Competence* (Social Work in Practice Series). Bristol: Policy Press

Gammell, C. (2008) 'Religious registrar', *The Weekly Telegraph*, 16 July – 22 July.

Garbutt, R. (2008) 'Sex and Relationships for People with Learning Disabilities: A Challenge for People and Professionals', *Mental Health and Learning Disabilities Research and Practice*, 5: 266–77.

Garrett, P.M. (2003) *Remaking Social Work with Children and Families*. London: Routledge.

Gay and Grey in Dorset (2006) *Lifting the Lid on Sexuality and Ageing: A Research Project into the Needs, Wants, Fears and Aspirations of Older Lesbians and Gay Men*. Bournemouth: Help and Care Development Ltd.

General Social Care Council (2002a) *Code of Practice for Social Care Workers and Code of Practice for Employers of Social Care Workers*. London: General Social Care Council.

General Social Care Council (2002b) *Accreditation of Universities to Grant Degrees in Social Work*. London: General Social Care Council.

Gershon, P. (2004) *Releasing Resources to the Front line: Independent Review of Public Sector Efficiency*. London: HM Treasury/HMSO.

Gibson, A. (1991) 'Erikson's lifecycle approach to development', in J. Lishman (ed.), *Handbook of Theory for Practice Teachers in Social Work*. London: Jessica Kingsley Publishers. pp. 36–47.

Giddens, A. (1992) *The Transformation of Intimacy: Sexuality, Love and Eroticism in Modern Societies*. Cambridge: Polity.

Gilligan, P. and Furness, S. (2006) 'The role of religion and spirituality in social work practice: views and experiences of social workers and students', *British Journal of Social Work*, 36: 617–37.

Glendinning, C., Clarke, S., Hare, P., Kotchetkova, I., Maddison, J. and Newbronner, L. (2006) 'Outcome-focused services for older people', *Adults' Services Knowledge Review 13*, Bristol: Policy Press with the Social Care Institute for Excellence.

Goldberg, A.E. (2010) *Lesbian and Gay Parents and their Children: Research on the Family Life Cycle*. Washington: American Psychological Association.

Golding, J. (1997) *Without Prejudice: The MIND Lesbian, Gay and Bisexual Mental Health Awareness Research*. London: Mind Publications.

Golombok, S. (2000) *Parenting: What Really Counts?* London: Routledge.

Golombok, S. and Tasker, F. (1996) 'Do parents influence the sexual orientation of their children? Findings from a longitudinal study of lesbian families', *Developmental Psychology*, 32: 3–11.

Golombok, S., Spencer, A. and Rutter, M. (1983) 'Children in lesbian and single parent households: psychosexual and psychiatric appraisal', *Journal of Child Psychology and Psychiatry*, 24: 551–72.

Golombok, S., Perry, B., Burston, A., Murray, C., Mooney-Somers, J., Stevens, M., Golding, J. (2003) 'Children with lesbian parents: a community study', *Developmental Psychology*, 39: 20–33.

Gorman, H. and Postle, K. (2003) *Transforming Social Care: A Distorted Vision?* Birmingham: Venture Press.

Government Equalities Office (2009) *Equality Bill – Equality Impact Assessment*. London: Government Equalities Office.

Gray, M. (2008) 'Viewing spirituality in social work through the lens of contemporary social theory', *British Journal of Social Work*, 38(1): 175–96.

Gray, M. and Webb, S. (2009) *Social Work Theories and Methods*. London: Sage.

Greater London Council (1986) *Danger: Heterosexism and Work*. London: Spider Publications.

Greater London Council and the Greater London Council Gay Working Party (1985) *Changing the World: London Charter for Gay and Lesbian Rights*. London: Strategic Policy Unit.

Greenslade, R. (2008) 'Vicar uses newspaper column to apologise for his "sodomy tattoo" jibe at gays', *The Guardian*, 14 October. www.guardian.co.uk/media/greenslade/2008/oct/14/theregions-pressandpublishing/ (Accessed 14.10.2008).

Greenstreet, W. (ed.) (2006) *Integrating Spirituality in Health and Social Care: Perspectives and Practical Approaches*. Oxford: Radcliffe.

Greenwood, P. (2007) 'Crucible of hate', *The Guardian*, 1 June. www.guardian.co.uk/world/2007/jun/01/gayrights.poland/print (Accessed 03.12.2008).

Gulland, A. (2009) 'Direct payments let down gay service users', *Community Care*. www.communitycare.co.uk/Articles/2009/02/09/110663/direct-payments-and-lesbian-and-gay-older-people.html (Accessed 27.10.2009).

Hafford-Letchfield, T. (2008) 'What's love got to do with it?: Developing supportive practices for the expression of sexuality, sexual identity and the intimacy needs of older people', *Journal of Care Services Management*, 2(4): 389–405.

Halstead, J.M. and Lewicka, K. (1998) 'Should homosexuality be taught as an acceptable alternative lifestyle? A Muslim perspective', *Cambridge Journal of Education*, 28(1): 49–64.

Hanscombe, G.E. and Forster, J. (1982) *Rocking the Cradle: Lesbian Mothers, A Challenge in Family Living*. London: Sheba Feminist Publishers.

Hart, J. (1980) 'It's just a stage we're going through: the sexual politics of casework', in M. Brake and R. Bailey (eds), *Radical Social Work and Practice*. London: Edward Arnold. pp. 43–63.

Hart, J. and Richardson, D. (eds) (1981) *The Theory and Practice of Homosexuality*. London: Routledge and Kegan Paul.

Hasler, F., Campbell, J. and Zarb, G. (1999) *Direct Routes to Independence: A Guide to Local Authority Implementation and Management of Direct Payments*. London: Policy Studies Institute.

Healy, K. (2000) *Social Work Practices: Contemporary Perspectives on Change*. London: Sage.

Healy, K. (2005) *Social Work Theories in Context*. Basingstoke: Palgrave Macmillan.

Heaphy, B., Yip, A.K.T. and Thompson, D. (2004) 'Ageing in a non-heterosexual context', *Ageing and Society*, 24: 881–902.

Herek, G.M. (1987) 'Religious orientation and prejudice: a comparison of racial and sexual attitudes', *Personal and Social Psychology Bulletin*, 13: 34–44.

Hicks, S. (2000) '"Good lesbian, bad lesbian": regulating heterosexuality in fostering and adoption assessments', *Child & Family Social Work*, 5(2): 157–68.

Hicks, S. (2005a) 'Sexuality: social work theories and practice', in R. Adams, L. Dominelli and M. Payne (eds), *Social Work Futures*. Basingstoke: Palgrave Macmillan.

Hicks, S. (2005b) 'Lesbian and gay foster care and adoption: a brief UK history', *Adoption and Fostering*, 29(3): 42–56.

Hicks, S. (2008) 'Thinking through sexuality', *Journal of Social Work*, 8(1): 65–82.

Hicks, S. (2009) 'Sexuality', in R. Adams, L. Dominelli and M. Payne (eds), *Practising Social Work in a Complex World*. Basingstoke: Palgrave Macmillan.

Hicks, S. (forthcoming 2011) *Queer Genealogies: A Sociology of Lesbian and Gay Parenting*. Basingstoke: Palgrave Macmillan.

Hicks, S. and McDermott, J. (eds) (1999) *Lesbian and Gay Fostering and Adoption: Extraordinary Yet Ordinary*. London: Jessica Kingsley Publishers.

Hill, M. (1987) 'Child rearing attitudes of black lesbian mothers', in Boston Lesbian Psychologies Collective (eds), *Lesbian Psychologies: Explanations and Challenges*. Urbana: University of Illinois Press. pp. 215–26.

HM Government, Local Government Association, Association of Directors of Adult Social Services, NHS and Department of Health (2006) *Our Health, Our Care, Our Say: A New Direction for Community Services*. London: Department of Health, HMSO.

Hodge, D. (2005) 'Epistemological frameworks, homosexuality, and religion: how people of faith understand the intersection between homosexuality and religion', *Social Work*, 50(3): 207–18.

Holloway, J. (2002) *Homosexual Parenting – Does it Make a Difference? A Re-Evaluation of the Research with Adoption and Fostering in Mind*. Newcastle upon Tyne: Christian Institute. www.christian.org.uk/html-publications/homosexualparenting.htm (Accessed 03.12.2008).

Holloway, M. (2007) 'Spiritual need and the core business of social work', *British Journal of Social Work*, 37(2): 265–80.

Home Office (1998) *Supporting Families: A Consultation Document*. London: Home Office.

Homer, S. (2005) *Jacques Lacan*. Oxford: Routledge.

Hubbard, R. and Rossington J. (1995) *As We Grow Older: A Study of the Housing and Support Needs of Older Lesbians and Gay Men*. London: Polari Housing Association.

Hudson, W. and Ricketts, W. (1980) 'A strategy for the measurement of homophobia', *Journal of Homosexuality*, 5: 357–72.

Humphries, B. (2004) 'An unacceptable role for social work: implementing immigration policy', *British Journal of Social Work*, 34(1): 93–107.

Hunt, R. and Jensen, J. (2007) *The School Report: The Experiences of Young Gay People in Britain's Schools*. London: Stonewall.

Husband, C. (1980) 'Culture, context and practice: racism in social work', in M. Brake and R. Bailey (eds), *Radical Social Work and Practice*. London: Edward Arnold. pp. 64–85.

Jack, G. (1997) 'An ecological approach to social work with children and families', *Child and Family Social Work*, 2: 109–120.

Jennings, R. (2007) *A Lesbian History of Britain: Love and Sex Between Women Since 1500*. Oxford: Greenwood World Publishing.

Jewell, A. (ed.) (1999) *Spirituality and Ageing*. London: Jessica Kingsley Publishers.

Jeyasingham, D. (2008) 'Knowledge/ignorance and the construction of sexuality in social work education', *Social Work Education*, 27(2): 138–51.

Jimenez, J. (2006) 'Epistemological frameworks, homosexuality, and religion: a response to Hodge', *Social Work*, 51(2): 185–7.

Jones, R.L. and Ward, R. (2009) *LGBT Issues: Looking Beyond Categories*. Edinburgh: Dunedin.

Jordan, B. (1990) *Social Work in an Unjust Society*. Hemel Hempstead: Harvester Wheatsheaf.

Kempe, S. and Squires, J. (1998) *Feminisms*. Oxford: Oxford Paperbacks.

Killin, D. (1993) 'Independent living, personal assistance and disabled lesbians and disabled gay men', in C. Barnes (ed.), *Making Our Own Choices: Independent Living and Personal Assistance*. Belper: British Council of Organisations of Disabled People and Ryburn Press.

King, M., Earner, E., Ramsay, J., Johnson, K., Cort, C., Wright, L., Blizard, R. and Davidson, O. (2003) 'Mental health and quality of life of gay men and lesbians in England and Wales: a controlled, cross-sectional study', *British Journal of Psychiatry*, 183: 552–8.

King, M., Semlyen, J., See Tai, S., Killaspy, H., Osborn, D., Popelyuk, D. and Nazareth, I. (2007) *Mental Disorders, Suicide, and Deliberate Self Harm in Lesbian, Gay and Bisexual People: A Systematic Review*. London: NIMHE.

Knocker, S. (2006) *The Whole of Me.*, London: Age Concern.

Kohli, H.K and Faul, A.C. (2005) 'Cross-cultural differences towards diversity issues in attitudes of graduating social work students in India and the United States', *International Social Work*, 48: 809–22.

Lacan, J. (1977 [1958]) 'The signification of the phallus', in *Ecrits: A Selection*. Trans. A Sheridan. London: Routledge. pp. 281–91.

Langan, M. (2002) 'The legacy of radical social work', in R. Adams, L. Dominelli and M. Payne (eds), *Social Work: Themes, Issues and Critical Debates* (2nd edn). Basingstoke: Palgrave. pp 209–17.

Langan, M. and Lee, P. (eds) (1989a) *Radical Social Work Today*. London: Unwin Hyman.

Langan, M. and Lee, P. (1989b) 'Whatever happened to radical social work?', M. Langan and P. Lee (eds), *Radical Social Work Today*. London: Unwin Hyman. pp. 1–18.

Lavin, N. (2008) 'Care settings and the home', in A. Fannin, L. Fenge, C. Hicks, N. Lavin and K. Brown (eds), *Social Work Practice with Older Lesbians and Gay Men*. Exeter: Learning Matters.

Laythe, B., Finkel, D.G., Bringle, R.G. and Kirkpatrick, L.A. (2002) 'Religious fundamentalism as a predictor of prejudice: a two-component model', *Journal for the Scientific Study of Religion*, 41(4): 623–35.

Lesnik, B. (ed.) (1998) *Countering Discrimination in Social Work: International Perspectives in Social Work*. Aldershot: Arena.

Lindgren, K. and Coursey, R. (1995) 'Spirituality and serious mental illness: a two part study', *Psychological Rehabilitation Journal*, 18(3): 93–111.

Llewellyn, A., Agu, L. and Mercer, D. (2008) *Sociology for Social Workers*. Cambridge: Polity Press.

Lloyd, M. (1996) 'Philosophy and religion in the face of death and bereavement', *Journal of Religion and Health*, 35(4): 295–310.

Lloyd, M. (1997) 'Dying and bereavement, spirituality and social work in a market economy of welfare', *British Journal of Social Work*, 27(2): 175–90.

Lloyd, M. and Smith, M. (1998) *Assessment and Service Provision under the new Community Care Arrangements for People with Parkinson's Disease and their Carers*, Research Report No. 13. Manchester: University of Manchester.

London Borough of Hounslow (2009) *Caring with Confidence*. London: London Borough of Hounslow.

London Borough of Islington (2008) *Towards One Islington: Sexual Orientation Equality 2008–2011*. London: Islington Council. www.islington.gov.uk/ DownloadableDocuments/CommunityandLiving/Pdf/equalitydocs/Sexual_ Orientation_Scheme.pdf (Accessed 15.01.2010).

London/Edinburgh, Weekend Return Group (1980) *In and Against the State*. London: Pluto Press.

Lorde, A. (1996) 'The master's tools will never dismantle the master's house', in A. Lorde, *The Audre Lorde Compendium: Essays, Speeches and Journals*. London: Pandora. pp. 158–61.

Lovell, A. (1995) *When Your Child Comes Out*. London: Sheldon Press.

Macpherson, W (1999) *The Stephen Lawrence Inquiry*. London: The Stationery Office.

Malik, K. (2009) 'Social work values and ethical practice: moving beyond ADP', *Moral Maze*, BBC Radio 4, first broadcast 8 July 2009.

Malin, N. (ed.) (1996) *Services for People with Learning Disabilities*. London: Routledge.

Mallon, G. (1999) *Let's Get this Straight: A Gay and Lesbian-Affirming Approach to Child Welfare*. New York: Columbia University Press.

Mallon, G. and Betts, B. (2005) *Recruiting, Assessing and Supporting Lesbian and Gay Carers and Adopters*. London: BAAF.

Manchester City Council, Children, Families and Social Care (2007) *Practice Guidance on Assessing Gay and Lesbian Foster Care and Adoption Applicants*. Manchester: Manchester City Council.

Manthorpe, J. (2003) 'Nearest and dearest? The neglect of lesbians in caring relationships', *British Journal of Social Work*, 33(6): 753–68.

Mason-John, V. and Khanbatta, A. (1993) *Lesbians Talk: Making Black Waves* London: Scarlet Press.

McCarthy, M. (1996) 'The support needs of people with learning disabilities: a profile of those referred for sex education', *Sexuality and Disability*, 14(4): 265–79.

McCarthy, M. (1999) *Sexuality and Women with Learning Disabilities*. London: Jessica Kingsley Publishers.

McCarthy, M. (2002) 'Going through the menopause: perceptions and experiences of women with intellectual disabilities', *Journal of Intellectual and Developmental Disability*, 27(4): 281–95.

McCarthy, M. (2003) 'Drawing a line between consented and abusive sexual experiences: the complexities for women with learning disabilities', *Journal of Adult Protection*, 5(3): 34–40.

McCarthy, M. and Millard, L. (2003) 'Discussing the menopause with women with learning disabilities', *British Journal of Learning Disabilities*, 31: 9–17.

McCarthy, M. and Thompson, D. (1994) 'HIV/AIDS and safer sex work with people with learning disabilities', in A. Craft (ed.), *Sexuality and Learning Disabilities*. London: Routledge. pp. 186–201.

McCarthy, M. and Thompson, D. (1998) *Sex and the 3 R's. Rights, Responsibilities and Risks* (2nd edn). Brighton and Hove: Pavilion Press.

McDonald, A., Postle, K. and Dawson, C. (2008) 'Barriers to retaining and using professional knowledge in local authority social work practice with adults in the UK', *British Journal of Social Work*, 38(7): 1370–87.

McLaughlin, H. (2009) 'What's in a name: "client", "patient", "customer", "consumer", "expert by experience", "service user" – what's next?', *British Journal of Social Work*, 39(6): 1101–17.

McLaughlin, K. (2005) 'From ridicule to institutionalization: anti-oppression, the state and social work', *Critical Social Policy*, 25(3): 283–305.

Meads, C., Pennant, M., McManus, J. and Bayliss, S. (2009) *A Systematic Review of Lesbians, Gay, Bisexual and Transgender Health in the West Midlands Region of the UK Compared to Published UK Research*, DPHE Report 7. Birmingham: West Midlands Health Technology Assessment Collaboration Unity of Public Health, Epidemiology and Biostatistics, The University of Birmingham.

Melendez, M.P. and LaSala, M.C. (2006) 'Who's oppressing whom? Homosexuality, Christianity and social work', *Social Work*, 51(4): 371–7.

Millar, M. (2008) '"Anti-oppressiveness": critical comments on a discourse and its context', *British Journal of Social Work*, 38: 362–75.

Milligan, D. (1975) 'Homosexuality: sexual needs and social problems,' in R. Bailey and M. Brake (eds), *Radical Social Work*. London: Edward Arnold. pp. 96–111.

Mills, R., Trumbach, R. and Cocks, H.G. (2007) *A Gay History of Britain: Love and Sex Between Men since the Middle Ages*. Oxford: Greenwood World Publishing.

Mind (2010) 'Lesbians, gay men and bisexuals and mental health – Factsheet'. www.mind.org.uk/help/people_groups_and_communities/lesbians_gay_men_and_bisexuals_and_mental_health#mentalhealth (Accessed 15.01.2010).

Mitchell, V. (2010) *Lesbian Family Life, Like the Fingers of a Hand: Under Discussed and Controversial Topics*. London: Routledge.

Moir, J. (2009) 'A strange, lonely and troubling death…', *Daily Mail*, 16 November. www.dailymail.co.uk/debate/article-1220756/A-strange-lonely-troubling-death-.html (Accessed 07.02.2010).

Morrow, D.F. (2006) 'Gay, lesbian, bisexual and transgender adolescence', in D.F. Morrow and L. Messinger (eds), *Sexual Orientation and Gender Expression in Social Work Practice: Working with Gay, Lesbian, Bisexual, and Transgender People*. New York: Columbia University Press.

Morrow, D.F. and Tyson, B. (2006) 'Religion and Spirituality', in D.F. Morrow and L. Messinger (eds), *Sexual Orientation and Gender Expression in Social Work Practice*. New York: Columbia University Press. pp. 384–404.

Moss, B. (2005) *Religion and Spirituality*. Lyme Regis: Russell House Publishing.

Mule, N. (2006) 'Equity vs. invisibility: sexual orientation issues in social work ethics and curricula standards', *Social Work Education*, 25(6): 608–22.

Mullaly, B. (1997) *Structural Social Work: Ideology, Theory and Practice* (2nd edn). Oxford: Oxford University Press.

Myers, S. and Milner, J. (2007) *Sexual Issues in Social Work*. Bristol: Policy Press.

Nash, M. and Stewart, B. (eds) (2002) *Spirituality and Social Care: Contributing to Personal and Community Well-being*. London: Jessica Kingsley Publishers.

National Equality Panel (2010) *An Anatomy of Economic Inequality in the UK: Report of the National Equality Panel*. London: Government Equalities Office.

National Institute for Mental Health in England (NIMHE) (2003) *Inspiring Hope: Recognising the Importance of Spirituality in a Whole Person Approach to Mental Health*. Leeds: NIMHE.

Nicholson, V. (2003) *Among Bohemians: Experiments in Living 1900–1939*. London: Penguin.

O'Connor, N. and Ryan, J. (1993) *Wild Desires and Mistaken Identities: Lesbianism and Psychoanalysis*. London: Virago.

Oliver, M. (1990) *The Politics of Disablement*. London: Macmillan.

Oliver, M. (1999) 'Capitalism, disability and ideology: a materialist critique of the normalization principle', in R. Flynn and R. Lemay (eds), *A Quarter-century of Normalization and Social Work Valorization: Evolution and Impact*. Ottawa: University of Ottawa Press. pp. 163–73.

Oliver, M. (2004) 'The social model in action: if I had a hammer', in C. Barnes and G. Mercer (eds), *Implementing the Social Model of Disability: Theory and Research*. Leeds: The Disability Press.

Oliver, M. and Sapey, B. (2006) *Social Work with Disabled People* (3rd edn). Basingstoke: Palgrave Macmillan.

Olson, L. (2007) 'Religious affiliations, political preferences and ideological alignments', in J. Beckford and N. Demerath (eds), *The SAGE Handbook of the Sociology of Religion*. London: Sage.

Ottosson, D. (2007) *State Sponsored Homophobia: A World Survey of Laws Prohibiting Same Sex Activity Between Consenting Adults*. Brussels: International Lesbian and Gay Association. www.ilga.org/statehomophobia/State_sponsored_homophobia_ILGA_07.pdf (Accessed 03.12. 2008).

Parekh, B. (2006) *Rethinking Multiculturalism: Cultural Diversity and Political Theory* (2nd edn). Basingstoke: Palgrave.

Park, A., Curtice, J., Thompson, K., Phillips, M., Clery, E. and Butt, S. (2010) *British Social Attitudes Survey: 26th Report*. London: Sage.

Parrott, B., MacIver, A. and Thoburn, J. (2007) *Independent Inquiry into the Circumstances of Child Sexual Abuse by Two Foster Carers in Wakefield*. Wakefield: Wakefield County Council.

Partners in Advocacy (2004) *People with Disabilities and Same Sex Relationships: Results of a Study Undertaken in Edinburgh in 2004*. Edinburgh: Partners in Advocacy. www.siaa.org.uk/documents/Learningdisabilitysame-sexrelationships-accessiblereportsummary.pdf (Accessed 14.01.2010).

Parton, N. (1994) '"Problematics of government", (post) modernity and social work', *British Journal of Social Work*, 24: 9–32.

Parton, N. (2006) *Safeguarding Childhood: Early Intervention and Surveillance in a Late Modern Society*. Basingstoke: Palgrave Macmillan.

Parton, N. and O'Byrne, P. (2000) *Constructive Social Work: Towards a New Practice*. Basingstoke: Macmillan.

Patterson, C.J. (2006) 'Children of lesbian and gay parents', *Current Directions in Psychological Science,* 15: 241–4.

Patterson, C.J. and D'Augelli, A.R. (1998) *Lesbian and Bisexual Identities in Families: Psychological Perspectives*. Oxford: Oxford University Press.

Patterson, C.J. (2004) 'Gay fathers', in M.E. Lamb (ed.), *The Role of the Father in Child Development* (4th edn). New York: John Wiley. pp. 397–416.

Patterson, C.J. (2005) *Lesbian and Gay Parenting*. Washington: American Psychological Association.

Payne, M. (2005a) *Modern Social Work Theory* (3rd edn). Basingstoke: Palgrave Macmillan.

Payne, M. (2005b) *The Origins of Social Work*. Basingstoke: Palgrave/Macmillan.

Pearson, G., Treseder, J. and Yelloly, M. (1988) *Social Work and the Legacy of Freud*. London: Macmillan.

Pease, B. and Fook, J. (eds) (1999) *Transforming Social Work Practice: Postmodern Critical Perspectives*. London: Routledge.

Perrin, E. and Committee on Psychosocial Aspects of Child and Family Health (2002) 'Technical report: coparent or second-parent adoption by same sex parents', *Paediatrics*, 109(2): 341–4.

Phillipson, C. (1982) *Capitalism and the Construction of Old Age*. London: Basingstoke.

Pollack, D. (2007) 'Sexual orientation and religion from the perspective of the code of ethics', *Social Work*, 52(2): 179–80.

Places for People (1999) *Housing Needs of Older Lesbians and Gay Men in the North East*. Preston: Places for People.

Press Association (2008) 'PC Sacked for suggesting gay sex was sinful', *The Guardian*, 27 November 2008.

Pugh, S. (2005) 'Assessing the cultural needs of older lesbians and gay men: implications for practice', *Practice: Social Work in Action*, 17(3): 207–18.

Quality Assurance Agency (2000) *Subject Benchmark Statement for Social Work*. Mansfield: QAAHE/Linney Direct.

Quality Assurance Agency (2008) *Subject Benchmark Statement for Social Work*. Mansfield: QAAHE/Linney Direct.

Rapaport, J., Manthorpe, J., Hussein, S., Moriarty, S. and Collins, J. (2006) 'Old issues and new directions: perceptions of advocacy, its extent and effectiveness from a qualitative study of stakeholder views', *Journal of Intellectual Disabilities*, 10 (2): 191–210.

Repper, J. and Perkins, R. (2003) *Social Inclusion and Recovery: A Model for Mental Health Practice*. London: Bailliere Tindall.

Richardson, D. (1981) 'Lesbian mothers', in J. Hart and D. Richardson (eds), *The Theory and Practice of Homosexuality*. London: Routledge and Kegan Paul.

Rights of Women Lesbian Custody Group (1986) *Lesbian Mothers' Legal Handbook*. London: The Women's Press.

Riley, D. (1983) *War in the Nursery: Theories of the Child and Mother*. London: Virago.

Rivers, I. (2000) 'Long-term consequences of bullying', in C. Neal and D. Davies, *Issues in Therapy with Lesbian, Gay, Bisexual and Transgender Clients*. Maidenhead: Open University Press. pp. 146–59.

Robb, G. (2006) 'Marriage and reproduction', in H.G. Cocks, and M. Houlbrook (eds), *The Modern History of Sexuality*. Basingstoke: Palgrave Macmillan. pp. 87–108.

Rowbotham, S. (1972) *Women, Resistance and Revolution*. London: Penguin.

Rowbotham, S. (1973) *Women's Consciousness, Men's World*. London: Penguin.

Ryan, J. with Thomas, F. (1987) *The Politics of Mental Handicap* (revised edn). London: Free Association Books.

Saffron, L. (1994) *Challenging Conceptions: Planning a Family by Self-Insemination*. London: Cassell.

Sale, A.U. (2007) 'Secrets in the care sector: homophobia in the social care sector', *Community Care*, 9.8.07. www.communitycare.co.uk/Articles/2007/08/08/105387/homophobia-in-the-social-care-sector.html (Accessed 01.05.2009).

Sapey, B. (2009) 'Engaging with the social model of disability', in P. Higham (ed.), *Post-Qualifying Social Work Practice*. London: Sage. pp. 89–102.

SCIE, Social Care T.V. (2010) *Working with Lesbian, Gay, Bisexual and Transgendered People with Mental Health Needs – Alison's Story*. London: SCIE. www.scie.org.uk (Accessed 01.02.2010).

Scott, S. (2002) *Research Briefing: The Impact on Children of Having Lesbian or Gay Parents*. Barkingside: Barnardo's.

Scottish Council for Voluntary Organisations (2003) *Working – Equality Work Across the Strands: Equalities Briefing October 2003*. www.scvo.org.uk/Equalities/resource_base/mainstreaming/working_together.htm (Accessed 06.02.2010).

Scottish Institute for Residential Child Care (2006) *The Contemporary Role and Future Direction of Residential Care for Children and Young People in Scotland*. Glasgow: SIRCC.

Scourfield, J., Roes, K. and McDermott, L. (2008) 'Lesbian, gay, bisexual and transgender young people's experiences of distress: resilience, ambivalence and self-destructive behaviour', *Health and Social Care in the Community*, 16(3): 329–36.

Sedgwick, E.K. (1990) *Epistemology of the Closet*. Berkeley: University of California Press.

Seebohm Report (1968) *Report of the Committee on Local Authority and Allied Personal Social Services*. London: HMSO.

Seidman, S. (ed.) (1996) *Queer Theory/Sociology*. Cambridge, MA: Blackwell.

Sellick, C., Thoburn, J. and Philpot, T. (2004) *What Works in Adoption and Foster Care?* Barkingside: Banardo's.

Sheldon, B. and Macdonald, G. (2009) *A Textbook of Social Work*. London: Routledge.

Shepherd, G., Boardman, J. and Slade, M. (2008) *Making Recovery a Reality*. London: The Sainsbury Centre for Mental Health.

Singer, I. (1973) *The Goals of Human Sexuality*. London: Wildwood House.

Skeats, J. and Jabri, J. (eds) (1988) *Fostering and Adoption by Lesbians and Gay Men.* London: London Strategy Unit.

Slade, J. (2006) *Safer Caring* (2nd edn). London: Fostering Network.

Smail, D. (2007) 'The cultural and community dimension of recovery', in P. Watkins (ed.), *Recovery: A Guide for Mental Health Practitioners.* Philadelphia: Churchill Livingstone Elsevier.

Smith, M. (2009) *Rethinking Residential Child Care: Positive Perspectives.* Bristol: Policy Press.

Social Perspectives Network (2007) 'Reaching the Spirit: Whose Recovery is it Anyway?' Paper 11, from Social Perspectives Network Study Day in partnership with the Delivering Race Equality Programme, Social Care Institute for Excellence, and the Sexual Orientation and Gender Identity Advisory Group. www.scie.org.uk/publications/misc/recovery.pdf (Accessed 25.10.2009).

Stainton, T. (2009) 'Learning disability', in R. Adams, L. Dominelli and M. Payne (eds), *Critical Practice in Social Work* (2nd edn). Basingstoke: Palgrave. pp. 346–55.

Stanley, N. (1999) 'The institutional abuse of children: an overview of policy and practice', in N. Stanley, J. Manthorpe and B. Penhale (eds), *Institutional Abuse: Perspectives Across the Life Course.* London: Routledge. pp. 16–43.

Statham, D. (1978) *Radicals in Social Work.* London: Routledge and Kegan Paul.

Stewart, D. and Ray, C. (2001) *Ensuring Entitlement: Sex and Relationships Education for Disabled Children.* London: Sex Education Forum, National Children's Bureau/Council for Disabled Children.

Stone, L. (1977) *The Family, Sex and Marriage in England, 1500–1800.* London: Weidenfeld and Nicolson.

Stonewall (2006) *Tackling Homophobia in Our Schools: Spell It Out Teachers' Guide.* DVD. London: Mayor of London/Stonewall.

Stonewall (2009) *Pregnant Pause: A Guide for Lesbians on How to Get Pregnant.* London: Stonewall.

Stonewall Cymru (2009) *Double Stigma: The Needs and Experiences of Lesbian, Gay and Bisexual People with Mental Health Issues Living in Wales – Summary Report.* Cardiff: Stonewell Cymru.

Stott, A. (2009) 'Adoption register overview: experience of the adoption register regarding lesbian and gay adopters', Sharing Evidence, Overcoming Resistance – Celebrating the Role of Lesbian and Gay Carers, BAAF Conference, 11 May, London.

Strega, S. (2007) 'Anti-oppressive practice in child welfare', in D. Baines, *Doing Anti-Oppressive Practice: Building Transformative Politicized Social Work.* Winnipeg: Furnwood Publishing. pp. 67–82.

Strommen, E. (1990) 'Hidden branches and growing pains: homosexuality and the family tree', in F.W. Bozett and M.B. Sussman (eds), *Homosexuality and Family Relations.* New York: Harrington Park Press. pp. 9–34.

Stryker, S. and Whittle, S. (2006) *Transgender Studies Reader.* New York: Routledge.

Sung Lim, H. and Johnson, M.M. (2001) 'Korean social work students' attitudes toward homosexuals', *Journal of Social Work Education*, 37: 545–64.

Swain, J., French, S., Barne, C. and Thomas, C. (eds) (2004) *Disabling Barriers: Enabling Environments* (2nd edn). London: Sage.

Swinton, J. (2001) *Spirituality and Mental Health Care*. London: Jessica Kingsley Publishers.

Tanyi, R. (2002) 'Towards clarification of the meaning of spirituality', *Journal of Advanced Nursing*, 39(5): 500–9.

Tasker, F. (2005) 'Lesbian mothers, gay fathers and their children: a review', *Journal of Developmental & Behavioral Pediatrics*, 26: 224–40.

Tasker, F. and Bellamy, C. (2007) 'Reviewing lesbian and gay adoption and foster care: the developmental outcomes for children', *Family Law*, 37: 473–570.

Tasker, F. and Golombok, S. (1995) 'Adults raised as children in lesbian families', *American Journal of Orthopsychiatry*, 65: 203–215.

Tasker, F.L. and Golombok, S. (1997) *Growing Up in a Lesbian Family: Effects on Child Development*. London: The Guilford Press.

Tasker, F. and Patterson, C.J. (2007) 'Research on gay and lesbian parenting: retrospect and prospect', in F. Tasker and J.J. Bigner (eds), *Gay and Lesbian Parenting: New Directions*. Binghamton: The Haworth Press. pp. 9–34.

Telegraph (2009) 'Catholic charities breaking law on homosexual adoption', *The Telegraph*, 3 June. www.telegraph.co.uk/news/newstopics/religion/5433917/ Catholic-charities-breaking-law-on-homosexual-adoption.html (Accessed 04.06.2009).

Tharinger, D. and Wells, G. (2000) 'An attachment perspective on the developmental challenges of gay and lesbian adolescents: the need for continuity of caregiving from family and schools', *School Psychology Review*, 29(2): 158–73.

Thomas, C. (2007) *Sociologies of Disability and Illness: Contested Ideas in Disability Studies and Medical Sociology*. Basingstoke: Palgrave Macmillan.

Thomas, M. and Pierson, J. (eds) (1995) *Dictionary of Social Work*. London: Collins.

Thompson, D. (1994) 'Sexual experience and sexual identity for men with learning difficulties who have sex with men', *Changes: An International Journal of Psychology and Psychotherapy*, 12(4): 254–63.

Thompson, N. (1993) *Anti-Discriminatory Practice*. Basingstoke: Macmillan.

Thompson, N. (2001) *Anti-Discriminatory Practice* (3rd edn). Basingstoke: Palgrave Macmillan.

Thompson, N. (2003) *Promoting Equality: Challenging Discrimination and Oppression* (2nd edn). Basingstoke: Palgrave Macmillan.

Thompson, N. (2006) *Anti-discriminatory Practice* (4th edn). Basingstoke: Palgrave Macmillan.

Thompson, N. (2008) 'Anti-discriminatory practice', in M. Davis (ed.), *The Blackwell Companion to Social Work* (3rd edn). Oxford: Blackwell. pp. 102–9.

Timms, N. (1964) *Principles and Practice*. London: Routledge and Kegan Paul.

Tirosh, B.A. (1998) 'An experimental attitude change: social work students and homosexuality', *Journal of Homosexuality*, 36(2): 59–71.

TOPSS (2002) *National Occupational Standards for Social Work*. Leeds: TOPSS England.

Trenchard, L. and Warren, H. (1984) *Something to Tell You*. London: London Gay Teenage Group.

Trotter, J. and Gilchrist, J. (1996) 'Assessing DipSW students' anti-discriminatory practice in relation to lesbian and gay issues', *Social Work Education*, 15(1): 75–82.

Trotter, J. and Hafford-Letchfield, T. (2006) 'Let's talk about sexuality', *Community Care*, 9.11.06: 36–7.

Trotter, J. and Leech, N. (2002) 'Linking research, theory and practice in personal and professional development: gender and sexuality issues in social work education', *Social Work Education*, 22(2): 203–14.

Trumbach, R. (1978) *Rise of the Egalitarian Family: Aristocratic Kinship and Domestic Relations in Eighteenth Century England* (Studies in Social Discontinuity). Burlington: Academic Press Inc.

Tully, C.T. (2000) *Lesbians, Gays and the Empowerment Perspective*. New York: Columbia University Press.

Tutu, D. (2004) 'Homophobia is as unjust as that crime against humanity, apartheid', *The Times*, 1 July. www.timesonline.co.uk/tol/comment/columnists/guest_contributors/article451901.ece (Accessed on 30.11.2009).

Van Voorhis, R. and Wagner, M. (2001) 'Coverage of gay and lesbian subject matter in social work journals', *Journal of Social Work Education*, 37(1): 147–60.

Ward, A. (2006) 'Models of "ordinary" and "special" daily living: matching residential care to the mental health needs of looked after children', *Child and Family Social Work*, 11(4): 336–46.

Warner, J., McKeown, E., Griffin, M., Johnson, K., Ramsay, A., Cort, C. and King, M. (2004) 'Rates and predictors of mental illness in gay men, lesbians and bisexual men and women: results from a survey based in England and Wales', *Journal of British Psychiatry*, Dec, 185, pp. 479–85.

Watkins, P. (2007) *Recovery: A Guide for Mental Health Practitioners*. London: Churchill Livingstone/Elsevier

Weale, S. (1993) 'Lesbian couple win three year struggle to foster young children but victory provides no charter', *The Guardian*, 21 April.

Webber, M. (2008) *Evidence-Based Policy and Practice in Mental Health Social Work*. Exeter: Learning Matters.

Weeks, J. (1993) 'Rediscovering Values', in J. Squires (ed.), *Postmodernism and Principled Positions*. London: Lawrence and Wishart. pp. 189-219.

Weeks, J. (2003) *Sexuality* (2nd edn). Oxford: Routledge.

Weeks, J. (2007) *The World We Have Won*. London: Routledge.

Weeks, J., Heaphy, B. and Donovan, C. (2001) *Same Sex Intimacies: Families of Choice and Other Life Experiments*. London: Routledge.

Weir, A. (1975) 'The family, social work and the welfare state', in S. Allen, L. Sanders and J. Wallis (eds), *Conditions of Illusion*. Leeds: Feminist Books. pp. 217–28.

Weston, K. (1991) *Families We Choose: Lesbian and Gay Kinship*. New York: Columbia University Press.

Wilkinson, R. and Pickett, K. (2010) *The Spirit Level: Why Equality is Better for Everyone*. London: Penguin.

Wilson, E. (1977) *Women and the Welfare State*. London: Tavistock Publications Ltd.

Wilson, K., Ruch, G., Lymberry, M. and Cooper, A. (2008) *Social Work: An Introduction to Contemporary Practice*. Harlow, Essex: Pearson Education.

Wilton, T. (2000) *Sexualities in Health and Social Care: A Textbook*. Buckingham: Open University Press.

Wise S. (2000) '"New right" or "backlash"? Section 28, moral panic and "promoting homosexuality"', *Sociological Research Online* 5(1). www.socresonline.org.uk/5/1/wise.html (Accessed 06.02.2010).

Wisniewski, J.J. and Toomey, B.G. (1987) 'Are social workers homophobic?', *Social Work*, 32: 454–5.

Wolfenden, J. (1957) *Report of the Departmental Committee on Homosexual Offences and Prostitution,* CMND247. London: HMSO.

Wolfensberger, W. (1972) *The Principle of Normalisation in Human Services*. Toronto: National Institute on Mental Retardation.

Wong, Y. and Vinsky, J. (2009) 'Speaking from the margins: a critical reflection on the "spiritual-but-not-religious" discourse in social work', *British Journal of Social Work*, 39: 1343–59.

Wright, S.L. and Canetto, S.S. (2009) 'Stereotypes of Older Lesbians and Gay Men', *Educational Gerentology*, 35: 424–52

Yelloly, M. (1980) *Social Work Theory and Psychoanalysis*. London: Van Nostrand Reinhold.

Yip, A.K.T. (2007) 'Sexual orientation discrimination in religious communities', in M.V. Lee Badgett and J. Frank (eds), *Sexual Orientation Discrimination: An International Perspective*. New York: Routledge. pp. 209–24.

Index

Research Methods Books from SAGE

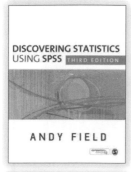

DISCOVERING STATISTICS USING SPSS THIRD EDITION

ANDY FIELD

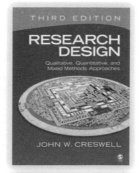

THIRD EDITION

RESEARCH DESIGN

Qualitative, Quantitative, and Mixed Methods Approaches

JOHN W. CRESWELL

Robert K. Yin

Case Study Research

Design and Methods

Fourth Edition

APPLIED SOCIAL RESEARCH METHODS SERIES

Second Edition

QUALITATIVE INQUIRY & RESEARCH DESIGN

Choosing Among Five Approaches

John W. Creswell

Doing a Literature Review

Chris Hart

STATISTICS for People Who (Think They) HATE STATISTICS

3.

NEIL J. SALKIND

SECOND EDITION

INTERVIEWS

Learning the Craft of Qualitative Research Interviewing

Steinar Kvale
Svend Brinkmann

THE QUALITATIVE RESEARCHER'S COMPANION

A. MICHAEL HUBERMAN
MATTHEW B. MILES

Basics of QUALITATIVE RESEARCH 3e

Juliet Corbin
Anselm Strauss

www.sagepub.co.uk

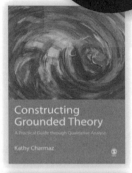

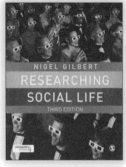
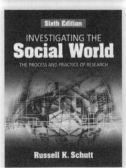